CHRISTIANITY,
THE PAPACY,
and
MISSION
IN AFRICA

CHRISTIANITY,
THE PAPACY,
and
MISSION
IN AFRICA

Richard Gray

Edited with an Introduction by
Lamin Sanneh

ORBIS BOOKS
Maryknoll, New York 10545

Founded in 1970, Orbis Books endeavors to publish works that enlighten the mind, nourish the spirit, and challenge the conscience. The publishing arm of the Maryknoll Fathers and Brothers, Orbis seeks to explore the global dimensions of the Christian faith and mission, to invite dialogue with diverse cultures and religious traditions, and to serve the cause of reconciliation and peace. The books published reflect the views of their authors and do not represent the official position of the Maryknoll Society. To learn more about Maryknoll and Orbis Books, please visit our website at www.maryknollsociety.org.

Library of Congress Cataloging-in-Publication Data

Gray, Richard, 1929–2005.
    Christianity, the papacy, and mission in Africa / Richard Gray;
edited with an introduction by Lamin Sanneh.
      p.   cm.
    Includes bibliographical references (p. 189).
    ISBN 978-1-57075-986–4 (pbk.); 978-1-60833-221-2 (e-book)
    1. Africa – Church history. 2. Catholic Church – Africa – History.
3. Missions – Africa. I. Sanneh, Lamin O.   II. Title.
BR1360.G69 2012
282'.6–dc23   2012010960

Contents

Introduction:
Foresight in Hindsight

Lamin Sanneh

Ecce Homo

Before his death in 2005 after a short illness, Richard Gray had been engaged on a pathbreaking inquiry into the history of Christianity and papal initiative in Africa beginning in the early fifteenth century. Gray was professor of African History at the School of Oriental and African Studies, University of London, where he had been a graduate student following his undergraduate career at Cambridge University. Although he had published several essays based on that research, including his *Black Christians and White Missionaries* (1990), he left the work largely unfinished as he continued his meticulous reconnoitering of Vatican libraries and archives as well as those of the Istituto Storico Francescano in both Rome and Bergamo, in Lisbon, and at the Correr in Venice. Nevertheless, so significant are the issues and the research implications of the project that scholars who had knowledge of it felt that no effort should be spared to salvage whatever could be salvaged of the work in order to bring it to the attention of the student and the general public, and that feeling received the enthusiastic support of Richard Gray's widow, Gabriella, and family, as well as the generous encouragement of the Lundman Family Foundation. With all the limitations of transition and sequence of the essay style, even a collected volume of papers as this one needs little justification beyond the obvious: few scholars had a better and a firmer grasp of the materials conveyed here. Gray's surefootedness over a range of sources and their diverse ramifications gives the essays the authority and clarity of an original work. Besides, the essays provide a crucial backdrop to the twenty-first century manifestations of Christian resurgence in Africa and elsewhere. In light of that, I am convinced that the publication of the essays represents a significant contribution of scholarship, of historical continuities as well as of interpretation.

1

These collected essays represent more than simply a tutorial tribute, though it is that, too. With students and colleagues alike Gray was consistent in declining accolades for himself. Instead he sought them for others. When the work of others was concerned he was uncharacteristically lavish in his praise, and his excitement was contagious enough to carry you along. He went to faculty meetings after a great deal of preparation because a colleague's career was at stake. He anguished much when he was faced with having to recommend one person for a job for which several applied. He would rush to be present when a student of his was making a presentation, taking a back-row seat so as not to be a distraction. Yet his judgment was always made with the highest regard for integrity. Because he kept these matters to himself, those whose career he promoted seldom knew the degree of assiduousness with which Gray applied himself on their behalf.

When his students acknowledged his help by thanking him, Gray would typically respond, "Nonsense," turning the attention away from himself. He was never so engaged and engaging as when he was helping others, which largely explains why he was unable to finish the book he planned over several decades. On his favorite casual stroll to Kenwood House on Parliament Hill in Hampstead Heath, for example, Gray would broach the subject of his unfinished research without the slightest hint of complaint or disappointment even though he was in the early stages of his illness. Alongside the piles of notes accompanying these essays were files and folders of correspondence with students, former students, colleagues, and friends whose work he generously promoted even if that meant neglecting his own. He devoted as much care and attention to a student who was a prominent Marxist voice of his day as he did to one of his last students who as a Catholic priest was a crucial voice in service to Church and country in his native Nigeria. Gray made no invidious distinctions in his scholarship. His staunch loyalty to all these people was legendary, and it is a good thing that hints of his generous spirit continue to resonate in these essays.

The essays represent installments from the fruit of the labor of a scholar whose skill and gifts defied his modesty, whose economical and understated erudition could not mask his brilliance and generosity, and whose scrupulous rigor made his humanity only the more approachable and the more admirable. These gifts of scholarship and humanity Gray carried lightly with quiet ease. One recalls him for this reason with a certain measure of trepidation for expressing in an acknowledgment a sentiment he would in all certainty have met with proverbial terseness with a simple "Nonsense." Gray was well practiced in the art of self-dispensability, except that in this case one must be grateful that he did not succeed in that entirely. In this sector of the scholarly life, Gray's work remains outstanding, distinguished by its subject matter and dependable for his sound judgments. He employed the scholarly craft to serve the cause of a wider humanity in which Africa and Africans loomed ever so large. Gray was never so ready to leap to his feet as he felt when Africa was at issue, and never more gracious than with those he disagreed with. This was certainly the case in the controversy of Rhodesia where the administration of Ian Smith declared him *persona non grata* for his criticism of its race policy.

Gray achieved scholarly eminence by seeming to avoid it. He lavished on his students the respect and reputation he never sought for himself, turning their trust into a teachable moment by appealing to their potential as leaders in the field. He made the academic challenge appear so easily within reach of anyone so inclined. He kept a folder of those students who gave up the life of the scholar and called it, "Those Who Fell on the Wayside," still hoping that they would turn up one day on his doorstep ready to resume from where they left off, such being his unflagging confidence in their potential. Without their knowing it, Gray was still rooting for them, because he just never gave up on anyone. It happened that many students landed on his doorstep seeking sustenance other than that of the academic kind. It is the reason also why those of us involved in this project of retrieval and restoration feel particularly fortunate that Gray's work on the subject can be assembled and presented under one roof. In spite of its great promise and rich resonance with more recent developments, the ground he covered is so rarely traversed in the normal scholarly foray.

Edifice

The thesis of the work as originally conceived was described by Gray in terms of a fresh perspective on the history of the Catholic Church, a perspective derived from developments in the field rather than from directives from Rome. The institutional history of the Church takes its orientation from official pronouncements and the activities of religious orders and foundations. In such histories what we learn of the societies affected, or of changes in policy and method, is understood in the light of the forms and styles introduced from outside. Gray was all too aware that this conventional structure of Catholic history is woefully inadequate to the true facts of practices and responses on the ground, and nowhere is this more the case than in the history of the papacy with respect to Africa. Papal engagement with the African mission was not based simply on sending down orders and directives and masterminding affairs from a remote distance, but on a greater sensitivity and acknowledgment of African demands than is generally recognized. In this picture we see evidence of a surprising degree of collegiality and responsiveness than what is represented in stereotype accounts. Gray's own words state his objective straightforwardly enough. He wrote:

> This study does not pretend to be a history of the Catholic Church in Africa. Its focus, the papal curia, is much narrower. And for most of the period from the fifteenth century to the early nineteenth century the popes and their curial officials could spare relatively few moments for the problems of Africa and the African slave trade. When I started to trace the development of papal interest in sub-Saharan Africa and to seek to understand the curia's policies and attitudes to that subcontinent, I assumed that the critical initiatives came from within Catholic Europe, or at least from its missionaries. I soon discovered, however, that the initiatives came from African Christians: from Ethiopia, its Christian tradition which stretched further than many parts of northern Europe; from Kongo, the first African kingdom to respond with a spontaneous enthusiasm to the Portuguese proclamation of the Gospel; from appeals to Rome by African Catholics attempting to reconcile their needs and their culture with the Christian laws brought to them by missionaries, and finally by slaves of

African origin from the New World protesting against the appalling discrepancy between Christian principles and the practice of slave traders and owners.

The substance of the essays develops this central argument in a consistent fashion across the centuries in diverse situations. Much of the struggles of formulating and implementing policy, recruitment and deployment of personnel, resource allocation, issues of identity, and achieving outcomes that are credible by local criteria can be explained on the basis of "initiatives from Africans." This is not the normal way of understanding the institution of the papacy, but Gray shows that it is the only credible way to take account of the significance of what happened on the ground. That point of view illuminates the motivation that was the driving force behind the meticulous details of events, personalities, and institutions, with lessons whose full implications became clearer with the passage of time. It is as if, while history does not repeat itself, it teems with ripe lessons for today. When, for example, the Church seems to be overtaken by events, and appears otherwise disconnected from prevailing currents, it rebounds with surprising vigor once a decision is taken to engage, at which point the Church gains the initiative that goes with the advantage of local responsiveness. The essays in this book provide convincing evidence of that fact, showing that in this sphere history is a living experience, not just conformity to official pronouncements.

Since 1402 Ethiopia had sent emissaries to Rome requesting missionaries to come to the country but without success. Ethiopian observers turned up at the Council of Florence in 1443, where their presence awakened Portuguese interest in Ethiopia and in Africa in general. Thus was laid the foundation of the Portuguese endeavor to embark on the maritime expansion. It coincided with the rise of Ottoman power, and after the fall of Constantinople in 1453 Portugal redoubled its efforts to escape the Ottoman stranglehold in the Mediterranean world. The Ethiopian overtures appealed to that motive, especially if such an alliance could offer strategic advantage to Europe. By the sixteenth century Ethiopia's appeals were bordering on the frantic, and papal strategists, confronted with the fallout of the Protestant Reformation and the reality of Ottoman ascendancy in the eastern

Mediterranean, started to pay attention to Ethiopia's overtures. Perhaps Ethiopia might after all be the missing link in the defense chain Catholic Europe needed to construct to avert serious decline.

The Spanish cleric Juan Bautista Vives drew up a memorandum for Paul V in which he recommended the creation of missionary seminaries and a new congregation as a direct challenge to Spanish and Portuguese patronal rights.[1] On April 18, 1617, Vives wrote to the emperor of Ethiopia proposing that the emperor should cooperate with the king of Kongo in opening a route between the two Christian states, a proposal that completely overlooked the realities of African geography and the prevailing poor state of communication. Vives had long been a friend of Jerónimo Gracián, who had organized the first Carmelite mission to Kongo, and that personal association may have been responsible for the idea of a Kongo-Ethiopia missionary axis.[2] Yet the idea was by no means a novel one. In a report written in 1578 by a young Venetian, Pietro Duodo, whose father, Francesco, had been captain general of the Venetian galleys at the defeat of the Ottoman fleet at the battle of Lepanto, it was alleged that some twenty-five years earlier, "two Genoese Negroni and Grimaldi" had sailed from Lisbon to the Kongo kingdom and from there "one month by river" had reached the imperial city of Ethiopia.[3] This was, however, no more than a figment of the imagination since no such voyage had taken place. But it does show in the early modern period evidence of growing interest in the mission to Africa.

These geopolitical considerations were an important motivation in inducing significant changes in the policies of church and state, and their ramifications in time altered the priorities of a Eurocentric church. Accordingly, the rise of the maritime powers of Portugal and Spain provided a channel and the motivation for the wider dissemination of ideas and practices of the African field. It showed the burdensome nature of the entanglement of Catholic missions with the anciens régimes, and it complicated considerably the church's efforts at trying to pursue a missionary course free of patronal interference from

1. Piras, *La Congregazione*.
2. Brásio, VI, 277–78.
3. BAV, Urb. Lat. 837, f.144.

Portugal. Indeed, overseas mission exposed the pitfalls and shortcomings of dependence on the state, but also equally importantly the limitations of European Catholic sovereigns in controlling the activities of their agents and subjects abroad. The notion of the uniqueness of Europe was proving impossible to sustain under the pressure of wider commitments.

The difficulties of the mission field reflected fledgling problems at home in Europe that would take time fully to become manifest, by which point the direction for events seemed irreversible. In both cases curial responsibility for Church and mission would require the creation of structures radically different from those envisaged under the *Padroado* system. In 1500, say, Europe had never been more Christian, and Christianity more European. Yet in the era before Europe's global outreach and while the dust of the Crusades was still settling, the symmetry of Church and society was achieved in relative confinement, thanks to the virtual blockade of the Mediterranean by Islamic power. As Ibn Khaldun expressed it, Christians could float not even a plank on the sea. Spain and Portugal were able to break out of their Islamic confinement by launching the maritime expeditions from Italy. Some of these expeditions, invested in the discovery of the New World, sailed via the west coast of Africa. In that cause, at the mouth of the Senegal River the emissaries of Prince Henry of Portugal, relieved with the prospects of gaining unhindered range, carved there Henry's arms and motto, *Talent de bien faire.* As recovering Crusaders, the Spanish and Portuguese thrones felt Islam nipping at their heels, noting that even in West Africa they could not escape the stranglehold the Arabs had on commerce.[4] The quest for a transatlantic escape route was joined in earnest.

The Portuguese built in 1482 a massive fortress, São Jorge da Mina, or Elmina, on the West African coast in the Gold Coast, modern Ghana. Of such feats, the chronicler Zurara (1410–1473/74) declared, "Of a surety, I doubt if since the great power of Alexander and of Caesar, there hath been any prince in the world that ever had the marks of

---

4. Alvise da Cadamosto, *The Voyages of Cadamosto and Other Documents on Western Africa in the Second Half of the Fifteenth Century*, trans. and ed. G. R. Crone (London: Hakluyt Society, 1937), 17.

his conquest set up so far from his own land."[5] Yet "marks of conquest," with the potential of deferred conflict with the Church, are scarcely an adequate way of undertaking the missionary enterprise, and it emboldened the maritime powers to make conquest the prerequisite of overseas mission. It landed the papacy in a historical dilemma of either embracing imperial subservience or adopting apostolic resistance. Meanwhile, the forces unleashed by the transatlantic slave trade, which laid the foundation of the Portuguese and Spanish seaborne empires, gave little time to plan a way out. The answer would eventually come, not from Rome but, appropriately, from the mission field.

Accordingly, by the eighteenth century Catholic missions had collapsed in their strongholds while Protestant missions were barely conceived, let alone organized and endowed. For Church strategists, the future of the faith lay beyond the balance of power in Europe, and, if missions could be assembled on a new foundation and launched at the opportune time, they could in theory compensate for the serious attrition of resources at home and shore up sagging morale. The realization began to dawn on Catholic thinkers that the Church was not a stationary institution tied to Europe by necessity, and that realization had unforeseen implications for Europe itself.

The hand of the papacy was strengthened when in the late sixteenth century an anonymous young Kongo princess sent an appeal that eventually stirred Rome to action. It played a not insignificant part in the establishment of the Sacred Congregation of Propaganda Fide in 1622. The trail began in 1577 when Teresa of Avila asked King Philip II of Spain if he could reform the Carmelite order and allow women to be nuns. The mission that ensued consisted of Carmelite nuns whom Philip dispatched to Kongo in 1584. The mission inspired an unnamed princess to aspire to enter the Order as a Carmelite nun, though it is not known what became of the princess's application to Mother Maria de San José, prioress of the newly founded convent in Lisbon, who responded by promising that she would try to meet her wishes. In the end little came of that though the interest it generated persisted.

_____

5. Gomes Eanes de Azurara (Zurara), *The Chronicle of the Discovery and Conquest of Guinea,* 2 vols. (London: Hakluyt Society, 1896, 1899; New York: B. Franklin, 1963).

All this was part of the growing engagement with Africa's Christian future and a sign that efforts in that direction would bear fruit. In that regard, Vives was determined to pursue a two-kingdom approach, a strategy that pointed emphatically away from the patronal arrangement with Portugal, away, that is, from the idea of the necessity of Europe. The matter was discussed in Rome and a memorandum subsequently submitted to Paul V on the subject by Girolamo Vecchietti who had also been involved in negotiations with the Coptic Church in Egypt.[6] Girolamo succeeded in obtaining the support of Cardinal Maffeo Barberini, the future Urban VIII, for his idea of a Kongo mission, though the Jesuits in Rome poured cold water on the scheme.[7] Yet about the time that Vives wrote to the emperor, the papal collector in Lisbon reported that Raffaello di Castro, a priest from Jacuman in New Spain, "a man of an enquiring mind (*uomo curioso*)," went to Ocanga on the northern frontier of Kongo and "passed far beyond it in order to obtain information regarding people who wore a wooden cross from the necks and came from the country of Prester John."[8] The enthusiasm for an African mission allowed fanciful exaggeration to creep into reports, yet the enthusiasm built a head of steam that moved popes and emperors to action. In his letter appointing Vives as his ambassador, for example, Alvaro II renewed the request that Rome send other missionaries.[9] In response to this royal request, Vives approached the Capuchins, who were already being used by the papacy for missions demanding skill and diplomacy. Together with Cardinal Trejo, a Spaniard who had been appointed in the Curia as Protector of the kingdom of Kongo, Vives assured the Capuchins that they would soon be able to obtain Philip III's support for this initiative. During a visit to the Iberian peninsular in 1619, Lorenzo da Brindisi, the influential Father General of the Capuchins, supported the intended mission to Philip III against opposition by defendants of the Padroado rights. In July 1620 Cardinal Borghese, Paul V's secretary of state, again urged the collector in Lisbon to take up the question. On March 19, 1621, barely a month

---

6. The memorandum by Girolamo Vecchietti is published by Beccari, *Rerum Aethiopicarum,* 11, 176–85.

7. Report by Girolamo Vecchietti, BAV, Vat. Lat. 6723, f. 6v.

8. Brásio, VI, 491–92.

9. Alvaro II to Paul V, 27.III. 1613, in Brásio, v. 6, 132.

after his election to the papacy, Gregory XV assured Alvaro III that the Capuchin mission would soon be leaving for Kongo, though he reckoned without the resistance of the Council of Portugal at Madrid that was dead set against any such independent move.[10]

Spanish Franciscans and Dominicans in the New World had been influential agents in tying mission into the colonial process. But that old-style Establishment system proved to be at the expense of the idea of mission as independent of the state. The Jesuits were the first to alert the papacy to the weakness of this policy of subservience to the colonial powers, by which time Rome had become all too aware of the perils of political sponsorship in the New World. The Padroado of 1514 was an ill-advised move, leading to a full-scale assault on the papacy. Charles V of Spain reacted harshly to the perceived papal interference in the affairs of empire, and in May 1527 the imperial troops invaded Rome and rampaged through the city, ransacking everything that lay in their path. It was a lesson in ecclesiastical subordination not easily lost on Rome: colonial entanglement might be unavoidable, but it could never be dependable, or even desirable in the final analysis. It would tie the hands of the Church in a domain central to apostolic authority. Undeterred, Pius III promulgated in 1537 the bull *Sublimus Deus* enjoining full recognition of the rights and humanity of the Indian populations. In an apostolic brief to the Archbishop of Toledo, the pope demanded recognition and respect for the rights of the native populations. Las Casas's forceful denunciations of colonial injustice in the New World had long made the moral case for mission as a friend but as an unavoidable foe of empire.

It is against this background that we have to understand how Francis Borgia, with his ambivalent relationship with Philip II of Madrid, took the initiative to break ranks with the old system. Although the attempt eventually of Pius V and Borgia to establish a permanent institution in the papal curia to direct Catholic missionary activities in Europe and overseas failed, it marked a point of no return. Mission as colonialism at prayer bestirred itself to claim its independence, and ultimately to repudiate the political interpretation of the apostolic mandate. It had a renovating effect on the Church.

---

10. Jadin in Metzler, I pt.2, 432.

These developments convinced Gregory XV to establish in 1622 the Sacred Congregation for the Propagation of the Faith, known as Propaganda Fide, an institution that became the most influential missionary organization in the history of the Church. The dogged appeals and unflagging aspirations of the remote, small community of Kongo Christians, with a precarious foothold in the royal family and court, had directly and consequentially contributed to the papal decision to confront the challenge of the overseas missions and the obstacles created by the Padroado. In that way, the checkered course of foreign mission had the unforeseen outcome of changing Church policy, and, indirectly, the role of the ancien régime in the Church. In that way the norms of reform and modernization of mission transcended purely European interests, with interesting long-term consequences for church-state relations in the colonial empire. Conceding Madrid's supreme control over the churches in Spanish America, Propaganda Fide turned its attention to other overseas areas.

Meanwhile, Francesco Ingoli, Propaganda Fide's first secretary, criticized Madrid for not appointing indigenous clergy, an issue that looms much larger for mission in Africa and Asia where Portuguese policy flouted this indigenous consideration. Portugal's limited manpower capability, furthermore, aggravated the indigenous question for mission in the more densely populated regions of the world, to reach a crisis point with the erosion of Portugal's seaborne mercantile monopoly that occurred long before the union of its crown with that of Spain in 1580. Dutch, English, and French Huguenot interlopers emerged to pose a far greater threat to Portuguese colonialism than to the Spanish New World, and the Protestant nature of the interlopers' threat reminded the papacy of the folly and unreliability of continuing to vest the direction of missions for Africa and Asia in Portuguese patronal rights.

The dilemma for Rome was clear. Access to the mission field could not be had without a maritime ally, but a maritime ally that wanted its monopoly protected would not, for that reason, tolerate international missions except as appendages of empire. Did that mean that mission was colonial endowment? Though Rome was slow or perhaps even unwilling to admit it, whatever its incidental advantages, colonial hegemony turned out to require paying little more than lip service to mission on the pretext that hegemony would serve its interest just as well. This situation could not be remedied by any cosmetic tinkering with existing rules of practice, whether they were of expedience or of principle. Accordingly, when in 1610 Paul V commissioned the Discalced Carmelites to embark on a mission to Kongo from Portugal, Philip III blocked the mission by preventing its departure from Lisbon. Asserting entitlement to the bait without the hook, a Portuguese official objected to the new papal policy, saying that "a monarchy that has lost its reputation, even if it has lost no territory, is a sky without light, a sun without rays, a body without a soul." The words could not be more apt also for an apostolic authority stripped of its missionary mantle. Portugal's defense of its patronage system was a more eloquent testimony of the thunder it wished to steal from the Church than of the political prerogative it felt entitled to.

Ground Rules

These obstacles notwithstanding, a significant Capuchin mission reached Kongo in 1645 to become the most important in Africa before 1700 with over a hundred missionaries despatched there by Propaganda Fide. Even at that early date Christian Kongolese were unwilling to let the missionaries have it all their own way, with King Garcia II, for example, insisting against missionary opposition that Christianity was not incompatible with indigenous customs and practices. Garcia II's defense represented a contestation of European influence in Christianity, an issue of much greater significance in later centuries. Slavery was a sticking point, and criticism by Christian Africans eventually reached the ears of Rome. Accordingly in 1686, following the appeal and intervention of an Afro-Brazilian, Lorenzo da Silva, the Holy See issued a strong condemnation of slavery and the slave trade. The Curia ranged itself firmly on the side of the liberty of Catholic Africans against Portuguese slave merchants, an example of the influence of converts exerted on changes in attitude and policy in Rome. It is instructive to reflect that, at least in the mission field, the conventional wisdom of the Church as rigidly authoritarian is not borne out by the facts.

In what marked the beginning of nearly two centuries of Capuchin involvement in Kongo, the Capuchins established schools in São Salvador and Soyo, learned kiKongo, and began systematic evangelization in the rural districts. They established confraternities among the Africans, among them the Confraternity of Our Lady of the Rosary, which was formed in Luanda in 1658 and which became a forum for promoting African rights. Between 1672 and 1700, thirty-seven Capuchin fathers recorded a total of 341,000 baptisms. Far from being merely a thin veneer of Catholicism and a pawn of imperial Portugal, as critics have argued, Soyo was a significant Christian African outpost. The claim that what remained of its Catholicism was syncretistic and fodder for crass Portuguese manipulation is belied by Soyo's efforts in inculturation by reconfiguring primal African concepts in Christian terms. Soyo showed its independence by preferring non-Portuguese missionaries, and by establishing trading relations with Portugal's archrival and ideological opponent, the Protestant Dutch. Other Capuchin missions were established on the Guinea Coast and in Sierra Leone in 1644, in Benin in 1647, and in the small state of Warri in the 1650s. Queen Nzinga of Matamba, in eastern Angola, embraced Christianity through the influence of a captured Capuchin priest. In 1656 she and a great number of her troops were received into the faith. She sought to create a Christian state, personally carrying stones for the building of the church of Our Lady of Matamba, which was completed in 1665, the year of her death. She was a distinguished example of women pioneers of Christianity in the ancient Church, as the following account of her role makes clear.

Queen Nzinga's personal example of devotion set the bar of faith for her people. At her encouragement baptisms multiplied, more churches were constructed, daily prayers of the rosary observed, and public processions held. After the communion service she distributed goods to her subjects and arranged for the poor to be fed. She crowned it all with displays of fireworks, music, and songs. It was the high-water mark of Catholicism in seventeenth century Kongo. Given this fact, the picture painted by critics of a superficial syncretism that passed off as Christianity in the Kongo kingdom is not accurate; it is a picture based on the assumption that the virtual extinction of Christianity in the area by the mid-nineteenth century must have been because the religion struck no genuine roots in its heyday. In fact Soyo was an outstanding Christian kingdom that assumed responsibility for the propagation and consolidation of the Church. Christian practice then showed depth and faithfulness, not failure and compromise.

After the Portuguese rounded the Cape, they set up colonies in East Africa, including fortified trading cities along the coast. The island-city of Mozambique became the main administrative center of Portuguese East Africa, with an estimated 2,000 Christians by 1586. The Dominicans held sway over the Mutapa Empire of Zimbabwe, whose kings accepted baptism. In the Zambezi Valley, the Portuguese crown made large grants of land (*prazos*) to settlers. Jesuits and Dominicans from Portugal accompanied the colonists, and in some cases the fathers owned *prazos*. According to a Portuguese Jesuit in 1667, there were sixteen places of worship pursuing missionary work in the lower Zambezi Valley—six conducted by the Jesuits, nine by the Dominicans, and one by a secular priest. The Jesuits in 1697 established a college at Sena for the children of both the Portuguese and African elite.

These initiatives showed that from the early to mid-seventeenth century, the prospect of Catholic Christianity gaining ground in Africa had never been brighter. A sticking point was Christianity's close ties with Portugal's imperial ambition, and that impeded the mission.[11] It is a lesson largely lost on historians that colonialism was a mixed blessing for the Church because anticlerical forces were no less powerful abroad than at home. In that respect, while many Africans embraced Christianity to please their Portuguese overlords, many others did so at real personal cost.

A graphic example bears this out. In 1631 the city of Mombassa was retaken by the Muslims led by Sultan Yusuf bin Hasan. Earlier, Yusuf bin Hasan had been adopted by the Portuguese as a protégé after his father was treacherously murdered by a renegade Portuguese captain. He was baptized as Jeronimo Chingulia and educated in Goa where he was made a knight of the Crusader Order of Christ. On his return to Mombasa Yusuf bin Hasan suffered ill treatment at the hands of the captain of the fort, and that experience gnawed at his resolve as

---

11. Anne Hilton, *The Kingdom of Kongo* (Oxford: Clarendon, 1985), 179ff.

a convert. In an act of vengeance, Yusuf bin Hasan had the captain and his guards murdered, and followed it with a full-scale attack on several Christians, who were offered a choice of accepting Islam or death. That seventy-two African men and women, known as the Martyrs of Mombassa, should have willingly accepted death along with their fellow Christian Portuguese rather than renounce their faith and embrace Islam testifies to their genuine faith and commitment. Another 400 defiant Africans were taken as slaves to Arabia in exchange for ammunition. Carrying the cross knew few bounds.

Action Reflux

By the early eighteenth century, however, the prospects for Christianity in Africa had dimmed markedly. Civil war shattered what was once the distinguished Christian Kongolese kingdom, and the power and authority of the king were irreparably damaged. The capital of São Salvador was sacked by a warring faction in 1678 and then was deserted for a quarter century. Reoccupied in the early eighteenth century, its twelve churches were in ruins, and only a single priest, Estavo Botelho, remained in the capital, by which time he had become a slave trader who lived openly with concubines. Of the several provinces of the kingdom, only the coastal province of Soyo retained a significant Christian population; it would be harsh to dismiss that remnant as mere syncretist chickens coming home to roost. In the end, the forlorn Capuchin mission in Kongo lingered with only two or three friars.

By 1750, the whole future of the Church rested on the weary shoulders of one Capuchin missionary, the remarkable Fr. Cherubina da Savona, who bravely carried on traversing the country from 1758 to 1774, baptizing some 700,000 during his lonely mission of twenty-seven years. Although later Capuchins attempted to carry on the mission, the last regular Capuchin priest withdrew in 1795. In some rural villages, the *maestri* continued to convey Christian teachings, and the people observed Christian rituals and chanted canticles. French missionaries discovered one such village north of the river Zaire in 1773, which tried to compensate for its remote, waning fortunes by means of a great cross. Without a regular priesthood empowered to baptize, however, such communities in time lapsed from their Christian faith. Despite periodic but short-lived bursts of mission in Warri and other kingdoms in West Africa, Christianity struggled under severe strains. In East Africa, the religious orders and secular priests increasingly restricted their ministry to the Portuguese ruling class, and by 1712, missions to Africans continued only in Zambesia. Soon these also died out. In subsequent eras, with the onset of colonial suzerainty, Christianity became a mere appendage of the imperial system, and the clergy chaplains to the colonizers and to their apprentices.

The reasons for the decline of missions were many and sundry, yet none is more telling than the ravages of the African slave trade. The ferocity of the trade had reached a new height in the eighteenth century. By 1448, according to Azurara, the number of Africans brought to Portugal as captives was only 927. In a matter of a few years, with the opening of the transatlantic channel, the traffic picked up, to reach epidemic proportions in the following centuries. Between 1741 and 1810, for instance, over 1.423 million African slaves were disembarked in the port cities of Bristol, Liverpool, and London, with Liverpool the dominant slave port. The slaves were then shipped off to the plantations of the Caribbean and Central and South America.[12]

For their part the rulers of Kongo gradually but inescapably came to the realization that while the slave trade enabled them to hold power and to enlarge and strengthen their kingdom, it also undermined them by making them dependent on the Portuguese slave traders for arms, supplies, and diplomatic recognition needed to avert enslavement, in turn, for their subjects—such being the cruel logic of the slave trade and of dynastic survival. Accordingly, Afonso I called on the help of Portugal and Rome to save his people and his kingdom. He pleaded with the Portuguese Crown, saying so great was the calamity caused by Portuguese trading factors that order was threatened, and with it the cause of the Gospel. "And we cannot reckon how great the damage is, since the mentioned merchants are taking every day our natives, sons of the land and the sons of our noblemen and vassals and our relatives.

---

12. Kenneth Morgan, "Liverpool's Dominance in the British Slave Trade, 1740–1807," in David Richardson, Suzanne Schwarz, and Anthony Tibbles, eds., *Liverpool and Transatlantic Slavery* (Liverpool: Liverpool University Press, 2007), 14–42.

. . . So great is the corruption and licentiousness that our country is being completely depopulated."[13]

The tripartite alliance of commerce, civilization, and Christianity in premodern Africa was turning out to be a deadly combination, as Afonso I discovered, and the European connection a mixed blessing at best. Infiltrated by agents from Lisbon, the Kongo kingdom found all alternative channels of contact with Rome virtually blocked or compromised, and so the kingdom languished in a noose of isolation. The interest the kingdom aroused in Rome led to the decision by the papal Curia to shift control of Catholic missions from Portugal and to create an indigenous priesthood. It was only under the pontificate of Gregory XVI, who as Cardinal Cappellari ran Propaganda Fide, that the papacy succeeded in regaining such control.

The waning power of Portugal undermined its ability to recruit and maintain missionaries, while at the same time it increased its suspicion of missionaries of other nationalities. Moreover, Rome experienced a declining interest in world mission during the eighteenth century, and, accordingly, the supply of missionaries gradually fell. There were never enough priests for the African mission field, and while many of the missionary priests were exemplary in their piety and commitment, others were appreciably less so. Often isolated and lacking regular episcopal supervision or encouragement, many grew discouraged, took concubines, or became slavers, bringing scandal and disrepute to their church and to their calling.

Missionaries succumbed to the African climate and fever. Of 438 known Capuchin fathers active in the mission to Kongo between 1645 and 1835, 229 died after a few years in the mission field—a 52 percent mortality rate—while others hobbled home in poor health. Portugal's decision in 1759 to expel the Jesuits from its colonial territories further reduced the number of missionaries, especially in Zambesia. Efforts to recruit and to educate an African priesthood produced meager results, and with the paucity of African priests went a decline in Catholic faith. To compound the problem, Capuchin priests, moreover, distrusted the lay *maestri* and failed to give them the necessary

---

13. Basil Davidson, ed., *The African Past: Chronicles from Antiquity to Modern Times* (Harmondsworth, Middlesex, England: Penguin Books, 1966), 194–95.

support. These problems and a failure of vision created a setback for Catholicism.

In spite of early promise, the Catholic involvement in the Ethiopian church hit a major stumbling block. When in 1622 the Jesuit Pedro Paëz succeeded in persuading the emperor Susenyos (1607–32) to join the Roman Catholic Church, everyone concerned believed that a new era had arrived for Abyssinian Christianity. But it was not long before those hopes were dashed by the willful and divisive policies of Paëz's successor, Alphonso Mendez, who arrived in 1626. Convinced that a price should be exacted for Ethiopia's belated admission to the Catholic fold, Mendez moved promptly to pursue the logic of the Counter-Reformation by trying to make Roman Catholicism the national faith of Ethiopia. Yet the implications of foreign domination in such a move antagonized Abyssinian Christians and reversed the desire for unity. Mendez adopted a collision course when he rammed through a thoroughgoing purge of the church by suppressing local customs, rebaptizing believers as if they were pagans, having their priests reordained and their churches reconsecrated, and introducing graven images and the Latin rite and calendar. Deeply rooted Jewish customs like circumcision, Sabbath observance, and lunar rites—long revered marks of identity—were proscribed. Ethiopian Christianity's Jewish roots had no analogues in Western Christianity, which viewed those roots as a sacrilege, so profound was the loss of the Jewish dimension of Latin Christianity.

In any case, the reforms of Mendez met with popular insurrection, and a fierce conflict erupted against the Catholic latinization "jihad" against Abyssinian Christianity. The bitter memories of foreign imposition left a century earlier by the jihad of Ahmad ibn Ibrahim al-Ghazi (1506–43), nicknamed Grañ, "the left-handed," were revived by the antagonism sparked by the Catholic attacks on the Abyssinian church. Many Christian chiefs declared that they would prefer a Muslim ruler rather than submit to Portuguese domination. The Muslim comparison must be appreciated for its rhetorical posture rather than taken literally. It was an attack on the Catholic purge of local customs by way of the Islamic analogy. In any case, Susenyos had no choice but to back down, and so he issued a proclamation reinstating the old faith. "We restore to you the faith of your forefathers. Let the former clergy return to the churches, let them put in their tabots, let them say their own liturgy; and do you rejoice."[14]

Fasilidas (r. 1632–67), Susenyos's successor, declared that the concessions to make peace with Roman Catholicism were, however, too little too late, "for which reason all further colloquies and disputes will be in vain."[15] The Jesuits were expelled, with Mendez transferring to India after sending a petition to the king of Spain calling for the conversion of Ethiopia and saying the only means for achieving that was military occupation of the country. Such ideas about the forcible conversion of Christian Ethiopia, it turns out, occurred also to Muslims nearer home, and in their case regional jealousies among Christians suggested that Christians, too, had an unsettling premonition of such future Christian defections to Islam. The period of rival regional sovereigns, called the *zamana masafent*, lasted from 1769 to 1855, and was profoundly shaped by the haunting specter of a surging Islam. One witness expressed in 1840 a sentiment that preserves much older attitudes: a widespread feeling prevailed that the nominally Christian Wallo passed their time in the repetition of prayers, while in the meantime a proverb and general belief circulated among them that their country could never be conquered by those who were not followers of the prophet Muhammad.

Edward Gibbon wrote that having slept for nearly a thousand years, Ethiopia became forgetful of the world by which it was in turn forgotten.[16] Yet under the shroud of mystery and far from the prying eyes of hostile neighbors, Ethiopia created from the second half of the twelfth century enduring monuments to its Christian heritage, such as the thirteen rock-hewn churches at the monastic settlement of Lalibela, set at an altitude of some 2,700 meters. Still a place of pilgrimage, Lalibela's architectural achievement is celebrated in legend as the place that angels built. The deep subterranean trenches, the open quarried caves, and the complex labyrinth of tunnels—narrow passageways

14. Job Ludolphus, *A New History of Ethiopia: Being a Full and Accurate Description of Abessinia* (London: Samuel Smith, 1682), 357; Balthazar Tellez, *Travels of the Jesuits in Ethiopia* (London: J. Knapton, 1710, 242).

15. Ludolphus, *A New History*, 364.

16. Edward Gibbon, *The Decline and Fall of the Roman Empire*, 3 vols. (New York: Modern Library, n.d.), ii, 863.

with interconnecting grottoes, crypts, and galleries—all shrouded in a soft and solicitous holy silence that is filtered with the faint echoes of monks and priests at prayer, justifies Lalibela's steadfast reputation as a historical wonder.

Catholic missions in other parts of the world confronted similar difficulties, without, however, the collapse they experienced in sub-Saharan Africa. What was distinctive about Africa was the social devastation the slave trade caused. While slavery and the slave trade had coexisted with Christianity in the past, in Africa the sheer scale of the trade was unprecedented. From the mid-seventeenth century, tens of thousands of Africans were shipped off each year to plantations in the Americas. Portugal's African empire became, above all, a slave quarry. In order to feed the growing demand for human labor, the slavers began seizing whole villages and devastating and depopulating whole districts, which in turn contributed to civil war and social breakdown. It is estimated that 40 percent of the total number of slaves that crossed the Atlantic came from the Kongo–Angola area, a figure out of all proportion to the population of the region, and one of the main reasons for the disintegration of the Kongolese kingdom.

It is a bitter irony, too, that some of the clergy in Africa owned slaves and engaged in the slave trade. For example, Fr. Pedro de S.S. Trinidade, who lived at Zumbo on the Zambezi between 1710 and 1754, owned 1,600 slaves and worked a gold mine. He was a larger-than-life figure, and his memory, appropriately, survived in local folklore as a rain-making divinity to whom people offered sacrifices in times of drought. Nearly all the clergy benefited financially from the slave trade. Yet, the prevailing climate of opinion notwithstanding, many members of the clergy launched a vigorous attack on slavery and the slave trade. Given its vast scale and momentum the slave trade continued unabated in spite of such opposition, with ruinous consequences for African societies and for missions until well into the early nineteenth century. By that time abolitionist sentiment had gained the upper hand: Parliament abolished the slave trade in 1807, and slavery in 1833, acts that had a domino effect on the stacked pieces of African slavery.

When the famed Scottish missionary David Livingstone reached Angola in 1854 on his trek across the continent, the only evidence of

Jesuit and Capuchin churches he saw was in ruins, and Christianity among the Africans nothing more than a folk memory. In 1750 the Jesuits and the Dominicans had decided to baptize converts no more because, acknowledging defeat in the face of the ignorant lifestyle of the people, they said that Christianity would only bring the people condemnation, not salvation. The last Dominican priest there died in 1837. Mission drifted in the surging mercantile tide, raising a disquieting question about the viability of Christianity as a link with commerce and civilization. The recovery of the Catholic missions would come, but because of a new calculation based on the rehabilitation and restoration of former slaves and ex-captives rather than continuing the policy of seeking a Carolingian model of the church.

Feedback

The nineteenth century witnessed the major breakthrough that altered the nature and direction of Catholic missions henceforth. Catholic strategists had recognized the challenge of interlopers, not so much to the balance of mercantile power as to the question of Protestant colonial ascendancy in Asia and Africa. The ambivalent experience of Catholic missions in Spanish America would be further complicated, on the one hand, by the demands of non-Catholic colonial powers, and, on the other, by African demands for an Africanized Christianity. The pressure from the top was for the colonial co-option of Christianity, in effect, for Christianity as a facet of the Western discovery of non-Western societies, while the pressure from below was for an indigenous valorization of the religion, that is to say, for Christianity as an aspect of African self-understanding. In the nineteenth and twentieth centuries the priority of local reception and adaptation took increasing precedence over the demand of European transmission and direction. Local Christian initiatives determined the course of the religion's development. Whereas, as Gray put it, the goal in the nineteenth century was for strategists "to mobilize for the defense of the papacy the liberated energies of a global Christianity," the goal now was to appreciate the importance of a resurgent grassroots post-Western Christianity for the worldwide church. Europe was once the faith's heartland.

Twentieth-century developments revealed the new bipolar reality of unprecedented attrition in Europe and a corresponding unprecedented acceleration in Africa and Asia, among other places. The faith's new heartlands moved Europe to the unforeseen and unaccustomed position of a new margin.

The accelerated pace of expansion took dramatic forms with the emergence of charismatic and Pentecostal groups, and it shows that the African discovery of Christianity was not merely a simple case of native takeover; it was, rather, a process of deep transformation of what Gray calls the religious cosmology. The formative revival period between 1918 and 1930, for instance, was when a spell was broken and dormant Christian ideas were revived to convulse whole communities and to realign the cultural landscape accordingly. Christianity became firmly lodged in the ethnic folk memory there to compete with ancestral institutions and practices. The outcome was by no means a foregone conclusion, yet the point of the message was clear: it cannot be doubted that God exists, or that God is powerful and will answer all personal needs, including the need for healing and for security of person and estate. The confusion and tragedy of the modern world had an answer in Christianity's ancient message. Those who could read were able to read not only about the bad news that engulfed their world but also about the good news of a God who knew their troubles, spoke their language, and could now heal and restore them. It represented a fundamental and permanent encryption of the African religious template.

Matters came to a head with the global economic slump of the 1920s, which spread panic and hardship among local people, requiring the government to adopt measures deemed highly unpopular. Contemporary with that, the city of Lagos was ravaged by bubonic plague between 1924 and 1926, increasing the demand for applied Christianity, a demand the new religious leaders met with charismatic gifts: prayer, dreams, visions, healing, and a sense of community. In addition, there was a severe famine in 1932.

Christianity's translated status was a boon in these hard, scrappy times as new local leaders presided over the ferment of revival and renewal. Bearers of charismatic good tidings burst upon the scene announcing their message and acting the part: wild, fidgety, strange, ecstatic, and earnest. In the hands of the new leaders Christianity defied denominational boundaries to become a religion of the open road. The spontaneous response was belated validation of Bible translation: all the critical vocabulary of a rallying narrative was derived from the vernacular Bible, with the commentary of life and experience providing the canon of interpretation. In his seminal work, *The History of the Yorubas* (1897), Samuel Johnson, a Yoruba born in Freetown, described the coming of Christianity as a watershed. Echoing a sentiment once expressed by Anexagoras about the ancient Greeks, Johnson said all things were in chaos when the Gospel arrived and brought light and order, lifting the age-long siege of internecine hatred. Oluwa Olorun Alaye: God begets life out of death, and would make apostles out of slaves. Jesus knew the way out of the grave, and that gave people reason to grasp at faith in the teeth of adversity.

In spite of sporadic resistance, conversion had consequences for all society. Religious activity became a paradigm of ferment and change. Accordingly, the Yoruba national sentiment spurred the emergence within Yoruba society of numerous separatist churches, which did not recognize the authority of a central structure. In the second place, recruiting African agents from one part of the continent for work in another part provoked local ethnic reaction. Third, vernacular translation by nonlocal experts did not succeed in stemming ethnic ill-feeling. No translation is perfect, and with mother tongues mistakes and errors quickly assume the guise of fault lines. In Yorubaland and in the Niger Delta the landscape was pockmarked by ethnically precipitated eruptions of separatist groups. Without the magistrate's power to bind and to loosen in the religious sphere, only Christian charity helped to smother this flammable ethnic force and to prevent a damaging social meltdown. African initiatives played a key role in bringing Christianity into the fundamental calculations about the meaning and value of life, and the imperative of a future possibility.

Several stages are evident in the evolution of African Christianity. The first is separation from the missions and the establishment of independent churches. It should be noted, however, that a similar indigenizing process occurred within the mission churches, with the advancement of Africans to positions of leadership, including recognition of their role as primary evangelizers. For example, it was the receptive Christian agents who as ministers, teachers, and traders were the pioneer evangelists in southern Nigeria and the neighboring areas beginning in the nineteenth century.

The second stage was the encounter between Christianity and indigenous beliefs, rituals, and customs that involved an ongoing process of interpretation, evaluation, and integration. Missionaries had typically ignored or scoffed at the traditional concerns, including the hopes and fears of Africans, but now a movement was mounted to redress that failure. Through a process of trial and error, Christian teachings were applied to the challenges spawned by the encounter with the modern West and the rapid social change it induced. By meeting explicit African needs, Christianity developed new characteristics, attained to new insights, and offered a fresh idiom of believing and belonging.

The encounter with evil was a major frontline of Christianity's indigenous course. Sorcery and witchcraft were a standard African response to the experience of evil. The proclamation of the Gospel was interpreted by Africans to mean that Christ's salvation was the beneficent antidote to the power of evil, with the vernacular scripture the infallible oracle of assurance and guarantee. In 1882 a ruler of the Yao at Masasi in Tanzania "hailed as a grand and certain result of Christianity spreading into his country the fact that witchcraft would be driven out before it." A chief wrote to a missionary informing him that the chief and his people had accepted Christianity but felt in need of instruction. His reason for asking for help was because he viewed Christianity as a defense against the devil. Terrified at the thought of the devil's imminent return the chief begged for urgency: "To avoid the devil visiting us any more, we pray that your Church supplies our need by sending a teacher here before the close of the month."[17]

In his concluding reflections on the rising convergence of Christianity and African needs, Gray paid close attention to this cosmological issue, carefully noting its role in evangelization and in the acclimatization of the religion in the African environment. While a major force in the rise of Christianity in Africa, the appeal of cosmology, however,

---

17. Charles W. Armstrong, *The Winning of West Africa* (London: Wesleyan Methodist Missionary Society, 1920), 41.

has generally been ignored by historians whose preoccupation with colonial rule and with the science of development economics has rendered them tone deaf to African continuities with the Christian message. It seems too high a price to pay only to be left with the religion's colonial reputation without appreciation for its considerable enduring African continuities and analogues.

Sometimes this saving aspect of "Christianity" assumed drastic and horrendous forms. In 1925 Tomo Nyirenda, who had been influenced by the millenarianism of Jehovah's Witnesses, embarked upon a career of identifying and slaughtering witches, but to the Lala people in Zambia he appeared as "before all else the bearer of Christianity . . . a Mission like any other" (Ranger, 1975: 45, 50). This example of the traditional takeover of Christianity was in time modified to renounce violent retribution as the answer to evil and reclaiming faith in Christ's power to muzzle evil forces.

Christianity came into contact with traditional cosmologies by a process of recognition, evaluation, and integration, helping the Christian churches to develop plausible hermeneutics of spirit mediation that modern Western missionaries had been inclined to ignore. When, for example, African Christians read the New Testament they discovered that Christ and the Apostles worked in spiritual healing. By the end of the nineteenth century most Western missionaries were committed to the benefits of medical science when some African groups were exploring relations with Pentecostal groups in North America and Europe who were directing attention to programs of spiritual healing. The message and influence of the call to purification and healing emerged almost automatically as a dominant aspect of the Gospel in Africa. The Church in Africa stands on the frontline of proclaiming the spiritual Gospel as a matter of urgent relevance, and in the process challenging the West's reliance on technology as the final and exclusive answer to the human predicament.

In my hearing Gray cited Vatican insiders who reported that Pius XII reminded the European bishops gathered for a meeting in Rome of growing evidence that the future of the Church lay in Asia and Africa. The pope was reflecting on the coming tribulation of war and its grisly secular aftermath. Yet even he could not have foreseen the scale of Catholicism in the current surge, nor imagined the corresponding responsibility for this extraordinary development.

By the time of his death Gray was gratified to see his protégés and former students assuming important and academic and leadership positions that were coming into being, thanks to the speed and scale of the Christian movement in Africa. He kept close tabs on the civil war in Sudan, but never lived to see South Sudan emerge into nationhood in 2011. Yet he had a premonition of coming events when he willed his library to the future University of Juba. It was more than a token of his faith in the phoenix he believed would emerge out of the ashes of war and enmity; it was a symbol of his lifelong dedication to the cause of peace and reconciliation. Giving up was never part of Gray's nature, and it demonstrates his tough-mindedness that he never allowed setbacks and disappointment to weaken his fundamental hope in a better future and in the goodness of others.

In his review of a book manuscript of mine, Gray challenged me not to settle for chronological criteria to define the boundaries of scholarly responsibility—lesser mortals such as I are all too inclined to fall prey to that. In circumstances of challenge and uncertainty, the historian, he pleaded, must raise his or her eyes above the horizon to glimpse yet the hope and promise that alone make the human endeavor worth its name. Even the safe and secure walls of the guild cannot be excuse enough not to be involved in life; the search for truth will never make social justice dispensable. In retrospect I felt in that admonition the pulse that animated Gray's scholarship. The copious notes and correspondence with students, colleagues, and friends he left behind attest to the truth that Gray was not bound by a narrow understanding of the academic life, but, rather, by a lavish, commodious view of the value of the work of others.

"The key to [his] unique contribution to the study of Christianity in Africa must surely lie in the extraordinary breadth and depth of his ecumenical encounters. [We have] in this remarkable book, the testament of an outstanding scholar who himself took a leading role in many of the more recent developments described in it." These words Gray inscribed to the memory of Bengt Sundkler, the Swedish Protestant missionary/scholar, and yet they are particularly appropriate when applied to their author himself.

1

The African Origins of
the *Missio Antiqua*

The *Missio Antiqua* of the Capuchins to the kingdom of Kongo was by far the most important mission sent to Africa by Rome before the middle of the nineteenth century. A distinguished line of scholars from Cavazzi in the seventeenth century have notably traced its fortunes and illuminated its significance. The volume by Teobaldo Filesi and Isidoro de Villapadierna is, and will long continue to be, the essential guide to the abundant sources of information for historians of Africa contained in the letters and reports written by so many of these pioneer missionaries. Forty years ago when I began to explore some of the archival sources in Rome, Louis Jadin generously gave me much initial guidance and imparted his enthusiasm for the history of the Kongo kingdom; twenty years later, when I began at last to turn my attention to this theme, Father Isidoro welcomed and initiated me into the riches of the Istituto Storico, which he with his confreres have so greatly fostered. Those of us who have had the fortune to benefit personally from his wide guidance, unending patience, and kindness, are deeply grateful that the contribution of the Capuchins to an understanding of African and ecclesiastical history has been so notably maintained.

The remote story of the Missio Antiqua might seem irrelevant to the opportunities and challenges which today face the Church in Africa. Yet this tradition of scholarly interest has kept alive the memory of this early endeavor with all its mutual misunderstandings, errors, and, on both sides, its redeeming sacrifices. Two major recent studies have notably underlined the significance of these early centuries for the whole theme of inculturation and the history of Christianity in Africa.[1] As the third millennium of Christianity approaches, it is also a source of

---

1. Adrian Hastings, *The Church in Africa 1450–1950* (New York: Oxford University Press, 1994); John K. Thornton, *The Kongolese Saint Anthony* (New York: Cambridge University Press, 1998).

hope and joy to discover the extent to which the growth of the Church in Africa has been not merely a matter of European endeavors, but a cooperative undertaking in which Africans took important initiatives from the very first moment. Two African Christian kingdoms played a major part in mobilizing papal interest in Kongo and thus in launching the Capuchins on their costly and sacrificial enterprise.

By seizing the imagination of papal strategists, Ethiopia was the first African kingdom to summon Christian Europe to a joint endeavor. In the early fifteenth century, when the papacy was to reestablish itself in Rome after the period of exile in Avignon, Ethiopian rulers and monks were seeking to strengthen their tenuous contacts with western Europe. Already in 1402 an embassy from King Dawit was received in Venice. They brought rare and expensive gifts, four leopards, a large pearl, and aromatic gums, and they took back with them a group of artisans and probably a silver-gilt chalice.[2] Five years later Ethiopians were reported in Bologna, and also subsequently at the Council of Constance, which recognized Martin V. This pope, who took the risky yet momentous decision to return to Rome, gave safe-conduct passes to three Ethiopians in 1418. King Yishaq in 1428 sent to Alfonso V in Valencia an ambassador, who received a warm and fruitful response, about which the pope was kept informed by Cardinal de Foix, who reported that Yishaq had seventy-two rulers subject to him, of whom sixty were Christian.[3]

These persistent contacts were but a prelude to the impact made by the Ethiopians at the Council of Florence in 1443. This encounter, it has been plausibly argued, was directly responsible for Portuguese interest in the lands of Prester John, providing a strong, and perhaps at times even a predominant, motive for the further vigorous exploration of Africa's Atlantic coast.[4] Early Ethiopian attempts to establish close

---

2. Taddesse Tamrat, *Church and State in Ethiopia 1270–1527* (Oxford, 1972), 257. See also M. E. Heldman, "A Chalice from Venice for Emperor Dawit of Ethiopia," in *Bulletin of School of Oriental and African Studies* 53 (1990): 442–45.

3. R. Lefevre, *"Presenze etiopiche in Italia prima del Concilio di Firenze del 1439,"* in *Rassegna di studi etiopici* 23 (1967–68): 5–26; C. de la Roncière, *La découverte de l'Afrique au Moyen Age,* vol. II Cairo, 1924–27, 115s.

4. F. M. Rogers, *O Sonho de unidade entre cristãos ocidentais e orientais no século XV,* Bahia 1960; id., *The Travels of the Infante Dom Pedro of Portugal* (Cambridge Mass., 1961); id., *The Quest for Eastern Christians. Travels and Rumour in the Age of Discovery* (Minneapolis, 1962).

contacts with European Christendom reached a high point under King Zara Yaqob. Following his defeat in 1445 of the Muslim ruler of Adal, Zara Yaqob sent an embassy to Europe, which was received by Pope Nicholas V in 1450. The embassy was given books and *"scripturis,"* an unusual specific, which, de Witte suggested, might indicate some theological documents setting out Catholic positions, and early in 1451 Nicholas authorized sending a messenger to Ethiopia, possibly taking advantage of the artisans and technical experts subsequently supplied to Zara Yaqob by Alfonso. These early relations between Ethiopia and Europe, rightly described by Taddesse Tamrat as "precarious, but nonetheless continuous," began to replace legend with facts in European minds. They enabled, for instance, Fra Mauro in Venice, subsidized by Alfonso, to incorporate much new information concerning the Ethiopian highlands in his *Mappamondo* (1460). They also laid a firm basis for an enduring interest in the papal Curia concerning this potential Christian ally.[5]

The first foundations of an increasingly authentic knowledge in Europe of an extensive African Christian kingdom situated beyond Muslim Egypt and, it was thought, commanding the waters of the Nile, had been laid almost entirely as a result of Ethiopian initiatives. It was the Ethiopians who had persistently attempted to improve their contacts with Europe and the papacy. After the Ottoman conquest of Constantinople in 1453, Ethiopia suddenly began to assume an urgent, critical potential strategic interest for the papacy. The immediate results of this interest were to be negligible, but its significance was to endure for centuries.

Frustrated in its attempts to mobilize, among the Italian states and more widely in Western Europe, a united response to the threats of Turkish expansion, the papacy found that at least it could encourage further Portuguese attempts to explore the sea route to Ethiopia. The

---

5. Tamrat, *Church and State in Ethiopia,* 264–67. C. M. de Witte, "Une ambassade éthiopienne à Rome en 1450, in *Orientalia Christiana Periodica* 21 (1956): 286–98. Tamrat's argument that Zara Yaqob's "strong monophysite stand rules out any theological and doctrinal reasons for his envoys calling at the papal court" (p. 265), perhaps surprisingly suggests that the court of Zara Yaqob had a far clearer view than western Catholics of the theological differences which then separated the Ethiopian Orthodox Church from Rome.

Portuguese crown was given extensive grants of ecclesiastical patronal rights and responsibilities (the Padroado) in its overseas possessions and the lands of the "new discoveries." Papal weakness in Europe was mirrored by the decline of royal power in Ethiopia following the death of Zara Yaqob and the consequent growth of the rival Muslim power of Adal. The hope in Rome of effecting an alliance and even union with these remote African Christians remained slender, but later in the fifteenth century the popes established a hospice for Ethiopian visitors to Rome attached to the church of S. Stefano Maggiore close to St. Peter's.

Ethiopian interest in creating closer ties with Christian Europe was expressed with increasing urgency in the early sixteenth century. In response to another royal invitation sent from Ethiopia in 1513, a Portuguese embassy reached Ethiopia by sea in 1520. Subsequently it brought back to Lisbon letters from King Lebna Dengel calling for a closer military relationship based on a common faith. "If I had a Christian king for a Tripol," the king wrote to John III of Portugal, "I would never part from him for an hour," and Lebna Dengel also urged the pope to exhort the Christian kings of Europe to help him "for from all sides of my frontiers the Muslims, an evil people, surround me."[6] Two decades later, harassed by the victorious Muslims, King Galawdewos sent a message to Lisbon in 1545, which was interpreted as a request for the appointment of a Catholic patriarch for Ethiopia. In Rome the response to this apparent opening was taken up by the Jesuits, and especially by their founder. Ignatius showed exceptioanl interest in the preparations for a mission to Ethiopia, and in October 1546 he wrote to John III in Portugal saying that he himself wanted to go on "the enterprise of Ethiopia" should he be chosen. He read Alvarez's account of the earlier Portuguese embassy, and he discussed the project with Pedro, an Ethiopian monk resident in Rome since 1540.[7]

Early in 1549 Ignatius learned that Pedro was asking the papal Curia to send five bishops to Ethiopia, leaving Galawdewos to select which one should be patriarch. The Portuguese ambassador in Rome

---

6. Merid Wolde Aregay, *The Legacy of Jesuit Missionary Activities in Ethiopia from 1555 to 1632,* in Getatchew Haile et al. eds., *The Missionary Factor in Ethiopia* (Frankfurt, 1998), 33s.

7. P. Caraman, *The Lost Empire* (London, 1985),10.

was doing his best to frustrate Pedro's plan, and in a letter Ignatius insisted that John III should hasten to make an appointment and hence assert the right to nominate to this position "in those lands not very distant from his India."[8] His letter illustrates the extent to which the Jesuits were becoming, in this instance, allies of the Portuguese Padroado. It may have been in many ways a realistic assessment of the situation, for the most practical way of reaching Ethiopia from Europe in the mid-sixteenth century was on board a Portuguese vessel. Yet it underlined the dependence on Portuguese control, even regarding an area which was in no way a Portuguese conquest.

John III had in fact already revealed his power. In 1547 when told of the proposal to appoint Broët, a French Jesuit, as patriarch, John had vetoed the idea on the grounds that Broët was a foreigner, and, even worse, a Frenchman.[9] It was not until July 20, 1553, that John informed Ignatius that he had decided to send a Jesuit as patriarch to Ethiopia, but then he went on to demonstrate the extent of his patronage. When the mission eventually sailed from Lisbon on April 1, 1554, it contained the largest group of Jesuits until then to sail for any mission. The king spent the colossal sum of 100,000 cruzados on its expenses, a sum equivalent to about one-fifteenth of the total regular papal annual revenue.[10]

Ignatius had a keen sense not only of the strategic importance of this endeavor but also of its difficult nature. He dictated pages of detailed instructions concerning the mission's approach to its task, demonstrating a good deal of sympathetic understanding of the people of Ethiopia and of their culture. Yet despite these preparations and high hopes, the Jesuits failed to bring the Ethiopian church into communion with Rome. Indeed, their efforts ended in creating fresh barriers between the two churches. Many factors contributed to this failure, and it would be incorrect to attribute too great a responsibility to Portuguese pride and imperialist ambitions, but the close interde-

8. *S. Ignatii de Loyola Soc. Jesu fundatoris epistolae et instructions* (Monumenta Ignatiana, Ser. Ia, II; Roma 1904), 304s.

9. F. Rodrigues, *História da Companhia de Jesus na Assistência de Portugal*, I/2 (Porto, 1932), 572.

10. Rodrigues, *História*, III, 581. K. R. Stow, *Taxation, Community and State* (Stuttgart, 1982), 16, for papal revenue estimate.

pendence between the mission and the Padroado was certainly by no means a minor factor.[11]

Yet if in Ethiopia the Iberian Jesuits failed to develop a firm understanding and union with these African Christians, elsewhere the exploits of Jesuit missionaries, notably those of Francis Xavier and his successors in Asia, were beginning to create an awareness in Rome of the potential ecclesiastical significance of the lands and peoples beyond Europe. Very gradually, the dangers inherent in leaving to royal Iberian patronage the development of the Church overseas were becoming apparent to the papacy. This burgeoning awareness was to prove of immense significance when eventually the appeals of a second Christian kingdom in Africa became known to the papacy.

The initial proposal to create a curial congregation in Rome to be concerned with the governance of overseas missions was made to Pius V in May 1568 by Francis Borgia, the third General of the Jesuits. Determined to carry through the reforming decrees of the Council of Trent, Pius fully recognized the value of the Jesuits and he entrusted them with special duties and missions. Six months after his election, the Imperial agent reported from Rome that "only monks and Theatines ([often confused in contemporary parlance with the Jesuits] go to the palace, and they think they can reform the world in a day." Pius especially supported their educational activities, and a Jesuit was even mobilized for the delicate task of attempting to persuade the Swiss Guards to marry their concubines. "It has rarely happened in a Pope," concluded Pastor, "that the sovereign has been so subordinated to the priest."[12]

Borgia sent Jesuits to Florida and other Spanish possessions in the Americas, and on many occasions discussed the needs of the overseas missions with Pius. In the spring of 1568, Cardinal Crivelli, a former nuncio in Spain, proposed that some Jesuits should be sent as visitors to the overseas territories. At the suggestion of Borgia, who was much closer personally to the royal court in Lisbon than to Philip II in Madrid, this particular proposal was discussed with Alvaro de Castro, the Por-

---

11. M. W. Aregay and B. Girma Beshah, *The Question of the Union of the Churches in Luso-Ethiopian Relations, 1500–1632* (Lisbon: Junta de Investigações do Ultramar and Centro de Estudes Históricos Ultramarinos, 1964).

12. L. von Pastor, *The History of the Popes* (Eng. trans.), XVII 66. See also pp. 139–43 and 95 for the Swiss Guards.

tuguese ambassador in Rome. Then on May 20, Borgia, his secretary Polanco, and Alvaro de Castro discussed with the pope the creation of a curial congregation for the conversion of the heathen. Pius decided to create the congregation, and the initiative was rapidly expanded on the advice of Peter Canisius, the Jesuit charged by the papacy with the major responsibilities in Germany, who proposed a similar congregation to deal with northern heretics. By early August, Borgia was passing information and suggestions to both bodies.[13] At last it seemed that a way had been found to build up an informed opinion in the Curia so that the papacy could begin to take a major role in the development of missionary work both in Europe and overseas.

The fact that Alvaro de Castro was willing actively to support a development which would have inevitably increased curial interests and influence in the areas of the Padroado, was a remarkable tribute to Borgia's excellent relations with Lisbon as well as reflecting the standing of the Jesuits at this time in Portugal. On this occasion, however, the defense of Iberian patronal rights rested not with Portugal but with Spain in the person of Phillip II. Whereas Charles V had seen his empire in terms of a dynastic rule embracing much of western Europe, his son saw it increasingly centered on Spain and its possessions; and whereas Charles, faced with Lutheranism, had at one time foreseen himself as presiding over attempts at accommodation, Philip was always convinced that the defense of Catholicism depended primarily on his own control of Spanish power. Even before he heard of the uprising in the Netherlands, he had instructed his ambassador in Rome to reassure Pius V that he did not intend, nor was he willing, "to be a lord of heretics."[14] Philip was convinced that if he was to defend the Church effectively, the rights of the crown had to be preserved. When therefore he learned that the pope wished to send someone to Spanish America "who would depend directly on the Holy See and have the authority of a nuncio," he took steps to strengthen royal control over ecclesiastical affairs in the Americas, and he informed the papal nuncio in

---

13. L. Lopetegui, "San Francisco de Borja y el plan misional de San Pio V," in *Archivum Historicum Societatis Iesu* 11 (1942): 5–8.

14. Philip II to Requesens, 12. VIII. 1566, quoted in K. M. Seatton, *The Papacy and the Levant*, IV (Philadelphia, 1984), 910.

Madrid that he had sent new officials there with instructions which he was confident would redound to God's service.[15] One of these officials, Francisco da Toledo, a close friend of Borgia, was appointed Viceroy of Peru, and by 1570 there were forty Jesuits in Lima.[16] Philip's action greatly strengthened the work of the religious orders in Spanish America, but effectively it blocked any immediate development of the curial congregation in Rome.

The intervention of the Jesuits had failed to create in Rome a permanent instrument for the control and guidance of all Catholic missions. Yet despite the brief existence of Pius V's congregation, its memory was kept alive in the papal Curia, notably by Antonio Santori, who in 1570, aged thirty-eight, was created a cardinal by Pius. Santori was entrusted by Gregory XIII in 1573 with the reform of the Greek-rite Catholics in Italy, and subsequently he expanded his activities to become Protector of the Orient, particularly concerned with increasing Rome's influence among Christian communities living under Ottoman rule and beyond. In 1584 Gregory sent Giambattista Vecchietti, a distinguished Oriental linguist, to Egypt and Persia to strengthen these contacts. Simultaneously he dispatched Giovanni Battista Britti to Ethiopia via Goa, charged with attempting to persuade the Ethiopian king to make a formal act of obedience to the see of St. Peter. Like Vecchietti, Britti was a layman, one of the papal camerieri or cibiculari, but he was killed while trying to land on the Red Sea coast.[17]

Santori entered the conclave of 1592 as a very strong candidate for the papal throne. Blocked by the opposition of one faction among

---

15. L. Serrano, *Correspondencia diplomática entre España y la Santa Sede durante el pontificado do S. Pio V* (Madrid, 1914), II 350s, 290 , and III, 42. See also, for the part played by the Franciscan friar, Alonso Maldonado de Buendía, and his contacts with Cardinal Crivelli: M. Mónica, *La gran controversia del siglo XVI acerca del dominio español in América* (Madrid ,1952), 159–63.

16. P. Suau, *Histoire de S. François de Borgia* (Paris, 1910), 425.

17. The details concerning Britti are in two memoranda written by Girolamo Vecchietti: one is published in C. Veccari, *Rerum aethiopicarum scriptores occidentales* (Rome, 1903–15), XI, 179, and the other, unpublished, is in cod. Vat. Lat. 6723, f. 6. Britti is described as "un gentilhuomo di cappa corta," and I am grateful to Father Mariano D'Alatri O.F.M.Cap. for the reference to G. Moroni, *Dizionario di erudizoione ecclesiastica* (Venice, 1841), VIII, 91, which states that the cubiculari wore a "cappa senza coda, con maniche larghe e corte."

the cardinals, he was nevertheless greatly respected by Clement VIII (1592–1605), who supported his initiatives. In 1593 Girolamo Vecchietti, younger brother of Giambattista, was sent to Egypt, and while he was there he contacted four Ethiopian monks. The following year Clement was reported to have established "the Congregation of Ethiopia" consisting of four cardinals, headed by Santori,[18] and throughout this period of intense negotiations with Copts in Egypt, contacts were maintained by Girolamo with Ethiopian clerics there. Girolamo was specifically instructed in 1595 that the Coptic patriarch should send to Ethiopia a copy of the proposed act of union with the papacy so that it could be published and observed in that country. Girolamo later claimed that after the act of union and obedience made by the Coptic delegation in Rome in 1597, notification of this was sent to Ethiopia.[19] Following these developments, Clement VIII formally appointed in 1599 a congregation of cardinals to be known as the Congregation of Propaganda Fide. Meeting regularly in Santori's palace, the congregation included two papal nephews and various prominent reforming cardinals, including Baronio, Federico Borromeo, and Bellarmine. Its discussions covered not only the area of Santori's greatest interest, but also Protestant Europe and the overseas missions. Clement's congregation, however, had merely a brief existence. Santori died in 1602,[20] and although the Congregation was reputed still to be functioning in 1605 at the beginning of Paul V's papacy, it appears to have achieved little after Santori's death.[21] Yet its organization and method of working clearly established a precedent for its eventual successor. Africans, in their continued summons and appeals from Ethiopia with the response they had evoked in the Curia, had begun to influence decisively papal missionary policy. This cooperative endeavor was to be strengthened immensely by the initiatives of a second African Christian kingdom.

After Santori's death, leadership in papal missionary initiatives devolved upon Pedro de la Madre de Dios, the gifted and outstanding

---

18. B.A.V., cod. Urb. Lat. 1062, f. 334 Avviso of 11.VI.1594.

19. B.A.V., cod. Vat. Lat. 6723, ff. 2–7v. Relazione d'Etiopia.

20. A. Castellucci, "Il risveglio dell'attività missionaria e le prime origini della S.C. de Propaganda Fide," in *Le Conferenze al Laterano* (*March-Aprile 1923*) (Rome, 1924), 168–69.

21. B.A.V., cod. Urb. Lat. 837, f. 464. Relatione.

Spanish member of the Italian province of the Discalced Carmelites. Deeply involved in the decision to send a Carmelite mission to Persia where Shah Abbas had defeated a Turkish army in 1603, Pedro was often called upon to advise Paul V on Middle East questions. He took a leading part in directing the negotiations with the Coptic Church in Egypt,[22] and in an undated memorandum to Paul V on the potential role which could be undertaken by the Franciscans in Jerusalem, he highlighted the importance of fostering relationships with the Ethiopian community at the Holy Sepulchre. Of "the six or seven" Christian groups in Jerusalem, he wrote, "the Abyssinians or Ethiopians of Prester John are the most open for they esteem to be united with the Church of Rome and to recognize the head Bishop of the Roman pontiff. These persons must be greatly cherished, and strongly confirmed in the union which they profess to have with the Holy Church." Pedro suggested that the Ethiopian monks at the Holy Sepulchre could be encouraged to elect an *abuna,* or bishop, who would then be confirmed the "the true," i.e., Latin, Patriarch of Alexandria, adding that "if it is true, as is reported, that Prester John is very dissatisfied with the present scandalous *abuna,*" he might be persuaded to ratify such an election.[23]

This intimate involvement in developing papal strategic thinking on the possibilities of outflanking the Ottoman empire suddenly in 1607 became clearly linked in Pedro's mind with a Carmelite interest in the kingdom of Kongo. By the end of the sixteenth century, a commitment to a Catholic identity had become an integral part of the legitimating ideology of the ruling elite in Kongo. In 1594 Antonio Vieira, a close relative of Alvaro II, the king of Kongo, had reached Lisbon charged with the task of negotiating the creation of a separate diocese for Kongo. Vieira had greatly impressed the papal representative in Lisbon, Fabio Biondi, both with his own understanding of the faith and his account of the Kongo court's commitment to Christianity. Biondi gave him every assistance, and Vieira returned to Kongo

---

22. V. Buri, "L'unione della Chiesa copta con Roma sotto Clemente VIII," in *Orientalia Christiana* 23 (1931): 237–53.

23. OCD archives in Rome, 281e cartapaccion f 27–27v. See also Buri, *L'unione della Chiesa copta,* 249–53.

not only with his mission successfully accomplished but also with a warm invitation from the papacy that King Alvaro should send an ambassador to Rome.[24] This ambassador, Antonio Manuele, a cousin of Alvaro II, reached Lisbon in November 1605 but soon found himself in great difficulties.

The embassy had been provided with the shell currency normally used for financial transactions in Kongo. This was perfectly adequate for use with the Portuguese in Luanda, but in Europe was valueless.[25] Even more difficult than this financial problem was the fact that the authorities in Lisbon and Madrid were most reluctant that he should go on to Rome, for they feared that this would result in a challenge to their patronal powers. They vigorously attempted therefore to persuade him not to proceed, but to entrust his affairs to their representatives in Rome. When Pedro in Rome learned of the ambassador's predicament, he saw this as an opportunity not only to resuscitate a Carmelite concern with Kongo but also to advance his plans for a papal mission to Ethopia.

At the invitation of Philip II, shortly after he had taken the crown of Portugal, a group of Spanish Discalced Carmelites had undertaken a mission to Kongo. Many in the reformed order in Spain were, however, hostile to accepting overseas missionary commitments, and the mission had been withdrawn.[26] One of the missionaries, Diego de la Encarnación, had retained a warm memory of Kongo Christians and he succeeded in contacting the beleaguered ambassador in Madrid. In a draft petition to the pope which Diego sent Antonio on January 1, 1607, Diego suggested that the Carmelites should be sent to Kongo and its neighboring areas from which one could reach out to "the great Emperor of Aetiopia who is called the Prester John."[27] From Rome, Pedro wrote to Tomás de Jesús, a young Spanish Carmelite whom Pedro hoped would take charge of the projected mission and

---

24. R. Gray, "A Kongo Princess, the Kongo Ambassadors and the Papacy," *Journal of Religion in Africa* 29, no. 2 (1999).

25. B.A.V., cod. Urb. Lat. 1076, f. 5v-6. Avvisi di Roma, 5.1.1608.

26. F. Bontinck, "Les Carmes Déchaux au royaume de Kongo (1587–1587)," in *Zaïre-Afrique* 262 (1992): 113–23.

27. A.S.V., Misc. Arm. I, 91, f. 215. Draft petition, January 1607, in the same hand as f188r-v, Diego to the Ambassadors, 1.1.1607.

from there "open a route to Prester John." Tomás had been primarily attracted to contemplative life, and he was set firmly against accepting this task, even when he was informed that the pope approved the proposal. Then, one day, when saying Mass, he became convinced that he should accept, and immediately he began to collect information concerning "the lands and languages of Congo and the Abyssinians."[28]

The belief in Rome that it might be feasible to open up a route between Kongo and Ethopia was not a new idea. Some thirty years earlier, a young Venetian, Pietro Duodo, had held long discussions with Don John, "a pure Ethiopian, a monk of the order of St. Anthony, about forty-two years old and an expert in the affairs of those states, who already, twice in the space of eight years, claims to have been in our lands."[29] We know nothing more about this Ethiopian, but Pietro Duodo came from a distinguished Venetian family renowned for their services to the republic's navy. His father, Francesco, had been captain-general of the Venetian galleys and had played a notable part in the victory at Lepanto. He had therefore grown up in an environment keenly conscious of the Ottoman threat, and when in 1578 he wrote a report on Africa his interest was largely focused on Ethiopia as an apparently powerful potential ally. In his discussion on the possible ways of reaching Ethiopia, Duodo reported that some twenty-five years earlier "two Genoese Negroni and Grimaldi" had sailed from Lisbon to the kingdom of Kongo and from there "one month by river" they reached "the imperial city of Zamber,"[30] which could be identified with Dambea, the province north of Lake Tana and a name sometimes applied to the lake itself. Almost certainly the report of this Genoese exploit is pure fantasy, but from the early sixteenth century an exaggerated idea of the southward extension of Ethiopia to the equator lent credence to the belief that the journey from Kongo to Ethiopia would be a relatively easy undertaking.

So in the mind of Pedro de la Madre di Dios the centuries'-long appeals from the Christian rulers of Ethiopia had become suddenly

---

28. Joseph de Santa Teresa, *Reforma de los Descalzos* (Madrid, 1684), IV, Libro XVII, cap 39.

29. B.A.V., cod. Urb. Lat. 837, f. 147r-v.

30. Ibid., f. 144.

fused with the predicament confronting Antonio Manuele, ambassador of the Catholic kingdom of Kongo. Not only did Pedro summon the Spanish Carmelites to assist the enterprise, but he also ensured that firm instructions should be sent to the papal nuncio in Madrid that the obstacles preventing the ambassador from coming to Rome should be overcome. As late as May 1607, Don Antonio believed that he would be unable to complete his journey to Rome. He envisaged that he would have to leave for Lisbon the following month, so that in September he could set sail for Kongo. By then he was a very sick man, severely stricken with gallstones and leaving the Mercedarians' house in Madrid only "to discuss the affairs of his embassy with the king or with his ministers." Later the Mercedarian provincial was to testify that the ambassador's behavior and way of life had given them all "a very great patience submitting himself to the Will of God."[31] Probably ignorant of the ambassador's state of health but aware of his despondent decision to abandon his journey to Rome, Pedro wrote to him on the July 24 from Rome reporting his discussions with the pope and the instructions sent to the nuncio, and urged Antonio to complete his journey, for without his actual presence in Rome little could be accomplished.[32] Already, however, early in June the ambassador had informed Diego de la Encarnación of his determination to complete his mission in Rome and by October he had begun his fateful journey.[33]

When he reached Rome, accompanied by Diego and lodged in the Vatican apartment recently occupied by Cardinal Bellarmine, he was at death's door, and he died on the eve of the feast of Epiphany 1608. Fabio Biondi, by then papal majordomo, presided over a magnificent funeral in Santa Maria Maggiore where his memorial bust is still to be seen, and Paul V took active steps to send a Carmelite mission to Kongo despite the protests of the Spanish and Portuguese representatives in Rome. A decisive challenge to the patronal pretensions of the Iberian powers had been initiated. The sacrificial death of this first

---

31. A.S.V., Misc. Arm. I, 91, f. 241. Certificate signed by the provincial, 10.X.1607. See also f.214 minutes of a letter by Antonio Manuel, 11.V.1607.

32. A.S.V., Misc. Arm. I, 91, f. 229 Pedro de la Madre de Dios to the Ambassador, 24.VII,1607.

33. A.S.V., Misc. Arm. I, 91, f. 220 Diego de la Encarnación to ambassador, Alcalá, 8.VI.1607 and f.253 deposition by Archbishop of Saragoza, 25.X.1607.

ambassador from an African Catholic kingdom was to have profound long-term consequences for the future governance of Catholic missions worldwide, but not immediately. The sudden death in August 1608 of Pedro de la Madre de Dios deprived the missionary enthusiasts in Rome of their leader, and the authorities in Lisbon, much to papal displeasure, were able to prevent Diego and other Carmelite missionaries from sailing to Kongo in 1611. For the moment, the Portuguese Padroado as it affected Kongo was preserved. The idea of reaching Ethiopia via Kongo continued, however, to be canvassed in Rome.

In October 1609, the former assistant of Santori, Girolamo Vecchietti, attempted to confirm papal interest in this route. His long memorandum submitted to Paul V surveyed the various routes to Ethiopia and urged the pope to whom was entrusted "the universal charge of the Church of God" to send a mission to Ethiopia. It is a fascinating, if somewhat fanciful, document, and since he almost certainly had discussed his ideas with Pedro it enables us to understand why the Carmelite leader in Rome espoused the Kongo mission with such energy and enthusiasm. In his memorandum, Girolamo emphasized, and almost certainly exaggerated, the resentment caused in the Ethiopian church by what he termed "the diabolical tyranny" exercised by the patriarchs of Alexandria. Fearing that the Ethiopians would subtract themselves from their jurisdiction, the patriarchs allowed the Ethiopians only one bishop or *abuna,* whereas "considering the extent of the country and the infinite and diverse multitudes of people who inhabit it," four hundred bishops would be too few.

Girolamo excluded both the normal routes to this promising field. In Egypt, he said, the Turks had expressly forbidden that any Latin emissary should be allowed to pass to Ethiopia. The route via Goa reached either from the Levant or from Portugal was very distant and, as Britti's death had illustrated, was extremely dangerous given the Turkish control of the Red Sea. Instead the Kongo kingdom, inhabited by a friendly and Catholic people, was, he maintained, separated from Ethiopia "by a small space of two hundred and fifty or three hundred miles at the most. It is true that it is not greatly frequented and there is no regular communication; nevertheless at a certain time of the year it is customary to hold a fair on the eastern borders of Congo, where many people come together to exchange goods, and from the inner-most parts of the land come some Christians who carry the cross in their hands and who are subject to the King of Ethiopia." Girolamo suggested therefore that the papal mission should attempt to travel in the company of these traders from Ethiopia, or that, at the request of the pope, the king of Kongo should open up this route and develop a regular traffic along it. Girolamo envisaged the establishment of a col-lege in Rome for more than a hundred Ethiopians from whom in the future could be promoted the bishops needed for so vast a territory. He even suggested that the Ethopians, enthused anew by the faith, would set out to convert other peoples, so that "extending to all parts of the great continent, they will even reach the ultimate point of the Cape of Good Hope."[34]

Evidently Girolamo had a fanciful imagination, but in 1609 he enlisted the support of none other than Cardinal Maffeo Barberini, the future Urban VIII, who, Girolamo later claimed, became "thoroughly apprised of the question and with a lively spirit wanted to push it for-ward," presenting the memorandum to Paul V. One of the strangest aspects of Girolamo's memorandum was its total absence of any ref-erence to the activities of the Jesuits in Ethiopia. When proposing a formal papal mission there, one might have expected that the author would have considered the possibility of building on this Catholic foundation. Although for several decades the results of the Jesuit mis-sion in Ethiopia had been relatively meager, it was precisely at this moment that Pedro Paëz and other Jesuits were strongly influencing Susenyos, formally crowned emperor in 1608. One can only speculate that in ignoring the Jesuit role in Ethiopia, Girolamo may have been reflecting an antagonism in at least some quarters in Rome towards the overseas activities of the Portuguese Jesuits, closely linked as they were with the maintenance of Portugal's patronal rights. Certainly the decisions by Clement VIII and Paul V to encourage the Carmelite missions to Persia and to Kongo were direct challenges to what were increasingly seen by some in Rome as pernicious Portuguese patronal pretensions, and it may be that in bypassing the Jesuits, Girolamo was

---

34. Girolamo Vecchietti's memorandum is published in Beccari, *Rerum anthiopi-carum scriptores occidentales,* XI, 176–85.

indicating the initial steps of a strategy which was later to be actively pursued by the Congregation of Propaganda Fide and its founding secretary, Francesco Ingoli. In 1609, however, Cardinal Maffeo, having presented the memorandum to the pope, became more cautious and discussed the proposal with the Jesuits in Rome who, Girolamo reported several years later, maintained that there was no need to take further action.[35]

Girolamo's proposal was therefore laid aside in 1609, but eight years later the idea of opening up a transcontinental route between Kongo and Ethiopia was formally proposed to the ruler of Ethopia by a remarkable Spaniard, Juan Bautista Vives, who had become the resident ambassador in Rome of the king of Kongo. Vives came from a family well established in Valencia since the early fifteenth century, a member of whom had been leading Renaissnce humanist, Juan Luis Vives. Juan Bautista was born in 1545, five years after the death in Louvain of his famous relative. Accounts differ as to the date of his arrival in Rome, but by 1584 he was a doctor in both civil and canon law and was already considered by his native Valencians to be a person of some influence in the Roman Curia, being entrusted by them with various petitions and causes. In 1591 Vives took minor orders as a subdeacon, and in the same year he opened a modest school for training missionaries in his residence in Piazza del Popolo. This was to be a forerunner of far greater things, for he was to be the founder of Propaganda's famous Collegio, but we do not know the origins of his interest in foreign missions. Possibly it was nurtured by his activities for the cause of the Dominican Fray Luis Bertrán, Apostle of New Granada, Colombia, with which the Valencians had entrusted Vives in 1586. Probably Vives had also been influenced by Jean de Vendeville, a professor at Louvain and subsequently bishop of Tournai, who in 1589 had suggested to Sixtus V the foundation of a missionary seminary. Certainly Juan Bautista's missionary interest and activity was strengthened by his friendship with the Carmelite Jerónimo Gracián, who had so actively

---

35. B.A.V. cod. Vat. Lat. 6723, f. 6v. The details concerning the fortunes of his 1609 memorandum are reported in this document written by Girolamo and now bound in a volume of memorandum almost certainly collected by Ingoli soon after the foundation of the new Congregation.

responded in 1580 to Philip II's invitation to send the Carmelites to Kongo, and to whom Vives was introduced in 1595 by Cardinal Deza, General Inquisitor and Protector of Spain.[36]

When the ambassador from Kongo reached Rome in January 1608, Vives was deeply involved in discussing missionary strategy with St. John Leonardi and Martín Funes, a Spanish Jesuit who had been sent to Rome from Colombia to attend the sixth general congregation of the Jesuits. Together the three men drew up a memorandum for Paul V proposing the creation of missionary seminaries in various parts of the world and the creation of a new pontifical congregation working in the Indies "tam Orientis quam Occidentis" as a direct challenge to Spanish and Portuguese patronal rights. This initiative was frustrated by Aquaviva, the Jesuit general, who wishing to respect Spanish rights and work for reforms through the royal council in Madrid, summarily ordered Funes to leave Rome.[37] With these ideas and contacts, Vives must have been brought quickly into contact with the strategists who, after the deaths of the ambassador and of Pedro de la Madre di Dios, were seeking to renew the Carmelite mission to Kongo. When it became obvious that the authorities in Lisbon would prevent the departure of that mission, Vives, at the behest of Paul V, summoned to Rome a man who had been pouring his wealth and energies into the establishment of the Discalced Carmelites in France and the Netherlands.

Brought into contact with St. Teresa's reform by Gracián in Seville in 1582 and subsequently informed that a young Kongo princess had expressed a desire to enter the order, Jean de Brétigny had preserved the dream of establishing Carmelite nuns in Kongo and had written to

---

36. R. Robres, *Vives y Marja, Juan Bautista*, in *Diccionario de historia eclesiastica de España*, IV (Madrid, 1975). See also Juan de Unzalu, "El Perlado Romano, Monseñor Juan Bautista Vives, in *Agencia Fides*, 1.VI. (1946): n.770, and 15.VI.1946, n.772. A. Castellucci, *Mons. Giambattista Vives*, in *Alma Mater,* II (Rome, 1920), 18–41. N. Kowalsky, *Juan Bautista Vives*, in *Enc. Cat. XII* (Città del Vaticano, 1954), 1566–1568. F. Bontinck, "Jean-Baptiste Vives, Ambassadeur des Rois de Congo auprè du Saint-Siege," in *Revue du Clerge Africain*, VII (1952): 258–64. Gracián in the proluge to his *Zelo de la propagación de la Fee* (Madrid, 1616), saluted Vives and on p. 281 praised him for his missionary work.

37. G. Piras, *La Congregazione e il Collegio di Propaganda Fide di J. B. Vives, G. Leonardi e M. de Funes* (Documenta Missionalia, 10; Rome, 1976).

the ambassador in June 1607 telling him of this plan and offering his assistance.[38]

Jean set out for Rome in March 1612 and stayed with Vives until September, offering Paul V very considerable financial assistance for a mission to Kongo. His generosity could not immediately be accepted, but his presence in Rome strengthened curial interest in Kongo, and the following year in a letter to Paul V, the king of Kongo formally appointed Vives as his ambassador in order that he could render obedience to the Holy See "with all solemnity that is customary for royal ambassadors."[39] It was nearly two years before Alvaro's letter was acted on in Rome, but on January 11, 1615, Vives wrote to King Philip III of Spain informing him that on that day the pope had declared him to be the ambassador of King Alvaro II. Vives explained that he would most willingly undertake this office "since this embassy deals solely with the propagation of the faith" and he requested Philip's assent to this appointment. Spanish approval was given finally in January 1616, and not until July 1618 did Rome receive a letter from Alvaro III, who had succeeded to the throne in August 1615, renewing the Kongo king's intention to render formal obedience to the papacy through Vives.[40]

Even before the arrival of Alvaro III's letter, however, Vives had taken two major initiatives. On April 18, 1618, he wrote to the ruler of Ethiopia proposing that he should cooperate with the king of Kongo in opening a route between the two states.[41] Unfortunately, there is no indication from the copy of his letter of the reasons which led Vives to raise this matter at this particular moment, nor is it stated by whom the letter was to be conveyed to Ethiopia. All we know is that about this time Accoramboni, the papal collector in Lisbon, forwarded to Rome an anonymous report concerning "the supposed route from the Kingdom of Kongo to that of Prester John." This report describes how "in our time" a priest called Raffaello di Castro, a native of Jacuman in New Spain, "a man of an enquiring mind (*uomo curioso*) and of great

---

38. P. Sérouet, *Jean de Brétigny (1556–1634). Aux origines du Carmel de France, de Belgique et du Congo* (Louvain, 1974). See also Gray, "A Kongo Princess."

39. Alvaro II to Paul V, 27.XI.1613, in A. Brásio, *Monumenta Missionaria Africana. Africa Occidental*, [I serie] VI (Lisboa, 1955), 128–30.

40. A. Brásio, *Momumenta Missionaria Africana*, VI, 186 and 288.

41. Ibid., 277s.

experience" went to the kingdom of Ocanga[42] and "passed far beyond it in order to obtain information regarding people who wore a wooden cross from the necks and came from the country of Prester John." The anonymous author of this report stated that he had been an eyewitness when Raffaello reported to the king of Kongo on this journey. He stated that he was "sure that, if His Holiness wishes this route to be opened, the king of Congo will immediately do so." He had sometimes heard the king discussing this possibility with his courtiers, and he added the intriguing comment that the opening of this route was "one of the principal matters which the ambassador, Don Antonio Manuele, who died in Rome" had been charged to discuss with the pope.[43] There is no mention of this question in the formal instructions given by Alvaro II to Antonio, nor in any of the correspondence concerning this embassy. Yet the ambassador certainly discussed this possibility, probably with Diego de la Encarnación. A report, written after his death and drawing on information supplied by Diego, states that it was learned from Antonio that "the greater part of these Xacchi" (i.e., Jaga), who previously had presented one of the principal obstacles to opening a route into the interior, "have received the faith."[44]

The letter of Vives to Ethiopia forcibly demonstrates the extent to which these two African Christian kingdoms had become closely linked in the minds of missionary strategists in Rome during the period leading to the foundation of Propaganda Fide. Although the victory at Lepanto had greatly reduced their maritime threat, the Ottomans still represented a major threat to Catholic Europe. The possibility of cooperating with what was still seen as a potentially powerful ally, a concept nurtured originally more than two centuries earlier by the initiatives of the Ethiopian rulers, was now dramatically reinforced by the fact that the kings of Kongo, anxious to enlist papal help against Portuguese patronal claims and the local threats from some Portuguese in Luanda, were manifestly willing to prove their diplomatic obedience, commitment, and loyalty to the papacy. Inevitably Vives' letter

---

42. Okango, on the lower Kwango, at the head of a route going towards the lower middle Kwilu, was a source of slaves from the last quarter of the sixteenth century. J. Vansina, *Paths in the Rainforests* (London, 1990), 201.

43. A. Brásio, *Momumenta Missionaria Africana*, VI, 492.

44. B.A.V., cod. Vat. Lat. 12515, f. 122.

was based on a great degree of ignorance concerning the geographical realities of equatorial Africa, and this particular diplomatic démarche from the newly appointed Kongolese ambassador was doomed to failure, but his other, second, initiative was destined to bring far more important consequences.

The Portuguese refusal to permit the Spanish Carmelites, charged with a papal mission, to set sail from Lisbon had caused considerable distress and anger at the Kongolese court. Their arrival had been eagerly awaited, and in the letter appointing Vives as his ambassador, Alvaro II renewed the request that other missionaries should be sent similar to the Carmelites who had gained "much fruit with their example, teaching, and charitable works." He contrasted this with the behavior of the Portuguese Dominicans sent in their stead, who, he complained, "concerned themselves with business alien to their order."[45] In response to this royal request, Vives approached the Capuchins, and on June 1, 1618, the general chapter of the Capuchin order formally decided to send to Kongo a visitor general with six other Spanish friars "to investigate the situation in that kingdom.[46]

Vives may have hoped to overcome Portuguese objections by relying on the strength and influence of the Capuchins in Spain and by working through his own Valencian contacts with them. Diego de Quiroga, the Capuchin provincial in Valencia, was present at the general chapter and was one of the Capuchins selected for the Kongo mission out of the four hundred Spanish Capuchins who applied for it. Diego was a man of considerable influence, and was later to become preacher and confessor to Philip III. Both Vives and Cardinal Trejo, a Spaniard who had been appointed protector of the kingdom of Kongo, assured the Capuchins that they would be able to obtain Philip III's support for this venture, and the Curia continued to take a lively interest in the proposal. During a visit to Portugal and Spain in 1619, the father general of the Capuchins, St. Lorenzo da Brindisi, recommended the intended mission to Philip III, and in July 1620 Cardinal

---

45. Alvaro II to Paul V, 27.III.1613 in A. Brásio, *Monumenta Missionaria Africana,* VI, 132.

46. Decision of the general chapter in A. Brásio, *Monumenta Missionaria Africana,* VI, 307.

Borghese, the secretary of state, again urged the collector in Lisbon to take up the question. On March 19, 1621, barely a month after his election to the papacy, Gregory XV assured Alvaro III that the Capuchin mission would soon be sailing, but already in Madrid the Council of Portugal had decided to prevent its departure.[47]

The *Missio Antiqua* of the Capuchins would have to wait two decades before finally being able to arrive in Kongo. As a result, however, of its African origins, of the initiatives and appeals of the two African Christian kingdoms, the mission went not primarily to convert the heathens but to bring the sacraments and papal support to what seemed in Rome to be a very notable and significant addition to the ranks of Catholic kingdoms. Doubtless, many other considerations also influenced Gregory XV's decision in 1622 to establish on exceptionally firm foundations the Sacred Congregation of Propaganda Fide, but the appeals from Ethiopia and the sacrificial death of the first Kongolese ambassador had also played their part.

---

47. L. Jadin, "L'oeuvre missionnaire en Afrique noire, in J. Metzler, ed., *Sacrae Congregationis de Propaganda Fide Memoria Rerun*, I/2 (Rome, 1971), 432.

2

A Kongo Princess,
the Kongo Ambassadors,
and the Papacy

With one most notable exception, relatively little is known concerning Christian women in the ancient kingdom of Kongo, whose importance for the history of African Christianity has been so notably demonstrated in Adrian Hastings's great history (Hastings, 1994).[1] Much of the seventeenth-century history of the neighboring kingdom of Matamba is dominated by the exploits of Queen Nzinga, but, apart from the dramatic, tragic, and much studied career of Beatrice Kimpa Vita, very little attention has been given to women in the study of Kongo's ancient history. Yet scattered across the documents from the sixteenth to the early nineteenth century are a number of indications that women played an important, and even at times vital, role in the maintenance and development of Kongo Catholicism. As early as the mid-sixteenth century, a Jesuit reported that the king had decided that "all the women should be gathered into a church called Ambiro," and that it was there that the Jesuits said Mass for them and "taught them to know Our Lord" (Wing, 40–41). A century later, the recognition by the Capuchin missionaries of Garcia II as a Catholic monarch was seriously endangered by his persecution of leading Christian ladies, who from the arrival of the Capuchins were reported to have "daily participated in all the spiritual exercises setting a great example and edification to the court" (Mateo de Anguiano, 365–69). At the end of the seventeenth century and well into the eighteenth, when the unity of the Kongo kingdom had been destroyed and its power dissipated among competing rulers, royal women continued to maintain the faith and warmly welcome Catholic missionaries. Hastings has recently drawn attention to the role of a former queen, Ana Afonso de Leão,

---

1. I am grateful to the Leverhulme Foundation and to the British Academy for assistance in undertaking research in the Vatican and Italian archives.

"a woman of great authority . . . politically responsible and devoutly Catholic" (Hastings, 1998, 151), and her importance, together with that of other Kongolese women, has been amply illustrated in John Thornton's recent, most valuable book (Thornton, 1998). In 1749 Bernardino Ignazio d'Asti reported how a royal widow had been recently visited by a Capuchin in "one of the most remote parts of Kongo." He had been overwhelmed there for almost a month, making four thousand baptisms and hearing the confessions of all the people "who had been prepared for the sacraments by that worthy lady."[2] So far as is known, however, the impact of all these notable Christian women was confined to Kongo itself. Yet in the late sixteenth century the fancy, perhaps fleeting, of a young Kongo princess, through the response which it evoked in Europe, played a part, minor yet significant, in the process which eventually persuaded the papacy to establish in 1622 the Sacred Congregation of Propaganda Fide, which was later to become the most powerful organization in Catholic mission history.

It is a strange story; church historians might even dare to call it providential. A series of fragile, brief, yet powerfully consequential, encounters established a network of Christian contacts which stretched across two continents. Perhaps the most extraordinary was the first: the audience given in the Escorial by Philip II of Spain to Teresa of Avila probably in December 1577. She herself described the meeting as follows:

"Imagine what this poor woman must have felt when she saw so great a King before her. I was terribly embarrassed. I began to address him; but, when I saw his penetrating gaze fixed on me—the kind of gaze that goes deep down to the very soul—it seemed to pierce me through and through; so I lowered my eyes and told him what I wanted as briefly as I could. When I had finished telling him about the matter I looked up at him again. His face seemed to have changed. His expression was gentler and more tranquil. He asked me if I wanted anything further. I answered that what I had asked for was a great deal. Then he said, 'Go away in peace, for everything shall be arranged as you wish . . .' I knelt to thank him for his great favor. He bade me rise, and making

---

2. Archives of Propaganda Fide, Scritture rif. nei Congressi, Angola, V. fol. 180. Memorandum by Bernardino Ignazio d'Asti, December 12, 1749.

this poor nun, his unworthy servant, the most charming bow I ever saw, held out his hand to me again, which I kissed" (Peers, 146). At that time the persecution of her reform was at its height, but within two years Philip recommended to Rome its recognition.

The next chain of events began with the death of King Sebastian of Portugal at the battle of Alcazar-el-Kabir, that total defeat in 1578 of the last attempt by European Christendom to reconquer North Africa by the force of crusading arms. Two years after this death, Philip II of Spain successfully asserted his rights to the Portuguese crown. With bullion from Spanish America already providing a major part of his finances, he was anxious to explore the potential mineral riches of his new African dominions. Additional forces were despatched to Mina to protect the export of West African gold, and the rumors of silver mines in the hinterland of Luanda attracted his attention. Together with these material interests, he was concerned to develop and deepen the Padroado, the ecclesiastical rights and responsibilities which the Portuguese crown had been granted by the papacy in the course of the fifteenth century. Philip was careful not to offend unnecessarily the susceptibilities of his new subjects, and Portuguese affairs in general continued to be administered separately. Yet for a mission to West Africa and Kongo in particular, Philip turned not to one of the orders which had previously sent Portuguese missionaries to the area, but to the order reformed by Teresa of Avila which was attracting some of the most ardent spirits of Spanish Catholicism.

Jerónimo Gracián, the young confidant of the aged saint, had just been elected provincial, and he was informed of the royal wish that the Discalced Carmelites should undertake this mission. By March 1582, five Spanish Carmelites were chosen, instructed by Gracián while their leader received words of encouragement from Teresa herself (Bontinck, 116). Philip himself went down to the port in Lisbon to see them set sail in April. The ship was lost at sea and the priests drowned. The following year a second group of Carmelite missionaries were captured by English pirates, but Philip encouraged Gracián to persevere and a third group set out from Lisbon in 1584. After eleven days of missionary work on the island of São Tomé, the missionaries joined another boat sailing with military reinforcements "sent by our king," as they reported, "to conquer a mountain of silver discovered" in the kingdom of Angola (Florencio, 13–35). The ship's passengers neatly illustrated Philip's parallel, and competing, concerns.

Directly after their arrival in Luanda, the Carmelite missionaries set out for Kongo. When they were near the royal capital, they informed King Alvaro I (r. 1568–87) that they were bringing with them a statue of the Virgin Mary and that they should therefore enter Mbanza Kongo in a solemn procession. Diego de la Encarnación, one of the missionaries, reported that a large crowd watched their entry. He estimated that more than thirty thousand people participated, including one hundred Portuguese merchants resident there. Immediately, he claimed, "a great devotion to the image of the Virgin" developed (Brásio, IV, 395–97). An unnamed princess, one of the four daughters of Alvaro and his canonical wife Dona Catalina, was swept up in this devotion. Seeing the statue clothed in the habit of a Carmelite nun, she asked the reason and was told that this was because the Virgin was the patron of the order of Mount Carmel, and that the nuns were so clothed. Listening to the preaching of the Carmelites, she developed a great desire to enter the Order as a Carmelite nun. She therefore sent a letter about this to Mother Maria de San Jose, prioress of the newly founded convent in Lisbon, who replied to her, promising that she would try to find some way of meeting her wishes.

We know nothing more about this princess, but one of the people to whom Mother Maria spoke about her request was Jean de Brétigny, a young man from Rouen, then the second-most-important town in France (Sérouet, 54). Jean belonged to one of the rich merchant families of Spanish, and often Jewish, origin who dominated the maritime trade of Rouen. His family came from Burgos, in northern Spain, and his relatives there continued to trade with Flanders and France. Jean's grandfather went to Rouen in 1510 and married into a family of Spanish origin, already well established in France, one of its members being a secretary to the king. Jean's father married into an old landed family and continued to prosper in trade. Jean, his eldest son, was born in 1556, but at the age of six he was sent to live with an uncle in Seville until 1570, probably to avoid the turmoil and violence of the religious wars in France. As a young teenager he returned to Rouen, and then in 1581 he was asked by his father to go back to Seville to undertake various business affairs for him. By this time, however, Jean was more interested in religion than in his family's business, and, with his father's consent, he first accompanied a group of Flemish Franciscan nuns to Lisbon, helping them to find a refuge there. Reaching Seville in 1582, he was introduced by a Spanish friend to Mother Maria de San Jose, then prioress of the Carmelite convent there. She sent him to Jerónimo Gracián, and for several months Jean attended the novitiate exercises of the Carmelites while also undertaking his father's business affairs. Under the influence of Gracián, Maria, and their colleagues, Jean began to learn that the ultimate aim of the Discalced Carmelites was not the individual perfection of their members, but the furtherance of the kingdom of God. Gradually they encouraged Jean to devote his considerable financial resources to this end (Sérouet, 2–51).

In 1584 Maria was sent to establish the convent in Lisbon, and soon Jean was entrusted with organizing, financing, and accompanying a caravan of reinforcements from Seville to Lisbon. While he was there in 1585, Maria must have informed him about the princess in Kongo, for Jean never forgot this plea from the princess. In 1585, however, there was little that either he or Mother María could do to respond to it immediately. By then St. Teresa had died, and in May Gracián was succeeded as provincial by Nicholas Jesús-María Doria, who did not share Gracián's enthusiasm for overseas missions. The Carmelites in Kongo, left with no reply to their requests for support and reinforcements, decided to return to Europe (Sérouet, 54–57).

The next initiatives came from Kongo, and there is one small but intriguing piece of evidence which indicates that the request of the princess may have been more than a fleeting fancy on the part of one individual. While Philip II had been encouraging the Carmelites to send a mission to western Africa, Alvaro I was instructing Duarte Lopez, a Portuguese trader who had been living at his court since 1578, to go as his envoy to Philip and also to the pope (Bal, 11). The instructions given to Lopez for his mission to Rome, signed by the king on January 15, 1583, reveal some of the motivations which led Alvaro to seek to enter into a closer relationship with the papacy.[3] Alvaro clearly recognized Rome as a major source of the spiritual power and strength with which he wished to surround his office and his people. His envoy was ordered "in the first instance to inform His Holiness in detail concerning what happens and takes place in these my kingdoms, to tell him the need that exists for ministers for so many Christian souls, and to ask for relics, indulgences and blessed objects so that with greater courage and devotion we may make progress in the service of God." In the case of many European embassies in the sixteenth century, such requests and petitions might indicate little more than a customary mode of approaching the papacy. In the case of Kongo, they represented an urgent and serious demand. In the continuous cosmological conflict with evil as experienced in this African kingdom, such requests to a new source of spiritual power had lost nothing of their validity and immediacy, as is indicated by other details in the instructions.

Lopez was told to negotiate "that matter which you have learned by heart from me in our discussions, in the hope that you will carry this through with diligence worthy of the trust in which I hold you." In all probability the hidden agenda thus committed to Lopez concerned the possibility of liberating Kongo from the restrictions and burdens of Portuguese patronal claims, particularly as exercised by the Portuguese bishop of São Tomé. Alvaro and his predecessors had come into conflict with the bishop and other Portuguese ecclesiastical emissaries, including the first Portuguese Jesuits in Kongo. Tension had arisen especially over Kongo practices which contravened canon law marriage. Alvaro clearly wished to have far greater control over the nature and development of Kongo Christianity. He also specifically raised the issue of indigenous religious orders. Lopez was told to insist that Alvaro should be given permission "to provide in these kingdoms orders of monks and nuns" and that suitable people in Kongo should be allowed to enter these orders. Lopez should also ask for papal bulls for the principal churches and confraternities, and for "an image of Our Lady, copied directly from one of the four painted by St. Luke" with

---

3. The original instructions were in Portuguese, but they are known to us only through an Italian translation held in the Vatican archives. They have been published by Brásio, III, 234–35, and by Filesi (1968) with a facsimile, 143–45.

the indulgences attached to it. Most probably this request referred to the thirteenth-century painting, popularly attributed to St. Luke, in the Basilica of Santa Maria Maggiore in Rome. We do not know who had told Alvaro about this, but in 1569 Francis Borgia had sent a copy of it to Queen Caterina in Portugal (Suau, 414), after whom Alvaro's canon-law wife, as opposed to his other wives, was named. His interest in this painting, and especially his specific request on behalf of Kongolese nuns, provides a fascinating background to his daughter's desire to become a Carmelite nun. It forcibly suggests that the idea of entering a religious order was not a novelty for women attached to the royal court at Mbanza Kongo.

When Lopez eventually reached Rome, the pope, Sixtus V, was unwilling to respond actively to Alvaro's initiative. Beset by the disastrous religious wars in France and many other problems, he was reluctant to challenge Philip's patronal rights. Doubtless he was also aware of the logistical difficulties of sending to Kongo an independent missionary expedition. The critical, ongoing contact with Rome was made by Alvaro II, who succeeded his father in 1587. Seven years later, his close relative, Antonio Vieira, arrived in Lisbon, charged with negotiating the creation of a separate diocese for Kongo. He quickly established a close and friendly relationship with Fabio Biondi, the papal representative in Lisbon. Vieira gave Biondi a lively, detailed account of the practice of the faith in Mbanza Kongo (Brásio, III, 502–3). Already the king and his notables were members of six lay confraternities, actively supporting and participating in their activities, which included attendance at a weekly Mass offered in part for the souls of previous members.[4] Kongo respect and veneration for the ancestors was gradually becoming subsumed into orthodox Catholic practice.

Above all, Biondi was deeply impressed by Vieira's Christian character and knowledge. An indication of the impact which the Kongolese ambassador made on Biondi can be glimpsed in the letters of recommendation that the papal collector wrote on his behalf when Vieira

---

4. I have stressed elsewhere (Gray, 1990, 45) the role of the confraternities in strengthening Christian commitment in late-seventeenth-century Soyo. Following Cavazzi's account, I had wrongly assumed that these confraternities were an innovation introduced to Kongo by the Capuchins.

was setting out from Lisbon for a visit to Madrid. Biondi informed the Archbishop of Evora that the ambassador merited a warm welcome on account of his personal qualities and "particularly for his religious commitment." He added that in view of the remoteness of Kongo, God should be praised that there were Christians there "of this quality." To the nuncio in Madrid, he affirmed that Vieira was "a very good Christian and devoted to the Apostolic See." On a later occasion Biondi admitted to being astonished at the fact that the ambassador was "very well instructed in Christian doctrine and in ecclesiastical history."[5]

As a result of these contacts, Biondi despatched in November 1595 a long and very optimistic report to Rome on the nature of Kongo Christianity, warmly supporting the request for a diocese to be created separate from that of São Tomé (Cuvelier & Jadin, 194–207). The Portuguese Mesa de Consciência in Lisbon also supported the request, and recommended to Philip that the bishop of São Salvador, or Mbanza Kongo, should be given by the crown the same salary as that of São Tomé (Brásio, III, 480–81). With this recommendation, the council maintained the assumption that Kongo, although an independent kingdom, fell within the Portuguese Padroado. Its members may well have thought that the presence of a Portuguese bishop, paid for by the crown, would not only strengthen the faith but also serve Portuguese interests, since Alvaro II, unlike his father, had already been involved in hostile exchanges with the Portuguese settlers in Angola.

Since Vieira's request was thus supported both by the papal representative and by Philip II, with the Portuguese crown meeting the expenses, the papacy had no hesitation in creating the new diocese of São Salvador, approved at the consistory held on May 20, 1596 (Brásio, III, 490). Already, however, Biondi's links with Kongo, and his admiration for its people, had been strengthened. A letter written by Alvaro II in the previous September had just reached him in Lisbon. In it Alvaro thanked the pope for "the favors and honors" shown by the papal collector to his ambassador, and asked, as a result of a letter he had received from Biondi, for further assistance from the papacy (Brásio,

---

5. Vatican Archives, Fondo Confalonieri, 28, f. 401, Biondi to Archbp of Evora, 27.XI.1595, and f. 566v. to nuncio, same date, and f. 678-678v. to Silvio Antoniano, 31.VIII.1596.

III, 490–91). Biondi reported how the messengers carrying the letter had been seized by English "pirates" and taken to England. Ill-treated, only with difficulty had they been able to save the letter from destruction. The whole story prompted Biondi to a further affirmation of his interest and affection for the people of Kongo. Forwarding it to Cardinal Aldobrandino, the pope's secretary of state, Biondi said that "they were people of great common sense," and the ambassador and "those who come from that kingdom give a very good account of their faith, which for me is exceeding wonderful, having so great a lack of priests who can instruct them. One could well say that the harvest is plentiful but the laborers are few indeed."[6] His admiration was about to launch the papacy on a confrontation with the Padroado rights which was gradually, yet inexorably, to grow in intensity.

Pope Clement VIII read Alvaro's letter to all the cardinals in consistory, warmly invited him to send ambassadors to Rome, and also sent him a plenary indulgence (Brásio, III, 544). Vieira left Lisbon in March 1597, taking with him the papal brief and a long letter from Biondi to Alvaro II, congratulating the king on the fact that the Bishop of São Tomé would no longer have occasion to trouble him. Biondi warmly underlined the papal invitation to send an ambassador to Rome "as do all Christian Kings." This, wrote Biondi, would result in Alvaro's "great glory and elevation," and he assured the king that the ambassador would be "received and honored by His Holiness with every honour and paternal affection."[7] These phrases proved to be no mere diplomatic niceties, for Biondi was to be highly instrumental in turning them into reality.

On his return to Kongo, Vieira discussed with Alvaro the possibility of sending an embassy to Rome. Alvaro accepted the proposal, but during the preparations Vieira died, and it was not until June 1604 that another ambassador was finally given his formal instructions. Alvaro chose his cousin, Antonio Manuele Nsaku ne Vunda, a man in his early thirties, who was to be described in Rome by those who saw him

---

6. Vatican Archives, Fondo Confalonieri 27, f. 178v–79, Biondi to Aldobrandino, 11.V.1596.

7. Vatican Archives, Fondo Confalonieri 28, f. 495v, Biondi to Alvaro II, 18.IX.1596. See Confalonieri 27, ff. 203, 213, 227, 238 for letters from Biondi to Aldobrandino dated 31.VIII.1596 to 15.III.1597 concerning Vieira's plans and movements.

as someone "of noble manners and above all pious and devout, also endowed with strength and prudence in diplomacy."[8] The embassy arrived in Lisbon in November 1605, but then they encountered many delays. When the ambassador eventually reached Madrid, he was confronted by the authorities with stern and vigorous attempts to dissuade him from proceeding to Rome. The situation facing the ambassador was becoming desperate in the extreme. Alvaro was reported to have sent his embassy equipped with at least twenty-five attendants, but it was supplied merely with shell currency.[9] Although this was very effective when conducting commercial transactions with the Portuguese in Luanda, as soon as the embassy left the African coast it ran into financial difficulties. According to a petition, the embassy had left Lisbon with very considerable debts to traders there, and as late as June 1607 the authorities in Madrid still hoped that the ambassador could be persuaded to entrust his mission to the Portuguese and Spanish envoys in Rome (Brásio V, 261–63, 311). Antonio eventually found board and lodgings in Madrid with the Mercedarians, an order whose principal task was to redeem Christian captives taken by North African Muslim corsairs. But besides being a pauper, he was now a very sick man, suffering severely from gallstones. After Antonio had been in the house for three months, the Mercedarian provincial reported that his way of life had given them all "a very great example." He only went out of the house "to discuss the affairs of his embassy with the king or with his ministers. For the rest of the time he stayed in his room, suffering greatly "with very great patience submitting himself to the Will of God."[10]

At this critical juncture, the Discalced Carmelites intervened. Most members of the reformed order in Spain were still extremely hostile to Gracián's overseas missionary interests; indeed Gracián himself had been expelled from the order in 1592 by his successor Nicholas de Jesús-María. In Rome, however, the situation was completely different. Here the leader of the Discalced Carmelites was in the forefront

8. Vatican Library, Vat.Lat. 12516, f. 43v, a report almost certainly drawing on information from Biondi amongst others.

9. Vatican Library Urb.Lat. 1076, f. 5v-6. Avvisi di Roma, 5.I.1608.

10. Vatican Archives Misc. Armadio I, 91, f. 241. Certificate signed by the provincial, 10.X.1607.

of curial strategic planning. The menace of Ottoman expansion in the Balkans, which threatened Austria, Bohemia, and Poland, and also the Turkish raids on the Italian coast, which caused terror in Rome, powerfully influenced what papal interest there was in sub-Saharan Africa at this time. Beyond Ottoman power, long enshrouded in medieval myth, the kingdom of Prester John or Ethiopia had emerged in the minds of missionary strategists as a potential ally of very great significance. Toward the end of his life, St. Ignatius had devoted a great deal of time and energy in sending to Ethiopia the most extensive mission ever launched by the founder of the Jesuits. Later, the first major attempt in Rome to establish a curial congregation charged with supervising and organizing the propagation of the faith, under the able direction of the remarkable Cardinal Santori, had been very largely concerned with strengthening the ties between Rome and the Christian communities within or neighboring the Ottoman empire. And Ethiopia had a position of prime importance among these Christians on the underbelly of the Ottomans. Already it was believed that control of the Nile waters by its Christian emperor could be a key to the mastery of Egypt. After Santori's death in 1602 the nascent curial congregation was allowed to wither, but leadership of these papal and missionary strategies devolved upon Pedro de la Madre de Dios, the gifted and outstanding Spanish leader of the Italian province of Discalced Carmelites. Clearly involved in the decision to send a mission to Persia, whose ruler had defeated an Ottoman army in 1603, he was often called upon to advise Paul V on Middle Eastern questions. He took a leading part in directing the negotiations with the Coptic church in Egypt, and in an undated memorandum to the pope he highlighted the importance of fostering relations with Ethiopia through the Ethiopian monks in Jerusalem.[11]

Together with some of Santori's former assistants, Pedro had become deeply interested in investigating the feasibility of developing a transcontinental route from Kongo to Ethiopia. From the early sixteenth century an exaggerated idea of the southward extension of Ethiopia to the equator had lent credence to the belief that the journey from Kongo to Ethiopia would be a relatively easy undertaking.

11. OCD archives in Rome 281e Cartapaccio f. 27–27v. See also Buri, 237–53.

As soon as Pedro learned of Antonio Manuele's arrival in Madrid, he wrote to Tomás de Jesús, a leading young Spanish Carmelite who was already a key figure in the conflict between contemplative and missionary vocations within the reformed order. Tomás's primary objective had been to promote the hermetical way of life, but gradually the needs of the missions both in Europe and overseas were brought before him. Pedro told Paul V that he hoped Tomás would take charge of a projected mission to Kongo and from there "open a route to Prester John." At first Tomás remained firmly set against accepting this mission, even when informed of the pope's approval, but while saying Mass one day he became convinced that he should accept this challenge, and immediately he began to collect information concerning "the lands and languages of Congo and the Abyssinians" (Joseph de Santa Teresa, t.iv, libro xvii, cap 39). Pedro also contacted Diego de la Encarnación, a member of the 1584 mission to Kongo, ordering him to assist the ambassador in his attempt to reach Rome. The papal nuncio was also instructed to help, and eventually in October 1607 Antonio Manuele set out from Madrid, together with the nuncio, being joined en route by Tomás and Diego.

They reached Rome on January 3, 1608. As Adrian Hastings has said, there seemed at that moment "a great and not entirely illusory hope for the conversion of Africa ... well, if ambiguously, symbolized" by the ambassador's arrival "that strangest of events in our history" (Hastings 1994, 126–27). Antonio Manuele was in a pitiable state. All but four of his attendants had died, among them at Livorno a nephew to whom he was deeply attached. From Civitavecchia he had been carried to Rome, where Fabio Biondi, now majordomo to Paul V, had assigned to the ambassador the rooms in the Vatican palace recently used by Cardinal Bellarmine. The pope visited him on his death bed and administered the last sacraments. After his death on the eve of the Feast of the Epiphany, Biondi personally arranged and supervised a magnificent funeral in Santa Maria Maggiore (Filesi, 1970).

Even before the ambassador had arrived in Rome, the papacy was prepared for a public confrontation with Philip III over the patronal powers of Spain and Portugal. Paul V had instructed the secretariat of state to begin preparations for sending a Carmelite mission to Kongo

(Brásio V, 362–63), and had decided to receive the ambassador in public consistory "despite the opposition of the Spaniards who maintain that this kingdom is tributary to them."[12] Antonio Manuele's death, followed by that of Pedro de la Madre de Dios in August, delayed the preparations for the Carmelite mission, but eventually on October 4, 1610, Paul V informed Philip III that it was setting out and asked for assistance for it (Brásio V, 617–19). A year later Cardinal Borghese, the secretary of state, informed Diego de la Encarnación that the news that he and the other Carmelite missionaries had been prevented from leaving Lisbon for Kongo had caused the pope "great displeasure" (Brásio VI, 41). The papal collector at Lisbon was ordered to brush aside "the pretext for this impediment" and to emphasize to the authorities the damage that this would cause to Christianity in Kongo and "in preventing the conversion of neighboring kingdoms."[13] The nuncio in Madrid was reminded of "the irreparable harm" that this obstruction would involve, and he was told that "since the affair is public knowledge, it would damage the reputation of this Holy See" (Brásio VI, 42–43). Curial concern over Ethiopia and Kongo, the two Christian kingdoms in Africa, had thus become a matter of vital interest for the papacy. Rome lacked the ships, finance, and human resources immediately to turn its missionary interest in Kongo into reality. The desire to foster the development of Kongo Christianity had, however, become an integral feature of the papal challenge to the Portuguese Padroado. A critical fracture had opened between Iberian colonial expansion and Catholic missionary enterprise.

When it became obvious that this papal missionary initiative was being effectively blocked by the patronal powers, Paul V began the search for financial resources. He summoned Jean de Brétigny to Rome. Jean had by no means forgotten the plea of the Kongo princess about which he had been told by Maria de San Jose in Lisbon over twenty years previously. In the meantime he had devoted much time, and a large measure of his considerable financial resources, in a patient, persistent effort to bring the Discalced Carmelite nuns across

---

12. Vatican Library, Urb.Lat. 1076 Pt.1, f. 19, Avvisi di Roma, 9.I.1608. See also Brásio V, 367, for report by the Portuguese agent.

13. Vatican Archives, Confalonieri 43, f. 96v, Borghese to Collector, 12.X.1611.

the Pyrenees to France and to Flanders. Several of the Spanish nuns who had been intimate assistants of St. Teresa keenly supported his endeavors, but with the religious wars in France and the hostilities between the French and Spanish kingdoms, it was no easy matter. In 1594 he had failed to obtain permission from Philip II and the authorities of the Discalced order in Spain to allow the nuns to go to such hostile territory. In 1604, while Antonio Manuele was setting out on his mission to Lisbon, Madrid, and Rome, Jean de Brétigny, ably guided by Pierre de Bérulle, finally obtained authority to bring four Spanish nuns to found the Carmel of Paris. Three days after the formal foundation of the Paris Carmel in October, Queen Marie de Médicis thanked him warmly for the present which he had brought to France (Sérouet, 107–98). By 1607 several other convents had been established in France with Jean's help, and in June, when he first heard of the presence in Spain of the embassy from Kongo, he was in Brussels as confessor to the first convent just being founded in Flanders.

Immediately, on June 7, 1607, Jean sat down to write to the ambassadors of the "province of Guinea" as he loosely described the area from which they came. He poured out his soul in the letter. He told them how he had held "a special joy for a plan which for some years I have held for the salvation of souls in those areas of Guinea" (*un particular gozo por un desseo que de algunos anos a tengo ala salud de las almas de aquellas partes de Guinea.*) God had conserved within him "for twenty-two years" the idea of sending Discalced Carmelite nuns to those parts in order to instruct young girls (*las donzellas*), for he thought this was the best way to bring them to know and to love "as their husband Jesus Christ and to offer him their virginity and service" (*al esposo Jesu Christ y ofresçerles su Virginidad y servicio*). He told the ambassadors that he was ready to do all that was necessary and to go to Africa himself. He asked them to let him know if they agreed, or at least to reply to him when they had returned, sending their letters care of the convents at Lisbon, Seville, Madrid, or Salamanca. Antonio Manuele was never able to reply to this letter, but he took it with him to Rome along with many other treasured papers, which, on his death, were entrusted to Diego de la Encarnación, and are now in the

Vatican archives.[14] It was probably via this letter that Jean de Brétigny's interest in Kongo, inspired by the unknown princess, became known to the little group of missionary strategists gathered around Pedro de la Madre de Dios. The pope's summons to Jean was notified to him by a remarkable Spanish cleric, Juan Bautista Vives, who had long been a friend of Gracián and had developed a keen interest in the work of overseas missions. Jean set out for Rome in March 1612 and he lodged in Vives's house during the months that he stayed there. In two audiences with the pope, he promised very considerable financial support for a mission to Kongo, and offered to go there himself to help though he was then 56 years old (Sérouet, 286–88). His generous offers could not immediately be utilized, but his presence in Rome maintained and strengthened curial interest in Kongo. The following year in a letter to Paul V, dated November 27, 1613, Alvaro II formally appointed Vives as his ambassador in order that he could render obedience to the Holy See "with all the solemnity that is customary for royal ambassadors" (Brásio, VI, 128–30). The challenge to the Padroado involved in such a proclamation of Kongo's independence from Portugal would continue. Vives was to make the initial approach to the Capuchins to send a mission to Kongo, and he was to play a notable part in the events leading to the foundation of Propaganda Fide.

Many factors and many people had combined together to produce in Kongo a firm commitment to the papacy as the institution which provided the focus and final legitimation of their identity as African Christians. When eventually in 1645 Propaganda Fide managed to introduce its own emmisaries into Kongo, they went not as evangelists to a non-Christian country, but as dedicated priestly reinforcements, bringing the sacraments of salvation and committed to strengthening the link with Rome. The Capuchins immediately recognized that Kongo, as represented by Garcia II and its male and female ruling elite, was a Catholic kingdom. These missionaries, like their confreres in many of those areas still ruled by Catholic monarchs in Europe, would

---

14. Vatican Archives. Misc.Armadio I, 91, f. 222. Jhoan de quintana, uenas. The final five letters of his signature have been torn away, Brussels, 7.VI.1607. This letter provides further valuable proof of the sources quoted by Sérouet concerning the appeal of the Kongo princess.

find much to criticize and condemn in the faith and morals of the ruler and his subjects to whom they came as ministers. They rejoiced, however, to witness the strength of Kongo's loyalty to the pope. They even seem to have found it in no way remarkable that Garcia could believe that the papal monarch, so remote and difficult to contact, could be persuaded to alter radically, yet effectively, the established Kongo custom of electing and legitimating royal succession (Gray, 1997, 294-95).

The extraordinary hopes which the Kongo kings placed in the papacy were the result of much that had happened ever since Afonso Mvemba Nzinga had been baptized in 1491 by the Portuguese pioneers, who likewise accepted Rome as the final arbiter of their faith. The Catholic Church is nothing if not an institution, even if it may well be more than that. In that institution, the papacy has a position of undisputed primacy, however much its members may criticize and seek to manipulate or reform it. The ruling Kongo elite, like its Portuguese counterpart, did not dream of disputing the primacy of the pope. In cementing this linkage and the fundamental commitment to the papacy, the request of an otherwise unknown princess and the sacrificial death of an ambassador had played their part.

3

Ingoli, the Collector of Portugal, the "Gran Gusto" of Urban VIII, and the Atlantic Slave Trade

In numerous articles and in four chapters of his great work on the history of the Sacred Congregation of Propaganda Fide, a work which is the indispensable starting point for any serious study of Catholic missions in modern history, Father Joseph Metzler has clearly established the immense contribution of Francesco Ingoli, the Congregation's first secretary.[1] When founding the Congregation, Pope Gregory XV had given it great potential. Not only had he entrusted it with curial jurisdiction over all mission territories in Europe, the Middle East, and the lands of the new discoveries, but he had also taken the exceptional step of providing it with independent control of its own financial resources. That this potential was rapidly translated into reality was, however, almost entirely due to Ingoli.

Born in 1578 to a well-established family in Ravenna, as a clever canon lawyer Ingoli had worked for Cardinal Bonifacio Caetani, papal governor of the Romagna, who took him to Rome on the conclusion of his governorship. An able linguist, who included Greek and Arabic among his languages, with wide scientific and pastoral interests, Ingoli had become auditor to Cardinal Lancellotti on Caetani's death, and was appointed preceptor to Ludovico Ludovisi, the nephew of Gregory XV and who, on his uncle's accession to the papacy, had been created cardinal and appointed secretary of state. Ingoli was therefore already well known in Rome and particularly to the Ludovisi family when Gregory appointed him secretary to the newly formed congregation.[2]

1. J. Metzler, ed., Sacrae Congregationis de Propaganda Fide *Memoria Rerum* 11 (Rome, 1971),chapters II, III, V, VI.

2. J. Metzler, Memoria Rerum 1/1 200–203 N. Kowalsky, Il testamento di Mons. Ingoli primo segretario della Sacra Congregatione "de Propaganda Fide," in NZM (*Neue Zeitschrift für Missionswissenschaft*) XIX (Schoneck, 1963), 78.

Ingoli quickly established himself at the center of an unrivalled information network. One of his first actions was to request papal nuncios and all the heads of religious orders to report to the congregation on matters affecting the mission territories. As the reports came in, Ingoli single-handedly summarized them, seizing hold of the principal points. Supplementing these reports by personal contacts and correspondence with missionaries and others in Rome, he constructed a clear strategy for the congregation which in many essential ways it has continued to pursue until the present day.

One source of these reports was Lisbon, where since 1580 with the incorporation of Portugal in the Spanish crown, the papal representative was termed collector rather than nuncio. Ingoli was well served by the officers in this post. Antonio Albergati, appointed to Lisbon in 1621, had previously served as nuncio in Cologne since 1610. He had close contacts with the Jesuits in Portugal and a keen interest in their missions, including those in Africa.[3] But perhaps Lorenzo Tramallo was the collector who most assisted Ingoli, and some of his reports and their reception in Rome provide an interesting insight into the process by which Ingoli shaped the nascent policy of the congregation. Born at Portovenere on the Ligurian coast a year earlier than Ingoli, Tramallo became a protégé and vicar general of Cardinal S. Sisto. In September 1626 he was appointed Bishop of Gerace and on March 1, 1627, he became collector in Lisbon.[4]

Three years later, on March 26, 1630, Ingoli informed Tramallo that his letters of the previous year had been referred by Cardinal Teodoro Trivulzi to a meeting of the congregation held in the Quirinali Palace in the presence of Pope Urban VIII. The pope and cardinals had listened to the account with great pleasure and interest ("con gran gusto"). As

3. CP (Congregazione Particolari in the archives of Propaganda Fide) 1, f. 414–17, Albergati, Relatione delle missioni fatte per l'Asia, Africa e Brasil, Lisbon, March 4, 1623.

4. Enzo D'Agostino, I *Vescovi di Gerace-Locri* (Chiaravalle, 1981) 128–33. The author does not identify which cardinal held the title S. Sisto, but I assume he refers to the Genoese Laudivio Zacchia, who was created Cardinal of S. Sisto by Urban VIII earlier in 1626. G. Moroni, *Dizionario storico-ecclesiatica* CIII (Venice, 1861) gives the date as January 19, 1626. His title was changed to that of S. Pietro in Vincoli on September 17, 1629, but I presume that Ingoli's later reference to S. Sisto (see below) still refers to Zacchia.

the letters contained some very important points, Urban had ordered that they should be referred to Trivulzi and four prelates for very careful consideration in order that he himself and the congregation could decide on a reply.[5] Since Tramallo's letters were to raise some major issues involving the Spanish crown, the appointment of the young Trivulzi to lead this committee was of some significance. Of a well-known noble Milanese family, he had served in the army of King Philip III of Spain and had married a princess of Monaco, who died after bearing him a son. After further diplomatic service for Philip III, he took holy orders and on November 19, 1629, he had been created a cardinal when he was 32 years old. He also acted as minister for the king of Spain in Rome.[6]

What then were these points which had so aroused the interest of the pope and cardinals? The crucial letter, that of December 15, 1629,[7] was principally concerned with the issue of recruiting Indians into the priesthood and religious orders in the context of the diminished financial resources of Portugal and the expansion of the Muslim Mughul empire. After extensive discussions with missionaries from India, Tramallo was convinced that the slight progress of the faith in India arose from the refusal of these missionaries to ordain Indians. They alleged that Indians were unstable in character and they also claimed that Indians would not obey bishops from Europe. This would provoke schisms, and it would be more difficult to convert heretics than mere pagans. Against these arguments, Tramallo pointed out that the Christians of St. Thomas "had preserved the Christian faith for so many centuries in the midst of so many pagans without any assistance from Europe." He was certain that many Indians, used to fasting and abstinence, could be recruited into seminaries and colleges to be trained for the priesthood, and that they could propagate the Faith "in their own nations far more easily than could European priests."[8]

---

5. Lettere (Lettere in the archives of Propaganda Fide) 10, f. 8.

6. G. Moroni, *Dizionario storico-ecclesiatica*.

7. In his letter of March 26, 1630, Ingoli referred to letters from Tramallo dated September 20 and December 10, 1629, together with a copy of one dated September 9, 1628. The latter referred to a copy of the bull *Omnimoda* and that of September 20, 1629, was merely a reply to one from Cardinal Borgia (SOCG = Scritture Originali riferite nelle Congregazioni Generali in archive of Propaganda Fide 98, f. 53). The date of December 10 must be an error, for Tramallo's letter is clearly dated December 15.

8. SOCG 131, f. 385–86v.

Ingoli was already convinced of the vital significance of creating an indigenous clergy, and he had immediately minuted that Tramallo's letter was of great importance.[9] Urban VIII however, having listened with great interest to this report, directed attention to yet another aspect of the situation. While Trivulzi's committee was deliberating, the pope wanted the collector to report on the means by which revenue could be put together in the East Indies to sustain missions, not merely to convert pagans but also to oppose the progress of the Muslims.[10]

This request rapidly prompted a further batch of letters from Tramallo dated June 8, 1630. One dealt in detail with the financial problem. He began by reminding Rome that the church in the Indies had no revenue or property. Tithes were collected by the king who paid the salaries and made provision for bishops and clergy, but the royal revenue in India had greatly diminished following the Dutch incursion. He listed therefore a series of possible measures. He proposed that some of the funds due to Rome from Portugal might be applied to the Indies and that if, as seemed likely, the crown asked the papacy for a further tax on ecclesiastics, some of the proceeds might be reserved for the propagation of the faith. He suggested that although the king's ministers had almost extinguished the system of spoils, yet one could negotiate with the king that in the Indies, Angola, and Brazil, "where the church is primitive and placed in such need," the proceeds or at least half of them could be used for the missions. He considered that this system was "even more needed for the service of God and of souls than for its temporal benefit, great though that should be. For while bishops and ecclesiastics stay in the missionary territories with the desires of acquiring wealth and lands they forget the needs of souls."

This point led Tramallo to remark that it seemed to him that many members of religious orders went overseas to collect money rather than souls, and he proceeded to consider certain remedies. First of all he suggested that the other orders should follow the example of the Jesuits and send only volunteers overseas. "In all the other, to a great degree either Love or Hatred is often involved, since if a superior wishes to be rid of an odious subject, or grant a favor to a friend

9. SOCG 131, f. 387v.
10. Lettere 10, f. 28–28v.

unsuited for Europe, he imposed an obedience for India, where they pursue anything other than the service of God." Secondly, no religious should be allowed to send gifts home save with their superior's permission. Thirdly, he explained that, whereas in the first months after taking up the collectorship he had thought that religious should not be prevented from returning to Europe, now "experience has convinced me that this would be beneficial, since almost all those who return (if not for a public cause) come merely to bring back their gains." To enforce these remedies, Tramallo suggested that a congregation, subordinate to Propaganda Fide, should be established in Goa.[11]

In another letter of the same date, Tramallo sent Cardinal Trivulzi a wide-ranging survey of the problems facing the missions in India, Angola, and Brazil. He thought that in each of these areas a great pathway for the propagation of the faith was open, especially in India, not only because of its size but also because of "the ability and intellect of its cultured people."

Even if the Muslims were expanding, there were still many others with whom one could build "an immense church," and the Muslims there were not as actively hostile as those nearer Europe. In a memorable phrase, he asserted, however, that "that church will be forever a weak little girl [una Bambina senza forze] if the doors are not opened to the natives, and if seminaries and colleges are not established to train candidates capable of preaching the Gospel in their mother tongue."[12]

Turning to the situation in Angola, he thought that, although the king (presumably of Kongo) was a Christian, the faith was no longer advancing there. The bishops and perhaps the other ecclesiastics who were sent there set themselves to accumulate riches; the people, although definitely less civilized than in India, had, however, this good quality that "even if they fall back into their practices, generally they do not ever abandon the faith once they have accepted it, even if in an uninstructed form." Then abruptly he added the following fact:

---

11. SOCG 98, f. 91–93.

12. In view of the fact that Ingoli picked up this phrase some eight years later (see Metzler, *Memoria Rerum* 1/1, 178), it is interesting to note that the word "Bambina" was added by Tramallo in his own handwriting, his scribe having left a space, perhaps hesitant about the use of this term.

Every year twelve to fourteen thousand Negroes are purchased there, having been enslaved by those who are more powerful, or in their wars, or even sold by their own relatives for an extremely cheap price, and immediately baptized they are shipped to the Indies or Brazil to work in the mines and other undertakings in which they are rapidly consumed.[13]

Tramallo made no further comment on this appalling situation, yet his laconic statement, as we shall see, brought possibly for the first time the evils of the Atlantic slave trade to the attention of the pope and cardinals of Propaganda Fide.

Cardinal Trivulzi reported the receipt of these letters to a meeting of the congregation on September 6, 1630, and they were referred to a small committee of four cardinals,[14] for whom Ingoli prepared one of the series of influential memoranda which helped to shape the major strategy of the congregation towards the overseas mission territories. Ingoli firmly opposed the collector's suggestion that a subordinate congregation should be established in Goa. He maintained that this would inevitably carry the risk of introducing confusion and discord between missionaries of that congregation and those of Rome. He preferred that subordinate congregations should be formed in Lisbon and Madrid under the collector and nuncio respectively, for in this way "they would depend totally on the Apostolic See." In addition, he thought that "two Italian officials, delegated from the Holy See," could perhaps be sent to Goa and Mexico with limited powers.[15]

Even so limited an injection of influential foreigners into their patronal areas would, however, have encountered fierce opposition from the authorities in Lisbon and Madrid and Ingoli's response to the collector's main suggestion clearly illustrates the fundamental dilemma which confronted Propaganda Fide. If its powers would not be delegated effectively to local representatives, the long and tenuous lines of communication between Rome and the mission territories via Lisbon and Madrid resulted in its wishes, and even its commands,

---

13. SOCG 98, f. 77–79.

14. Acta (in archive of Propaganda Fide) 7, f. 132. No. 27 of September 6, 1630.

15. SOCG 98 f. 97v. In an earlier letter to Tramallo, Ingoli expressed the wish to see a congregation for the Indies meeting regularly every month under the collector: Lettere 10, f. 83–83v.

being disregarded to the point of continuing to inflict serious damage to the whole overseas missionary enterprise. On the other hand, if the congregation took the risk of delegating its powers, then they would in all probability be distorted and misused, since the members of the subordinate congregation would have to conform to local pressures, both secular and ecclesiastical. Propaganda Fide had been created to centralize control over the missions and thus to strengthen their evangelistic work, but the means at its disposal were far too meager to achieve this end effectively during the first two centuries of its existence.

Ingoli thought, however, that some of Tramallo's other proposals regarding finance could be taken up because Monsignor Vives says that it would "not be difficult to gain the King's agreement."[16] His is an interesting comment, for it highlights the standing and influence of this Spanish priest during the first decade of the congregation. From a well-known family in Valencia, Juan Bautista Vives had been appointed Scrittore delle Lettere Apostoliche by Sixtus V in 1589. He had developed a keen interest in training priests for the missions fields, and he donated the palace which eventually became the headquarters of the congregation.[17] Before putting the final touches to his memorandum, Ingoli had sent a draft to Vives who agreed that the points regarding finance made by the collector were useful.[18]

Concerning the issue of ordaining East Indians, Ingoli was sure that there was no difficulty, particularly as regards Brahmins and Japanese. "It is certain that in the primitive Church the apostles ordained bishops and priests for the local areas, and it is right to follow their practice as guided by the Holy Spirit." As regards those of the West Indies and the Americas, many are of the opinion "that they are unsuitable," but, Ignoli argued, "one can see on the contrary the potential in some as is proved by the gift they have in learning music, in making decorated cloths [*panni figurati*] and various artifices." He went on to declare roundly that the refusal of Europeans to accept Indians into religious orders "is a tyranny to prevent the Indians from breathing in order not to loose the riches which are reaped from the Indies. I would suggest

---

16. SOCG 98, f. 98v.

17. Metzler, *Memoria Rerum* 1/1, 76–77.

18. SOCG 98, f. 107. Ingoli to Vives, September 18, 1630, with notes added by Vives.

that a strict order is laid down in favor of the Indians so that in each convent there should be at least one-third of native Indians, and the other two-thirds could be Europeans, Creoles, or half-caste."[19]

Taking up Tramallo's remarks concerning Angola and Kongo, Ingoli thoroughly agreed that help for that kingdom had to be provided. He referred to the fact that some years previously there had been a suggestion of sending a mission there of twelve Capuchins, "but it was not carried out, because, it is said our people purchase little in that kingdom. Others suggested that youths of that kingdom aged about fifteen or sixteen years old who would not forget their language should be educated in Europe and then repatriated. The Augustinians, Jesuits, Franciscans, and Dominicans could recruit some, and having instructed them send them to that kingdom to found their orders there." As regards the slave trade, Ingoli, ever a realist where material interests were concerned, thought that "one could raise the matter with the king of Spain but without much hope of fruit, because the mines are too important for that crown."[20] In the midst of all the other preoccupations and concerns which were crowding into Propaganda Fide at this time, this issue, which for succeeding centuries was to lie at the heart of Europe's attitude to Africa, seemed if not a minor question, at least an affair that the Church could do little to solve. Propaganda Fide, in the person of Ingoli, had not yet recognized that it was here confronted with an evil of colossal dimensions, which required the mobilization of the people of God in a massive reassertion and clarification of basic human rights and dignities.

Ingoli finished this memorandum on September 25, 1630, and circulated it to Trivulzi, S. Sisto, and the two other cardinals. This committee formally met finally on November 18,[21] and its decisions were ratified at the meeting of the whole congregation held in the presence of the pope on November 22. They approved many of the suggestions

---

19. SOCG 98, f. 96–96v. The same year Matteo de Castro, a Brahmin, was ordained in Rome, Metzler, *Memoria Rerum* 1/1, 178.

20. SOCG 98, f. 96v. By "our people," Ingoli presumably means Italians. A. Brásio, *Monumenta Missionaria Africana*, VII (Lisbon, 1956), 634–35, prints a somewhat faulty copy from the Ajuda Library of these somments by Ingoli concerning Angola and the slave trade.

21. The minutes of this committee are in the Vatican Library, B.V. Ottob. 2536 f. 154.

regarding the Indies and finance, and Ingoli sent his friend and confidant, Giovan Battista Agucchi, nuncio of Venice, a copy of the resolutions made for the Indies "from which I hope great progress will be made."[22] The cardinals also agreed that help should be given to the missions in Angola. As regards the slave trade, however, the congregation took a firmer line than was indicated in Ingoli's memorandum. The cardinals, and here it was perhaps significant that they were led by Trivulzi with his close Spanish connections, condemned the trade as a scandal against the good reputation of the Spanish nation. They recommended that the slaves, whom they referred to as "hos paupers Mauros," should be commended to the Catholic king and that they should not be held in so severe a servitude or treated with such cruelty. This recommendation was approved by the congregation, and it was resolved that the pope should strongly condemn this custom as contrary to piety and the Christian religion.[23]

We do not know whether Urban took any immediate action on this. The index in the Vatican archives to the papal briefs shows nothing relevant for November or December 1630,[24] but this does not necessarily mean that a brief or even a papal bull was not sent either then or subsequently. It is also possible that Urban had this earlier condemnation in mind when on April 22, 1639, in the brief *Commissum Nobis*, he commanded the collector of Portugal to forbid, on pain of execution, all enslavement of the Indians and all slave trading in Indians. This order, however, like similar papal condemnations later in the seventeenth century, encountered the hard, vested interests which Ingoli had foreseen.[25]

---

22. Ingoli to Agucchi, December 28, 1630, in B.V. Ottob. 2536, f. 150.

23. Acta 7, f. 174v.

24. Index number 767.

25. J. F. Maxwell, *Slavery and the Catholic Church* (Chichester, 1975), 72. On an eighteenth-century copy in the archive of Propaganda Fide (Fondo di Vienna 56, f. 101) of the ruling of the Holy Office of March 20, 1686, concerning the Atlantic slave trade, there is a marginal note which refers to the briefs of Paul III and Urban VIII "che proibiscono il far schiavi gli Indiani Negri." For a discussion of the 1686 ruling and its consequences, see chapters 1 and 2 of R. Gray, *Black Christians and White Missionaries* (New Haven, 1990).

4

The Papacy and Africa
in the Seventeenth Century

The development of Christianity in Africa has often been presented as an aspect of the expansion of European influence and culture. It has been assumed that the major decisions, the essential initiatives, were taken not in Africa, but in Europe, and that Christianity was planted and developed in Africa by European missionaries. When one examines papal policy towards Africa in the seventeenth century, however, one discovers that the reality was far more complex. Many of the vital initiatives were taken by African Christians. Their appeals and embassies to Europe had a major influence not merely on papal policy towards Africa, but on Rome's plans to supervise and control the whole world-wide Catholic missionary enterprise. Similarly, when one looks at the development of Christianity in Kongo, the principal area in Africa of Catholic missions at that time, one is confronted with a collaborative process. The Capuchin mission to Kongo was unique in that from the first moment it was seen to be an attempt not primarily to convert pagans but to assist and strengthen a remote Catholic outpost. The labors and sacrifices of the missionaries, a high proportion of whom died in Africa, were complemented and often eclipsed by Africans who were appropriating Christianity, applying the faith to their own needs. Africans were bringing new insights and understandings of the relevance of Christianity and of its ethical demands. Africans were actively, not passively, participating in that unending search of what it means to be Christian.

African Embassies and the Creation
of Propaganda Fide

The interest of the papal Curia in sub-Saharan Africa had its origins not so much in European, primarily Portuguese, missionary initiatives but in appeals to Rome from two African Christian kingdoms. In the fifteenth century, Ethiopia, with its embassies and emissaries to Europe, and most notably to the Council of Florence, had evoked in the Curia the mirage of a powerful Christian state lying behind, and potentially threatening, the military might of the Ottomans. In the early sixteenth century, the ruler of the kingdom of Kongo had embraced Christianity with enthusiasm, taking at face value the Portuguese claim that their faith contained the secret of their political power and success.[1] By the late sixteenth century, embassies from Kongo, seeking to establish direct contact with Rome, were to be directly instrumental in leading the papacy to establish the Congregation of Propaganda Fide with responsibility for Catholic missions throughout the world.

The decisive contact between Kongo and the papacy was established in Lisbon in 1594 between Fabio Biondi, the papal collector in Portugal, and Antonio Vieira, a close relative of Alvaro II, king of Kongo. Vieira had been sent to negotiate the creation of a separate Kongo diocese. His request caused few if any difficulties. It did not seem to the royal authorities in Lisbon and Madrid to represent any threat to the patronal rights granted to the Portuguese crown by the papacy. The expenses of the diocese would be met by Portugal and, to a lesser extent, by the king of Kongo, and the Portuguese crown retained the right to nominate to the see. Vieira however astonished the papal representative with his knowledge of "Christian doctrine and ecclesiastical history."[2] Biondi was most impressed by him and developed a deep interest in Kongo Christianity, and Vieira took back to Kongo a strong recommendation that Alvaro should send an ambassador to Rome.

When this ambassador, Antonio Manuele, a cousin of Alvaro II, reached Lisbon in 1605, the authorities feared that a direct contact between Kongo and Rome might threaten the maintenance of Portuguese patronal rights over the area. For nearly two years the ambassador was delayed in Portugal and Spain, but at this critical juncture he was assisted by the Discalced Carmelites, who had undertaken a

1. The critical significance of Kongo Christianity in the sixteenth and seventeenth centuries is well established in Adrian Hastings, *The Church in Africa, 1450–1950* (Oxford, 1994).

2. A. V. Confalonieri 28, f.678–78v. Biondi to Silvio Antoniano, 31.VIII.1596. My research in the archives in Rome was facilitated by an emeritus fellowship granted by the Leverhulme Trust.

brief mission to Kongo in 1584–87.[3] He was joined in Spain by Diego de la Encarnación, who had been his confessor twenty years earlier. Both were strongly encouraged to come to Rome by Pedro de la Madre de Dios, the commissary general of the Italian province. A principal adviser on papal missionary strategy, in 1604 Pedro had organized the mission to Persia, the first direct papal mission into an area partly claimed by the Portuguese Padroado. He guided delicate negotiations with the Copts in Egypt, and in 1606 was responsible for papal instructions for a projected Capuchin mission there.[4] Keenly interested in Ethiopia, he hoped to open up a route there across Africa from Kongo. Pedro therefore did all in his power to help the Kongolese ambassador come to Rome. While delayed in Spain, however, Antonio Manuele had been afflicted by gallstones. When he eventually arrived in Rome on January 3, 1608, he was a very sick man and he died there on the eve of Epiphany.

Yet the arrival, death, and funeral of this ambassador created a sensation in Rome.[5] It greatly deepened papal interest in overseas missions, and notably increased the papacy's resolve to bring these missions under its direct supervision. Biondi had returned from Lisbon determined to foster Rome's interest in Kongo, and, appointed papal majordomo in 1605, he made the most of the opportunity presented by the arrival of the long-awaited embassy. He assigned to the ambassador the rooms in the Vatican palace recently used by Cardinal Bellarmine, and after Antonio Manuele's death, he personally arranged and supervised a splendidly magnificent funeral in Santa Maria Maggiore.

Even before the ambassador arrived in Rome, Paul V had instructed the secretariat of state to begin preparations for sending a Carmelite mission to Kongo.[6] As the embassy approached Rome, the Spanish ambassador and the Portuguese agent in Rome requested the pope to

3. F. Boontinck, "Les Carmes Déchaux au royaume de Kongo (1584–1587)," *Zaire-Afrique*, 262 (1992): 112–23.

4. V. Buri, "L'unione della chiesa copta con Roma sotto Clemente VIII," *Orientalia Christiana* xxiii/2, no. 72 (Rome, 1931): 237–39.

5. See the reports in T. Filesi, *Roma e Congo all'inizio del 1600.* Nuove Testimonianze (Como, 1968).

6. A. Brásio, *Monumenta Missionaria Africana. Africa Ocidental* (I serie), V, 362–63.

consult them regarding Madrid's wishes, but it became widely known that the Congregation of Rites had decided to receive the embassy in public consistory "despite the opposition of the Spaniards who maintain that this kingdom is tributary to them."[7] The papacy was prepared for a public confrontation with the patronal powers, even though Rome recognized that both countries were faithful Catholic bastions in Europe, and that under the Padroado Portugal had established so many Catholic outposts overseas. In its relations with Kongo, the papacy was beginning to explore and pursue a new realm of responsibility, and in the process it was also incidentally to emphasize and recognize the political independence of Kongo.

In September the Portuguese agent reported that the pope was demonstrating a "great desire" to send non-Portuguese Carmelites to Kongo, and in October 1608 the Spanish ambassador realized that Paul V was "very determined on this missionary question, saying it belonged to his office, and that it concerned the well being of souls and the propagation of the Catholic faith."[8] Evidently the issue was seen in the papal court to raise a fundamental principle. Previously in August, however, Pedro de la Madre de Dios had died, and the pope now had to encourage the Discalced Carmelites to renew their commitment to the mission. In May 1610 they were ready to undertake it, and on October 4, 1610, Paul V recommended the mission to Philip III.[9] The following year Cardinal Borghese, the secretary of state, told Diego da la Encarnación that the news that he and the other Carmelite missionaries had been prevented from leaving Lisbon for Kongo had caused the pope "great displeasure."[10] The collector at Lisbon was informed that "the pretext for this impediment" was vain, and he was ordered to do his utmost to overcome the difficulty, emphasizing the damage that it would cause to Christianity in Kongo.[11] The nuncio in Madrid was reminded of "the irreparable harm" that the obstruction of the mission would bring for Kongo and the neighboring kingdoms. Then in a most illuminating phrase, Borghese added that "since the affair is

7. B.V. Urb. lat. 1076 Pt.1, f.19 Avvisi di Roma, 9.1.1608.

8. Aytona to King, 14.X.1608 in Brásio, V, 473–5. Jose de Melo's report of 17.IX.1608 in ibid, 461–62.

9. Brásio, V, 147, 485, 585, 617–19.

10. Brásio, VI, 41.

11. A.V. Confalonieri, 43, f.96v. Borghese to Collector, 12.X.1611.

public knowledge, it would damage the reputation of this Holy See."[12] A few years later, the Spanish diplomat Zuniga argued that "a monarchy that has lost its reputation, even if it has lost no territory, is a sky without light, a sun without rays, a body without a soul."[13] If this was true for Spain, it was even more relevant for the papal monarchy.

Rome lacked the logistical resources to turn its missionary determination immediately into reality. But the challenge to what were now seen in the Curia as patronal obstacles and pretensions could not be postponed indefinitely. When the Kongolese ambassador had reached Rome in January 1608, a remarkable Spanish cleric, Juan Bautista Vives, was drawing up with two other missionary enthusiasts a memorandum for Paul V recommending the creation of missionary seminaries and a new congregation as a direct challenge to Spanish and Portuguese patronal rights.[14] Vives had long been a friend of Jerónimo Gracián, who had organized the first Carmelite mission to Kongo, and when it became obvious that Paul V's initiative was being blocked in Lisbon, Vives, at the pope's request, summoned to Rome Jean de Brétigny, who some thirty years previously had been deeply impressed by the report of a request from a young Kongolese princess to be permitted to join the Carmelite order. Subsequently Jean had spent much of his inheritance in establishing the reformed Carmelites in France and the Spanish Netherlands. He had retained, however, a keen interest in Kongo, and he contacted Antonio Manuele while the ambassador had been detained in Madrid. Immediately after receiving Paul V's summons, he set out for Rome in January 1612 and lodged in Vives's house, where he stayed until September. On two occasions in audiences with the pope, he offered considerable financial support for a mission to Kongo.[15] His generous offers could not immediately be utilized, but about the time he was in Rome it was suggested to Alvaro II in Kongo, probably by Jean or by Diego da Encarnación, that the king should appoint Vives as his official representative at the papal court. In a letter

---

12. Borghese to Carafa, 12.X.1611, in Brásio, VI, 42–43.

13. Quoted in J. H. Elliott, *The Count-Duke of Olivares* (New Haven, 1986), 58.

14. G. Piras, *La Congregazione e il Collegio di Propaganda Fide di J.B.Vives. G. Leonardi a M.de Funes* (Rome, 1976).

15. P. Serouet, *Jean de Brétigny (1556–1634). Aux origines du Carmel de France, de Belgique et du Congo* (Louvain, 1974), 286–88. See also Brásio, VI, 59 and 83.

to Paul V dated November 27, 1613, Alvaro formally appointed Vives as his ambassador in order that he could render obedience to the Holy See "with all the solemnity that is customary for royal ambassadors."[16] The challenge to the Padroado involved in such a proclamation of Kongo's independence from Portugal would be revived. On receipt of Alvaro's letter, Paul V declared Vives to be the ambassador of the king of Kongo, and Vives proceeded to take two major initiatives.

On April 18, 1617, Vives wrote to the emperor of Ethiopia proposing that the emperor should cooperate with the king of Kongo in opening a route between the two Christian states.[17] This idea was by no means novel. In a report written in 1578 by a young Venetian, Pietro Duodo, whose father, Francesco, had been captain-general of the Venetian galleys at the defeat of the Ottoman fleet at the battle of Lepanto, it was alleged that some twenty-five years earlier, "two Genoese Negroni and Grimaldi" had sailed from Lisbon to the Kongo kingdom and from there "one month by river" had reached the imperial city of Ethiopia.[18] This reported Genoese exploit is almost certainly pure fantasy, but it illustrates the way in which Italian fears of the continuing threat from Ottoman power and expansion could influence Rome's interest in both Ethiopia and Kongo.

In the minds of both Vives and Pedro de la Madre de Dios, the strategic and missionary significance of these two African Christian states was such that the hard realities of African geography and travel vanished before their enthusiasm. The possibility of opening a route from Kongo to Ethiopia had been one of the principal matters Don Antonio Manuele had been instructed to discuss in Rome during his embassy there, and the year after his death, a long memorandum had been submitted to Paul V on this subject by Girolamo Vecchietti. Together with his brother, a distinguished traveler and Oriental linguist, Girolamo had been closely involved for several decades in the papacy's negotiations with the Coptic church in Egypt and with other potential allies against the Ottomans. Reviewing all the other possible ways of reaching Ethiopia, Girolamo concluded that the route via Kongo would

---

16. Brásio, VI, 128–30.
17. Brásio VI, 277–78.
18. B V Urb. Lat. 837, f 144.

be much the most promising.[19] He succeeded in enlisting the support of none other than Cardinal Maffeo Barberini, the future Urban VIII, but after discussing the proposal with the Jesuits in Rome, who maintained there was no need to take further action, the cardinal did not press the matter.[20] Yet about the time that Vives wrote to the emperor, the papal collector in Lisbon reported that Raffaello di Castro, a priest from Jacuman in New Spain, "a man of an enquiring mind [*uomo curioso*]," went to Ocanga on the northern frontier of Kongo and "passed far beyond it in order to obtain information regarding people who wore a wooden cross from the necks and came from the country of Prester John."[21]

We do not know whether Vives had seen this report, and it is difficult to believe that Raffaello in fact penetrated deep into equatorial Africa. Yet if this particular diplomatic move on the part of Vives was doomed to failure, his other initiative bore far more significant consequences. The Portuguese action in preventing the Spanish Carmelites from passing through Lisbon had caused anger in the Kongolese court, where their arrival had been eagerly awaited. In his letter appointing Vives as his ambassador, Alvaro II renewed the request that Rome should send other missionaries.[22] In response to this royal request, Vives approached the Capuchins, who were already being used by the papacy for missions demanding skill and diplomacy. Together with Cardinal Trejo, a Spaniard who had been appointed in the Curia protector of the kingdom of Kongo, Vives assured the Capuchins that they would be able to obtain Philip III's support for this initiative. During a visit to the Iberian peninsular in 1619, Lorenzo da Brindisi, the influential father general of the Capuchins, warmly recommended the intended mission to Philip III, but defendants of the Padroado rights caused delay, and in July 1620 Cardinal Borghese, Paul V's secretary of state, again urged the collector in Lisbon to take up the question. On March 19,1621, barely a month after his election to the papacy, Gregory XV assured Alvaro III that the Capuchin mission would soon be

---

19. The memorandum by Girolamo Vecchietti is published by C.Beccari, *Rerum Aethiopicarum*, XI, 176–85.

20. B.V. Vat. Lat. 6723, f.6v. Report by Girolamo Vecchietti.

21. Brásio, VI, 491–92.

22. Alvaro II to Paul V, 27.III.1613, in Brásio VI, 132.

leaving for Kongo, but already the Council of Portugal at Madrid had again decided to prevent its departure.[23]

Many other developments in Europe and elsewhere helped to persuade Gregory XV to establish the Sacred Congregation of Propaganda Fide in 1622. Yet it is an extraordinary fact that in these decades, which culminated in Gregory's decision to create what was to become the most influential missionary organization in the history of the church, the appeals and aspirations of the remote, minute community of Kongo Christians, centered precariously on their royal family and court, had directly and powerfully contributed to the papal determination to confront the challenge of the overseas missions and the obstacles presented to them by the Padroado.

The Capuchins and Kongo Christianity

Despite its significant role in the creation of Propaganda Fide, sub-Saharan Africa was at first of very minor importance for the new congregation. The radical guidelines concerning overseas missionary policy established by Ingoli, its first secretary, were drawn up in relation to Asia and Latin America. As far as Africa was concerned, Propaganda merely legitimized some minor expeditions to the West African coast by French missionaries, directed by Joseph de Paris working with Richelieu. Then, in response to a repeated royal request from Kongo conveyed again by Vives, Propaganda decided in 1640 to send Italian Capuchins to the area. This became by far the most important Catholic mission in Africa in the seventeenth century. More than two hundred Capuchin missionaries, organized and subsidized directly by Propaganda, were sent to the area before the end of the century, and Kongo was to be the mission in Africa where Ingoli's policy of creating an indigenous priesthood guided by independent vicars apostolic was first seriously considered.

This overseas mission was unusual, for it was directed primarily not to pagans but to fellow Catholics. The welcome given to the missionaries by large numbers of the common people together with their rulers, the eagerness with which they sought baptism for their

---

23. Jadin in Metzler, I pt.2, 432.

children, the fact that the rulers, while seeking to exploit the advantages offered to them by Dutch or English traders, resolutely refused to permit any dissemination of Protestant opinions or doctrines—all this demonstrated to the pioneer Capuchins that Kongo was a Catholic kingdom, and Kongolese attachment to the sacraments was at times compared favorably with the situation in the heartlands of Catholic Europe. Not surprisingly, however, there were points of sharp disagreement between the Capuchins and the Kongolese.

Propaganda's missionaries in Kongo were among the most committed exponents of Catholic reform in the seventeenth century. Their evidence concerning the nature of Kongo Christianity must therefore be read with this in mind. In France at the same time Catholic reformers were proclaiming a form of religion, which, it has been suggested, was "far beyond anything previously demanded . . . manifestly beyond the capabilities of most of the population. . . . French clerical writers came to assert with surprising accord that the great majority of the population were damned, sunk irreplacably in paganism, idolatry and concupiscence."[24] Prophets and reformers denounce the compromises and complacency of ordinary believers, and it is hardly surprising that the missionaries, largely ignorant of local cultural values, should find much in Kongo to criticize and condemn. Their identification with the poor at times distanced the Capuchins from the ruling elite. Their insistence on canon-law marriage was a far greater cause of disagreement and confrontation. More fundamental still was the issue of religious allegiance.

Kongo had in no way been a spiritual tabula rasa before the introduction of Christianity. The great questions of life and death, of prosperity, security, sickness, and suffering were determined ultimately by spiritual forces. To a large extent the missionaries shared this cosmology. The pope obliged when asked by the Capuchins to exorcise the locusts which were afflicting Kongo.[25] On the mission field the locusts were banished by the sign of the Cross, while rogue elephants were seen as men transformed into that shape, instruments of the Devil

---

24. R. Briggs, *Communities of Belief. Cultural and Social Tension in Early Modern France* (Oxford, 1989), 372.

25. Papal brief of 30.V.1648 in Brásio, X, 166–68.

seeking to drive out the missionaries.[26] Healing was achieved relatively often through miracles, divine guidance was given in dreams,
and chance played a much more restricted role than it did for many
of their successors in the twentieth century, though even in the 1930s
locusts were exorcised by a Jesuit in Rhodesia.[27] The Capuchins often
interpreted any recourse to other ritual experts as a deliberate, offensive rejection of the Christian Gospel. They saw Kongo as a battlefield
and expected Catholic rulers there to support them wholeheartedly.

Garcia II as a Catholic Ruler

For a variety of reasons, Garcia II, ruler of Kongo since 1640, had welcomed the arrival of the missionaries from Rome. He hoped they
would help him to persuade the pope to intervene and proclaim his
son as his successor. He thought they would succeed in persuading
Propaganda to appoint non-Portuguese bishops to his kingdom, and
doubtless he hoped that such appointments, by eliminating Portuguese interference, might facilitate royal influence and even control
over the church in Kongo. For like any Catholic ruler or politician in his
day, or subsequently, this was a major political objective.

By the time that Bonaventura d'Alessano, the able and saintly first
prefect of the mission, had died in 1649, both the king and the missionaries had become disillusioned with each other. As the Capuchins had
begun to speak and understand Kikongo, they had become increasingly aware of the extent to which pre-Christian rituals were still practiced in Kongo. "An infinite number of magicians, enchanters, and
sorcerers" publicly practiced their rites and "every day new superstitions were being uncovered," Bonaventura reported to Rome. The prophetic, holy rhetoric was beginning to form a stereotype.[28] When they
confronted Garcia with a dossier of complaints, he is reported to have
frozen "like a statue." Deeply disappointed by the Capuchins failure to

---

26. C. Piazza, *La prefettura apostolica del Congo alla metà del xvii secolo. La relazione inedita di Girolamo da Montesarchio* (Milan, 1976), 178, 234–38.

27. E. Isichei, *A History of African Christianity* (Grand Rapids, Mich.,1995, 88.

28. Memorial by Bonaventura d'Alessano to Propaganda Fide, 4.VIII.1649 reprinted
in Graciano Maria de Leguzzano's translation of Cavazzi, *Descrição Historica dos tres
reinos Congo. Matamba e Angola* (Lisbon, 1965), II, 313–14.

obtain his requests in Rome, he replied coldly that he would procure a remedy, but instead began to persecute their informants.[29]

Garcia's disappointment with the Capuchin alliance was not, however, total. Still less did it imply, as some missionaries reported, a rejection of Christianity. When he learned that a new Capuchin prefect, Giacinto da Vetralla, had arrived in Luanda in May 1652, Garcia urged him to come immediately to Mbanza Kongo and welcomed him with signal honors. He persuaded Giacinto of his desire "to see the Catholic faith not only proclaimed in all parts of his kingdom but also for it to be solidly established," and when he heard that the prefect carried with him a papal authorization for a jubilee with indulgences, Garcia insisted on solemnly proclaiming it himself. In a letter addressed to all his provincial rulers, officials and even village elders (*nkuluntu*), Garcia admonished them: "This is the moment to show yourselves true Catholics. Abandon concubinage, superstition, fetishes, idols, and all other vices, . . . Do not force me to use the sword and to issue penal laws. Do not oblige me to be a rigorous judge. I know that divine law proscribes that I should punish evil doers and recompense the good. If I do not do this, I myself will be punished. I am ready to exercise justice against those who practice superstitions contrary to the law of God and to the commandments of the church of Rome. I am ready to die for the faith even a thousand times if I have a thousand lives."[30]

Garcia was an able diplomat and Giacinto was then fresh and somewhat naive, but his account of the king's desire to send another embassy to Rome rings true. Garcia showed the prefect how large parts of his palace had recently been destroyed by fire. They included his treasury where he had accumulated two hundred specially selected ivory tusks to finance an independent embassy to Rome to be led by his eldest son. Evidently this mission was planned at least in part in response to the Capuchin failure to obtain papal support for the prince's right of succession. The king wondered whether the fire had not been started deliberately, and he declared that if his adversaries,

---

29. Serafino da Cortona to the Capuchin Provincial in Tuscany, 15.V.1652 in Brásio, XI, 191.

30. Giacinto's report of 20.VIII.1652 and Garcia's decree are published in *Analecta Ordinis Capuccinorum* 13 (1897): 89–96, and in Brásio, XI, 216–30.

including the Portuguese, sought to block such an embassy, he himself would suddenly and secretly undertake it.[31] Even if we discount Garcia's edict as designed primarily for Capuchin consumption, there seems no doubt that, despite the lack of tangible results obtained from his alliance with the missionaries, the king still placed the highest value on strengthening his links with Rome. For him, the pope manifestly possessed a legitimating authority in Kongo. Indeed his hope of papal intervention in his aim of radically setting aside the customary mode of royal succession in Kongo is an astonishing testimony of Garcia's belief in the potential power of the papacy to influence internal Kongo politics.

One could argue that Garcia in some ways took his Catholic allegiance perhaps as seriously as his young contemporary, later to become the most renowned Catholic monarch in the seventeenth century, Louis XIV.[32] Like Louis, Garcia was continually exposed to Catholic ritual and, like his predecessors, he insisted on taking a prominent role in it. After the reading of the Gospel at Mass, the missal was taken for him to kiss it, at the offertory he went to the altar to kiss the paten, and at the end of Mass he participated in various rituals.[33] While Louis was privileged to listen to some of the most learned, outspoken, and persuasive preachers of his day, Garcia also constantly heard the faith expounded and interpreted by his most prominent royal chaplain, Manuel Roboredo. Son of a Portuguese father, a nobleman according to some accounts, and of Eva, a Kongolese princess, Manuel was educated in Kongo by the Jesuits and ordained priest in 1637. Entrusted by Garcia with the initial contacts with the Capuchins, Manuel soon won their respect also. After more than four years close association with him, the sternly ascetic

---

31. Ibid. The use of ivory to finance this projected embassy is significant, since Alvaro II's famous embassy of 1605–8 had been seriously handicapped by its dependence on local *nzimbu* shell currency, valuable in Kongo but useless in Europe. Garcia's wish to send his son to Rome echoes Afonso I's desire in the early sixteenth century.

32. For a convincing analysis of Louis' religious development, see F. Bluche, *Louis XIV,* English trans. (London, 1990).

33. F. Bontinck, ed. and trans., *Brève relation de la fondation de la mission . . . au Congo* (Louvain, 1964), 126–27.

Bonaventura d'Alessano reported that he was "an esteemed priest . . . with a fervent spirit" and that he wanted to accept him into the Capuchin order.[34] Taking the name Francesco da São Salvador, he was formally admitted into the order by Bonaventura's successor in August 1652 and continued to play a major role in the relations between the Capuchins and the royal court.

Unlike the Capuchins, Garcia and many of his courtiers and officials did not see Kongo as a straightforward, sharply defined battleground between Christianity and paganism. The last thing that he wanted in religious matters was to be forced to "use the sword, to issue penal laws and become a rigorous judge." Despite his commitment to the papacy as an ultimate religious authority, he was anxious not to disrupt too forcefully the modus vivendi between Christianity and Kongo beliefs and customs. At the request of the Capuchins, he was sometimes willing to condemn established, pre-Christian practices, particularly if they did not affect his own authority. A striking example occured early in 1652. While serving in Nsundi, a major province northeast of Mbanza Kongo, Girolamo da Montesarchio discovered that the local *kitomi*, in charge of the territorial spirits of the area, played a vital role in the installation of the province's governor and in the provision of continued ritual support for him. The Capuchin wrote to Garcia requesting the king to prohibit a new governor from taking part in this customary installation ritual. Garcia sent him a courteous reply, stating that "as a Catholic king" he also disapproved of this practice and had given the requisite orders to the new governor. Distrusting this smooth assurance, Girolamo hurried to the capital in order to prevent "such a diabolic practice," and he obtained from Garcia written confirmation of his orders. The missionary found that the new governor, "being a good Christian," fully accepted the prohibition, despite desperate, furious reproaches from his wife who accused Girolamo of wishing to kill her husband. Her protest was supported by the governor's entourage, but her husband's resolution held firm, and Girolamo reported that "the governor

---

34. SOCG 249, f.38–43 Bonaventura d'Alessano, 4.VIII. 1649.

was much esteemed in Nsundi, all the land holders came to bring him tribute, and he ruled for many years."[35]

Another occasion on which Garcia supported the Capuchins in their aggression against rival religious specialists came when Georges de Geel, a Flemish Capuchin on a missionary tour in the province of Mbata, was killed by an angry populace while attempting to destroy a shrine and their charms. When news of his death reached Garcia, the king proclaimed in March 1653 that he had sentenced the missionary killers to slavery, and he reiterated that all officials should assist the Capuchins.[36]

The king, however, was equally ready to restrict Capuchin influence, and to give his favors to their ritual rivals. A faithful interpreter of the Capuchins, suspected of having revealed secrets to the missionaries, was executed, and two prominent royal princesses, who "from the beginning daily participated in all the spiritual exercises setting a great example and edification to the court," were sent into exile and their lives endangered. Many of the other interpreters were terrified and refused to go to church, but at this critical juncture Francesco da São Salvador began to hear confessions at the court. "With this help at such an opportune moment the spiritual exercises of the court were continued," though Francesco aroused Garcia's anger and was thought to have exposed himself to considerable personal danger.[37]

Dialogue between Christianity and Primal Religion in Kongo

Thus already in the 1650s the spectrum of Kongo response to the papal missionaries was becoming clear. At one extreme was a provincial ruler and those interpreters and catechists who were willing to incur popular wrath and even to risk their lives by identifying themselves

35. C. Piazza, *La prefettura apostolica del Congo*, 212-15. Girolamo's account of the installation ritual is one of the fullest descriptions which have come down to us. See A. Hilton, *The Kingdom of Kongo* (London, 1985), 47; W. MacGaffey, *Religion and Society in Central Africa* (Chicago, 1986), 196. Neither of these authors, however, refer to Girolamo's successful intervention.

36. P. Hildebrand, *Le martyr Georges de Geel* (Antwerp, 1940), 334-38, 393-96.

37. Mateo de Anguiano, *Misiones capuchinas en Africa. I. La mision del Congo* (Madrid, 1950), 365-69.

with the Capuchins' inflexible demands and their prophetic examples of a Franciscan way of life. At the other end of the spectrum were those pre-Christian ritual experts whose whole raison d'être seemed to be threatened by these intrusive aliens, many of whom inevitably had but the slightest understanding of Kongo customs, fears, and beliefs. Between these two poles lay most of the ruling elite exemplified by Garcia II, followed perhaps by an increasing mass of the general populace. Convinced of a Catholic identity, they remained, however, on the whole deeply content with the compromises and evasions which had enabled them to come to terms with the teachings of Christianity. It was here, in this middle ground of continually shifting allegiances, of dialogue between varying religious beliefs and practices, that the ministry of Francesco da São Salvador was of such potential significance. The fact that he was able to continue to exercise his ministry at the royal court at this time of crisis demonstrates his persistent patience, the fruit of an innate understanding of Kongo Christianity. One suspects that he may well have softened some of the missionaries' harshest precepts, adapting their understanding of the faith to the local environment, while at the same time deepening, reforming, and expanding the hold of Christianity in Kongo.

This patient process of dialogue, of what might now be termed gradual inculturation, demanded time as well as patience, but at this juncture time in Kongo was not provided. Garcia died in 1660. Soon afterward his successor was defeated by the Portuguese from Luanda and their Imbangala allies. At the battle of Ambuila in 1665, the king, his chaplain Francesco da São Salvador, some four hundred Kongolese nobility, and about five thousand warriors were slain. The kingdom of Kongo never recovered its unity. For the remaining decades of the seventeenth century, the coastal province of Soyo emerged as the most powerful political unit, but its ruler failed to establish his predominance over the rest of Kongo. In Soyo the Capuchins maintained an almost continuous presence for more than a hundred years, and at the end of the seventeenth century Soyo understandings of Christianity, and even the possibilities of dialogue, were brought briefly to the attention of the cardinals of Propaganda Fide. The predicament confronting Soyo Christians challenged the papacy on a point of fundamental missiological significance.

In 1692 Andrea da Pavia returned to Rome after three years in Soyo. He reported that a general assembly there, presided over by the ruler, had debated whether they "wished to observe the laws of God or their superstitious ceremonies." The response had been that "they firmly believed in God and in everything that was taught them, but that they also believed in their ceremonies and vain observances." Andrea asked Propaganda "if in some respects" the people of Soyo "could be excused, for in their ceremonies they do not make an explicit, or implicit, pact with the Devil, but they have a simple faith from which one tries to raise them as much as one can."[38] Andrea's assessment of their pre-Christian rituals showed a remarkable degree, for his time, of sympathetic understanding of their problems. As he pointed out, their "superstitious ceremonies" involved no worship of the Devil as many of the other missionaries had assumed. Rather they were attempts to summon supernatural assistance to combat their fears and experiences of evil. He was even tentatively suggesting that the missionaries might recognize some of the positive values in Soyo religion, the vital first step to any productive dialogue. His report was submitted to the Congregation by Cardinal Gaspare Carpegna, an eminent canon lawyer who a decade later was to take a leading part in Propaganda's momentous discussions concerning the problem of Chinese rites. Rome's decisions on that issue were to rigidify most Catholic missionary approaches until well into the twentieth century, but on this earlier occasion Carpegna was sympathetic to the issues raised by Fra Andrea's report. He suggested that certain rites such as benediction could be introduced to take the place of "superstitions." Given time, adaptation and possibly even a fruitful dialogue might have developed.[39]

Propaganda Fide and the Atlantic Slave Trade

Already, however, a far more immediate ethical challenge affecting the sufferings and survival of millions of people of African origin had been

38. SOCG 514, f471v, "compendiosa relatione . . . data da me F. Andrea da Pavia" considered on 6.IV.1693.

39. R. Gray, *Black Christians and White Missionaries* (New Haven, 1990), chapters 3 and 5.

forcefully and dramatically brought to the attention of the papacy. The Atlantic slave trade was first drawn to the attention of Propaganda Fide by a report from the papal collector in Lisbon in 1630. The secretary, Ingoli, thought that the matter could be raised with the king of Spain but, aware of the vested interests which Spain and Portugal had in the slave trade at this time, he correctly felt that little headway would be made. In the presence of the pope, however, the cardinals recommended that the slaves should not be held in so severe and cruel a servitude, and it was resolved that Urban VIII should strongly condemn this cruelty as contrary to piety and the Christian religion.[40]

Later the reports of the Capuchins provided Propaganda with the first detailed accounts of the system of domestic slavery and of the Atlantic slave trade. The first Capuchins in Kongo, like the vast majority of their contemporaries, both European and African, accepted slavery as an established institution. In fact the slaves with whose affairs Rome was most conversant in this period were the thousands of European captives held as slaves in the towns of North Africa. The missionaries thought that before the opening of the Atlantic trade the Kongo area had been densely populated, but by 1659 five to six thousand slaves were embarked every year for the Americas. By this time the political economy of Kongo was dominated by slavery and the slave trade. Within the kingdom, slaves were used as agricultural labor and as porters. Rich Kongolese travelled in hammocks carried by domestic slaves, and most Kongolese owned between four and six such slaves, and some owned twenty or thirty and upward. "Those who remain within Congo," a Capuchin reported, "have only the name of slaves, being little differentiated from their owners who do not beat them, and some slaves have other slaves dependent on them."[41] Domestic slavery of this sort raised little or no moral problems for the Capuchins. The Atlantic trade was different. The missionaries realized that the desire to capture slaves for export did foster local conflicts. It

40. R. Gray, "Ingoli, the Collector of Portugal, the 'Gran Gusto' of Urban VIII and the Atlantic Slave Trade," in *Ecclesiae Memoria. Miscellanea in onore del R.P. Josef Metzler O.M.I.*, ed. W. Henke (Rome, 1991).

41. SOCG 250, f.28. An unsigned memorandum, probably by Serafino da Cortona in late 1659 or 1660, entitled "Delli schiavi che si comprano e vendono nel Regno di Congo e come si possono Li Christiani vendere dopo Battezzati," ff.26–29.

also promoted the seizure of individuals and the levying of fines which involved the sale of local baptized children, who might then be sold to Dutch, English, and other Protestant traders. In 1660, as a result of their reports, the secretary of Propaganda wrote a formal letter to "The People of Congo" exhorting them not to sell their children as slaves, and the missionaries were ordered to admonish the Christians not to enslave other Christians.[42]

The Capuchins also reported the cruelties practiced by some owners of slaves in Angola and the high mortalities suffered on the journey to the Americas, but they did not immediately alert the papacy to the full-scale ethical challenge confronting the Church. A voice direct from the New World and keenly aware of the realities of slavery across the Atlantic was needed to awaken the cardinals in Rome with a sudden shock to the real horrors of the Atlantic slave trade. On March 6, 1684, the cardinals of Propaganda were confronted with a petition presented to the pope by an Afro-Brazilian, Lourenço da Silva de Mendonça. Claiming descent from the kings of Kongo and representing various black confraternities in Brazil and in the Iberian peninsular, Lourenço gave a graphic account of the "diabolic abuse" and cruelties inflicted on the slaves, which led to numerous suicides. His statements were confirmed by Spanish and Portuguese missionaries questioned in Rome, and the horrified cardinals immediately instructed the nuncios in Madrid and Lisbon to request that such inhumanity should be prohibited under the severest penalties.[43]

Lourenço's petition was directed primarily against the practice of perpetual slavery, especially when it involved baptized Christians. A year later, however, the cardinals considered a memorandum which went far beyond previous papal discussions of the ethics of the Atlantic slave trade. Incorporating the views of two Capuchins arrested and expelled from Havana for their protests against the owners of Negro slaves, it was concerned not merely with the fate of Christian

---

42. Brásio, XII, 312–13. Alberizzi to Popoli del Congo, 6.X. 1660.

43. R. Gray, "The Papacy and the Atlantic Slave Trade: Lourenço da Silva, the Capuchins and the Decisions of the Holy Office," *Past and Present* 115 (1987): 52–68, reprinted in *Black Christians and White Missionaries*. I am most grateful to Father Henrique Pinto Rema OFM for correcting my earlier reading of Mendonça and also for many helpful comments.

slaves, but with the flagrant violation of rights arising from a common humanity. Following Aristotle, the memorandum, submitted by the influential procurator general of the Capuchins, made no attempt to question slavery as an established, legitimate institution, but unhesitatingly the missionaries sought the condemnation of specific widespread abuses in the actual practice of the trade. The violent and fraudulent enslavement, sale, and purchase of innocent "Negroes and other natives" was to be condemned; traders and owners of such slaves should be forced to emancipate and compensate them, and the owners of any slaves should be forbidden to endanger, wound, or kill them on their own private authority. These propositions made not the slightest distinction between Christian and other slaves. Instead they were a radical plea for justice, motivated, as the Capuchins put it, "by Christian charity."

Propaganda Fide, although autonomous in other respects, did not possess the authority to decide theological or ethical questions. The propositions of the Capuchins were therefore forwarded the same day to the Holy Office for decision. No answer was received, and then on January 14, 1686, Lourenço da Silva launched a further, decisive appeal. His second petition was again concerned with the fate of Christians held in perpetual slavery, but, reminded of the Capuchins' wide-ranging memorandum, the cardinals of Propaganda wrote immediately to the Holy Office, which on March 20, 1686, formally declared its complete agreement with every proposition put forward by the Capuchins. The highest tribunal of the papal Curia thus formally condemned the Atlantic slave trade as it was currently practiced. Had its decisions been enforced, they would have made the trade totally impracticable just at the moment when it was entering its fullest extent. Potentially this must have been one of the most notable statements on human rights ever to have been published by the papacy.

The Catholic Church, however, was not only the church of the poor and the oppressed, whose concerns were represented by the petitions of Lourenço and the Capuchins. It was also the church of the conquistadores. Propaganda immediately communicated the decisions of the Holy Office to the nuncios in Spain and Portugal and to a range of Spanish and Portuguese bishops, but the vested interests in Europe and the Americas ignored this condemnation. The papacy could define its stand on ethical questions, but the implementation of its decisions depended on clerics and laity whose loyalties lay with the Padroado. Nor, amid the multitude of other concerns which demanded the attention of the congregation, was the slave trade at the top of Propaganda's agenda. On several occasions in the eighteenth century and as late as 1821, Propaganda appealed to the principles enunciated in 1686, but already the whole basis of the debate was shifting, as other Christians, notably the Quakers, began to attack the institution of slavery itself.

Conclusion

As the seventeenth century drew to a close, the concerns and challenges of Africa still occupied a minute place in the papacy's world-view. In its day-to-day operations, Propaganda Fide was mainly concerned with the problems which seemed to threaten the survival of Catholic Europe. On the one hand, there were the manifold consequences of the Protestant Reformation, which had virtually split Europe between north and south. On the other, there was the Ottoman empire which dominated so much of the Balkans and the Mediterranean world. Even these major threats were often obscured for the popes and their secretaries of state by the tasks of governing and defending the papal lands in Italy, which were seen as the bedrock of the papal monarchy's independence. The first flashes were discernible of an Enlightenment which, with its political and intellectual revolutions, was to shake this system to its ancient foundations. Yet already in the seventeenth century African Christians had begun to summon the papacy to a new vision of its role in the world. The condemnation of the slave trade in 1686 was potentially one of the most notable statements on human rights ever to have been published by the papacy, but other day-to-day concerns in Rome, together with the vested interests elsewhere involved in the trade, soon cast into obscurity this challenge to Christian ethics. Earlier, the embassies and appeals of the kings of Kongo had, however, successfully played an important role in the steps which led to the establishment of Propaganda Fide. Portuguese and Spanish patronal rights would continue for a time to obstruct the implementation of Propaganda's policies, yet within the Curia there now existed a potentially powerful organization which by the end of the nineteenth century vitally shaped the papacy's view of the world.[44] Meanwhile the attempts by Kongo Christians to apprehend and appropriate the faith from within the traditions of their primal religion were beginning to present some of the challenges of dialogue and inculturation to a Eurocentric missionary orientation. Africans were summoning the papacy not merely to a major new ethical perception of human rights, but also to a new responsibility in the world beyond Europe, and also to a fresh understanding of evangelism, and hence ultimately of the nature of Christianity itself.

---

44. C. Prudhomme, *Stratégie missionnaire du Saint-Siège sous Léon XIII (1878–1903)* (Rome, 1994).

5

Come Vero Prencipe Catolico:
The Capuchins and the Rulers of Soyo
in the Late Seventeenth Century

S tudents of Europe's contact with Africa have long regarded the
Christian missions in the ancient kingdom of Kongo as a pecu-
liarly potent symbol.[1] For some the conversion and subsequent reign
of Afonso I in the first half of the sixteenth century were a momentary
aberration, a false dawn quickly to be obscured by the realities of the
exploitation associated with mercantile capitalism and the horrors
of the Atlantic slave trade. For others, the story of these missions has
merely served to illustrate the continuing inviolability of indigenous
traditions. Kongo society, it is argued, accepted only a thin veneer
of Christianity, while its basic cosmology, practices, and beliefs,
remained unchanged.

> Christianity affected only a slim minority. For the majority of the
> people of the Kongo, its ceremonies, its symbolism, its churches, and
> its clergy were less pretexts for belief than occasions for imitation. It
> left a lasting impression only where it managed to become associ-
> ated with traditional usages. In trying to reach the people, it became
> an instrument of syncretism. . . . Alongside a Christianity which was
> weakly established and in constant danger, the traditional religious

1. The research on which this article is in part based was undertaken with the help
of an award from the British Academy. I am most grateful to Fathers Joseph Metzler,
OMI, and Isidoro de Villapadierna, OFM Cap., archivists respectively of Propaganda
Fide and the Capuchin Generalate, for their advice and many acts of kindness. I would
also like to thank for their comments and criticisms those who attended a conference
at the School of Oriental and African Studies at which an earlier version was discussed,
and those, especially Professor J. D. Y. Peel, who have read subsequent drafts. The following abbreviations are used for citations of documents from the archives of Propaganda Fide:
SOCG   Scritture originale riferite nelle Congregazioni generali.
SC Africa   Scritture riferite nei Congressi. Series Africa, Angola, Congo, etc.

94

pluralism and the syncretic cults oriented the religious life of the people of the Kongo from the sixteenth century on. (Balandier, 1968: 254-55)

These interpretations share a common assumption. Faced with what seems to be the virtual extinction of Christianity in the area by the mid-nineteenth century, scholars have assumed that the early missionary impact was fleeting and superficial, and that these missions met with insuperable difficulties or proceeded on false principles which inevitably involved them in failure. Yet the early influence of Christianity in Kongo cannot be usefully discussed without taking into account the fact that its impact varied enormously over time and space. At the capital, Mbanza Kongo or San Salvador, the role of Christian missionaries was very different in the reigns of Afonso I, or Garcia II (1641-61), or Pedro IV (1696-1718), while in the various regions of the kingdom there were even greater differences. If we take our standpoint in the late seventeenth century and consider carefully the evidence for that period, we are confronted in Soyo, a powerful, dominant region at that moment, not with failure but with an extraordinary depth and extent of Christian influence. Several factors distinguished Soyo from the rest of Kongo, yet so striking is the picture of Soyo's commitment to Christianity at this period that one is forced to reconsider the whole direction of religious change that was occurring at that moment. And, in doing so, one has to begin to reassess some of the previous interpretations of this major episode of Christian evangelism in Africa.

The Emergence of Soyo

Soyo (Sogno, Sohio) was distinguished from the rest of the kingdom of Kongo by its natural resources, its geographical location, and its historical development in the sixteenth and seventeenth centuries. According to a Capuchin from Pavia, Soyo was as large as the seventeenth-century state of Milan.[2] It stretched along the Atlantic coast northward from the River Mbridge to the mouth of the Zaire and inland along the southern bank of this vast estuary. It was a sandy,

---

2. SOCG 514, f.471, "Compendiosa relatione . . . data da me F. Andrea da Pavia" considered on April 6, 1693.

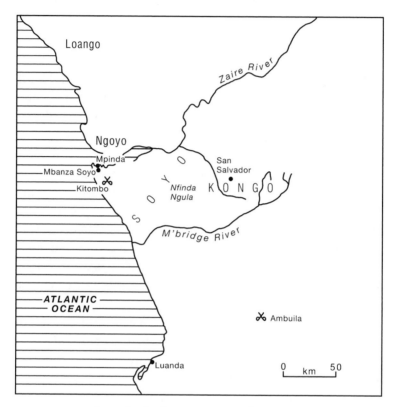

Soyo in the late seventeenth century

relatively infertile area, whose principal natural product was salt
obtained on the seacoast (Cavazzi, 1687: 4), but from the end of the
fifteenth century it was no longer a backwater. Its economic and strategic importance was suddenly transformed. The port of Mpinda, a few
miles within the Zaire estuary, provided the natural gateway for trade
and contacts with the Portuguese, and the capital of Soyo, Mbanza
Soyo, was established some three miles in the interior behind Mpinda.
By the seventeenth century the ruler of Soyo was asserting a degree of
independence which at times culminated in active revolt against the
king of Kongo. This insubordination was assisted by the existence of
the Nfinda Ngula, a large, forested wilderness which separated Soyo

from Kongo (Thornton, 1979: 41), but of even greater importance was the growth of trade with the Dutch.

After the Portuguese settlement in Luanda in the 1570s, the main commercial route of the *pombeiros* (trading agents of the Portuguese) between the Pool, San Salvador, and Luanda ran overland bypassing Soyo, but with the arrival of Dutch traders in the coastal kingdoms north of the Zaire and in the Zaire estuary in the 1590s, the fortunes of Soyo rapidly expanded. Unlike the Portuguese, the Dutch were willing to exchange firearms and ammunition for ivory, copper, and slaves (Wilson, 1978: 140–49). In the 1630s the army of Soyo defeated that of the king of Kongo on several occasions (Dapper, 1670: 565–66), and Soyo became a haven for defeated, dissident factions from San Salvador (Thornton, 1979: 131), but it was only in the last third of the seventeenth century that Soyo emerged as a dominant power in the Kongo kingdom.

In 1665 the Portuguese advancing from Luanda defeated the Kongo army, killing the king and many of his nobility at the battle of Ambuila. Only a few months later the ruler of Soyo seized his opportunity to ransack San Salvador and place his protégé on the Kongo throne, an intervention which was repeated in 1669. The following year the Portuguese governor in Luanda sent an army to invade and humble the upstart Soyo. After an initial defeat, however, the forces of Soyo rallied and, with Dutch armaments, smashed the Portuguese at Kitombo in October 1670, killing the Portuguese commander and taking many captives and much booty. It was a decisive victory. Not until the nineteenth century were the Portuguese again able to invade Kongo *(*ibid., 193). Yet Mbanza Soyo was never able to take the place of San Salvador: it never provided the central focus for the whole kingdom of Kongo, nor did its rulers ever attain the luxury, power, and lifestyle previously enjoyed by the powerful Kongo kings. There is nothing in the late seventeenth-century descriptions of Soyo to match the magnificence of Garcia II's reception of the Dutch envoys in 1642 (Dapper, 1670: 561–62). But by the 1680s Soyo was definitely thought to be the key to peace and prosperity throughout Kongo: its rulers were reported to be "very powerful" and "greatly feared" by the prominent people in Kongo.[3]

---

3. SC Africa I, f.573v, Giuseppe Maria da Busseto to Prefect, April 4, 1685.

The missionary records of the late seventeenth century give the impression that in Soyo local power was concentrated on the ruler and his court at Mbanza Soyo. The principal office holders were the ruler's close kinsmen, and if news of his illness became public a succession crisis could be feared. The ruler could appoint and dismiss the governors (*mani*) of dependent towns and villages at will, and after one serious armed dispute with the captain-general of his army, in which the Capuchins acted as mediators, he took care to demote his opponents (Merolla, 1692: 154, 236–48). Insofar as these sources provide an insight into the political structure and organization of Soyo in this period, they corroborate MacGaffey's opinion that "the precolonial Kongo chief was much like the 'Big Man' of Melanesia . . . a successful competitor in an unstable political system" in which, however, favorable conditions (as in late seventeenth-century Soyo) could for a period produce "centralized, hierarchical and relatively stable regimes," while in the exercise of such power the existence of a center was "much more important" than clear territorial boundaries (MacGaffey, 1970: 263).

The Capuchins' Advantages in Soyo

The Capuchins in Soyo were therefore probably correct in concentrating their efforts at Mbanza Soyo, and as the power of the rulers of Soyo increased, so was the commitment of Soyo to Christianity extended and intensified. When the first Capuchin missionaries arrived at Mpinda in 1645, Soyo was already in their eyes a Catholic country. They were welcomed amid scenes of great enthusiasm by the populace and ruler. A Dutch sea captain attempted to prevent their landing, but Soyo, together with the rest of Kongo as exemplified by Garcia II (Wilson, 1978: 304–5), showed little or no sympathy for Calvinist doctrines, however much the ruler and people of Soyo profited from Dutch commercial contacts. Hundreds of people brought their children and youths to be baptized, and the Capuchins throughout the seventeenth century did not hesitate to distinguish sharply Soyo and Kongo from their northern "pagan" neighbors.

As the missionaries subsequently attempted to enforce the precepts of canon law, they soon encountered in Soyo, as in the rest of the Kongo kingdom, widespread opposition. In Soyo, however, the Capuchins enjoyed peculiar advantages. In the first place, they were able to establish and maintain a continuous presence at Mbanza Soyo. Death and disease took a steady toll of the missionaries who arrived after 1645, and the arrival of reinforcements was sporadic after the first few years, so that elsewhere in Kongo, outside San Salvador, it was rare for any provincial center to have a resident missionary for more than a few years at a time, particularly after the 1650s. But in Mbanza Soyo there were always one or two Capuchin priests, ably assisted by a brother, one of whom, Leonardo da Nardo, through prolonged service obtained a deep knowledge of the people and their language (Cavazzi, 1687: VII, 123, 856).

Even more important than this uninterrupted ministry, however, was the fact that in Soyo the Capuchins had no rivals. When the Capuchin missionaries arrived at San Salvador, there were several secular priests, of both Kongo and of mixed race. With many of these local priests the Capuchins were involved in bitter disputes over ecclesiastical jurisdiction. Inevitably this rivalry weakened their influence both with the king and other laity (Jadin, 1964; Wilson, 1978). In Soyo, however, the Capuchins were the sole, unchallenged providers of Catholic sacraments, save for a few months in 1673–74 when Flemish Franciscans and a Kongolese priest briefly intruded into their monopoly (Jadin, 1966).

The Diplomatic Role of the Capuchins

Throughout the seventeenth century the Capuchins in Soyo, as in Kongo, derived some of their influence from the particular position they occupied in the wider diplomatic world. They had been sent to Kongo by Pope Urban VIII in response to repeated overtures from the kings of Kongo who had long been attempting to establish a direct contact with Rome. The kings wanted to receive missionaries who would be independent of the Portuguese Padroado, and it was no coincidence that the Sacred Congregation of Propaganda Fide selected the Capuchins for this task as theirs was the order most closely identified with this new, powerful curial organ by which the Vatican hoped to assert its influence over Catholic missionary activity. The first parties of Spanish, Flemish, and Italian Capuchins had slipped into Mpinda while the Dutch had temporarily occupied Luanda. After the reconquest of Luanda in 1648, the Portuguese crown was prepared to continue to admit Italian Capuchins to this mission field provided that they were not Spanish subjects and that they passed through Lisbon and Luanda. In Kongo the Capuchins became something of a diplomatic liability for Garcia II after 1648 (Wilson, 1978: 321–23), but the rulers of Soyo continued to appreciate the diplomatic benefits which could be drawn from these contacts with the missionaries from Rome.

Although the Portuguese in Luanda were defeated in their attempt to conquer Soyo in 1670, they still remained an ominous, hostile force, and the ruler of Soyo requested the pope to intervene on his behalf. As a result, the papal nuncio elicited from the king of Portugal an admission that the ruler of Soyo was an independent prince. The nuncio also received an assurance from the king that the hostility of the governor of Luanda towards Soyo did not reflect the policy of Lisbon.[4] Firearms and artillery obtained from Dutch traders were undoubtedly the principal external factor in insuring the survival of an independent Soyo, and, as will be seen, the rulers of Soyo thoroughly appreciated the crucial importance of maintaining access to these weapons. It is also clear, however, that the rulers were anxious not to become entirely dependent on the Dutch. The links with papal diplomacy provided Soyo with an independent access, however tenuous and slight, to the world of European diplomacy, and this brought distinct, if intangible, advantages.

The Capuchins also played a major role in the protracted negotiations which eventually led to a reestablishment of relations between Soyo and the Portuguese. As early as 1685 the vice prefect of the mission could report that the ruler of Soyo, "*Come vero Prencipe Catolico*," was prepared for the church to take a major part in this critical diplomacy.[5] While patiently assisting the Portuguese to strengthen their contacts with Soyo, the Capuchins steadfastly supported the ruler in his refusal to permit the Portuguese to establish a fort at the strategic

---

4. SC Africa I, f.365–66, Nuncio to Prefect, Lisbon, May 3, 1677.
5. SC Africa I, f.573v, Giuseppe Maria da Busseto to Prefect, April 4, 1685.

port of Mpinda. They seem to have accomplished this task with at least a touch of that skill and charity which enabled members of their order to play similar roles in the diplomacy of seventeenth-century Europe,[6] and for more than a decade the Capuchins were intimately involved in the execution of Soyo's foreign policy (Jadin, 1970: 387–89).

The Capuchins and the Soyo Authorities

The influence of the Capuchins in Soyo, however, was not solely, or even principally, due to their undoubted political and diplomatic value to the state. Far more fundamentally they possessed a basic, ritual significance. They were welcomed and respected as Christian priests who made accessible what were increasingly recognized as sacraments of salvation by Soyo's rulers and their subjects. As in any example of profound and extensive interaction between an African polity and Christian missionary activity, points of congruence were found between the new religion and the local social structures. In the Kongo kingdom as a whole the Capuchins occupied an ambivalent position. In most of the kingdom the points of congruence fluctuated and were unstable. At times, particularly for the first three years of their mission, the Capuchins saw themselves, and were seen by the ruler and people of Kongo, as allied to the king and his local representatives; at other times, especially when they later came into open conflict with Garcia II, they assumed some of the attributes of radical revolutionaries, seeking to take salvation to the poor, the marginal, and the oppressed, or at least they were seen as the opponents of hostile and "oppressive" rulers (Wilson, 1978: 328–35). In Soyo, although elements of tension between rulers and missionaries remained, as one might expect if evangelism preserved its potential prophetic challenge, the Capuchins were far more closely and continuously identified with the establishment, and in its turn, the ruling institution at the center of Soyo became far more thoroughly Christianized than was the case with the government centered on San Salvador in the seventeenth century.

Most of the principal public rituals in Soyo were becoming centered around the Christian calendar by the late seventeenth century. The festivals of Easter, Christmas, Pentecost, and All Souls had become major occasions, uniting ruler and subjects in colorful, enthusiastic displays of worship and rejoicing. On such occasions the ruler attended Mass splendidly arrayed in the white robes of the order of Christ. Even on weekdays (for he normally attended church at least three times a week, either for Mass or the rosary) he came specially attired, wearing on his breast a cross of solid gold, holding his rods of office and borne aloft in a hammock. He was accompanied by a crowd of attendants, who carried his velvet-covered chair, his faldstool, carpet, and cushion, and he was preceded by musicians sounding trumpets, double bells, and other instruments. During Mass, before the reading of the Gospel, one of his pages was given a lighted torch, and at the end of the Gospel the missal was brought to him to kiss. At the end of Mass he came forward to the altar to receive benediction and accompanied the priest into the sacristy (Merolla, 1692: 169–75).

Besides these regular occasions for regal splendor and royal ritual participation, two saints' days had become of great local political significance. As in Kongo every governor (*mani*) or headman of the towns and major villages of Soyo was obliged to present himself at Mbanza Soyo accompanied "by all his people" to hear Mass and to render obedience to the ruler on the feast of St. James on July 25. At a great ceremony held outside the Capuchins' church, the ruler, after receiving a blessing from the priest, executed two war dances. Then, seated on his throne in the shade of a magnificent tree, he watched while each official, from the captain-general down to the village headmen, first received a blessing from the priest and then executed a war dance, bringing also a symbol of the tribute which they were each obliged to offer the ruler. These ceremonies went on for a fortnight, during which time the missionaries were kept busy dispensing the sacraments of marriage, penance, and baptism, Fra Girolamo da Sorrento baptizing 272 people in one day alone (Merolla, 1692: 156–58; Jadin, 1970: 448–52). This ancient and well-established festival became matched in Soyo by the feast of St. Luke on October 18, at which the crushing defeat of the Portuguese in 1670 was commemorated with suitable devotion and pride in a crowded and joyous procession (Cuvelier 1953: 58). At Mbanza Soyo two of the town's six churches were particularly associated with rulers: one contained the tombs of the rulers and another was the royal chapel (Merolla, 1692: 168). By January 1702 the "Gram Principe de Sonho" had acquired an official seal: the symbolism consisted solely of a cross.[6]

Christian rituals and symbols thus provided an impressive component of the court's pomp and splendor. In these circumstances the excommunication of the ruler became, as will be seen, a matter of considerable political concern. But the alliance between missionary and ruler was by no means limited to their joint participation at Mass. It included an important element of legitimation by the spiritual powers, who were intimately concerned with the public ratification of the ruler's accession. MacGaffey remarks how the candidate chief in Kongo "had to submit to inspection by his peers to ensure that his spirit was appropriate to the role" ("Religious Commission," 1970: 30), and Fra Girolamo describes how, after the election of a ruler by nine electors, the missionary was immediately informed. If the choice "had fallen on a worthy individual, the priest approved it and announced it publicly in church to the populace, otherwise the election would be null and void" (Merolla, 1692: 153). The consent and ritual support of the missionaries was sought at other crucial occasions: before declaring war the ruler obtained the approval of the superior of the mission, and as his army went out to fight it was fortified by Christian rites (ibid., 119; Jadin, 1970: 457). On his side the ruler sent gifts of food to the missionaries, and he allocated land to the slaves and servants of the mission when they married (Merolla, 1692: 156).

The rulers of Soyo may well have had greater need than the kings of Kongo for the political support and legitimation provided by Christian rituals. They seem to have lacked a well-established indigenous tradition of legitimacy. Dapper's reference in his description of mid-seventeenth century Soyo to the fact that the area was divided among many chieftaincies who usually enjoyed independence but who by that time "lived under another sovereign power" (Dapper, 1670: 544), forcibly suggests the upstart nature of the Soyo ruling establishment as known to the Capuchins. Its fortunes in the seventeenth century largely rested, as we have seen, on a series of successful rebellions against San Salvador, followed by the eventual destruction of this once-powerful capital. The measure of legitimation bestowed by the new religion may well, therefore, have been highly valued for political reasons by the rulers of Soyo.

The Mission's Disciplining of the Ruling Elite

Until one can gain a clearer view of the rise of the ruling dynasty in Soyo, this aspect of the political significance of Christianity as the source of ritual legitimation must remain somewhat speculative. But it is already abundantly clear that by the last quarter of the seventeenth century the mission had come to occupy a central role in the training, formation, and even selection of Soyo's ruling elite. By that time the principal officials gained their education and training during a period of highly disciplined, committed, and privileged service in the work of the mission.

The creation of a nucleus of disciplined, committed Christians went back to the early days of the Capuchin mission. Cavazzi describes their bold, "inspired" decision to create congregations or confraternities (brotherhoods) for lay men and women in San Salvador and Mbanza Soyo, as "a stupendous act" taken in the face "of all human reason" (Cavazzi, 1687: III, 45, 342–43). The rules of these confraternities insisted that each member should hear Mass daily if at all possible; should make confession and communicate every first and third Sunday in the month taking part in public discipline; should fast every Saturday; should conduct prayers morning and evening and teach their families Christian doctrine; should shun dances, and persuade "concubines" to marry (Piazza, 1973: 54–56; Buenaventura de Carrocera, 1946–47: 123–24). Originally these confraternities were open to all, *Plebei e Nobili*, provided that they were of good reputation. In their early days, at least, they seem to have performed some of the functions of a purification or witchcraft-eradication cult: after the sermon "many would lie prostrate on the ground" voluntarily and publicly confessing their failings (Cavazzi, 1687: III, 45, 342–43). Gradually membership of these confraternities became a prerequisite for high office in Soyo. Already in the early 1660s it was customary for judicial officials to be selected from members of the confraternities,[7] and in 1674 it was reported that the ruler of Soyo was normally selected from among the Confraternity of St. Francis (Jadin, 1966: 290).

At the head of this Christian elite were the interpreters, or *Maestri delta Chiesa*. Eight or ten in number, these men of "noble" birth were, by the end of the seventeenth century, "not only the most cultured in the land, but also in good part relatives of the prince" (Zucchelli, 1712: 138). Since few of the Capuchins in late seventeenth-century Soyo had sufficient command of the vernacular, the main task of these interpreters was to assist the missionaries in hearing confessions, and like the priests, the interpreters operated under a seal of secrecy. The mission was thus incorporating into its structure the deep desires for purification spontaneously expressed in the early behavior of members of the confraternities, and by the last quarter of the seventeenth century hand-picked scions of the Soyo rulers, and of the Barreto da Silva patrilineage in particular, were intimately collaborating in this routinization of piety. The interpreters also prepared the altars and taught "the people the way of salvation" (ibid.). In return for these services they were relieved of military service, paid no taxes, enjoyed benefit of clergy in legal cases, and were buried with the missionaries. By the 1680s several of the principal officers of the court had served as interpreters, as had the two rulers elected in the 1690s (ibid., 141–42).

This training, together with membership of the confraternities and the obligations which this involved of observing a strict Christian discipline, added an inner, spiritual dimension to the alliance and relationship of missionaries and ruler. It was not simply a question of political necessity or convenient ritual legitimation. Again Cavazzi enables us to catch a glimpse of an early stage in this process. Soon after the formation of the confraternities in the 1640s the ruler of Soyo became suspicious of the activities of these groups and began personally to attend their meetings. In this way he himself became exposed to the detailed teachings of the Capuchins and, under their influence, he repented and decided publicly to adopt Christian marriage (Cavazzi, 1687: III, 47, 346–47). In the relatively scanty evidence which

---

7. SOCG 250, f.428v, Cristostomo da Genova's report, January 10, 1665, referring to conditions prior to his departure from Angola in July 1663.

is available it is difficult to trace this thread of inner conviction and to evaluate its influence on the relationship between the missionaries and the rulers; but, as will be seen, it occasionally surfaced, and the early training and service as interpreters and teachers undoubtedly brought missionaries and elite together in an intimate bond of what many of those involved would regard as deep Christian fellowship.

The Test Case of Christian Marriage

The depth and extent of Christian penetration into Soyo life and culture was, for the Capuchins, measured by their fortunes in two major areas of confrontation. The first was Christian marriage, as laid down by the Council of Trent. The evidence available suggests that here, somewhat unexpectedly, their efforts at imposing ecclesiastical discipline were being marked with increasing and substantial success. Membership of the Christian elite, the confraternities and the interpreters and teachers, naturally involved an acceptance of canon-law marriage. The Capuchins went on to use this example of the ruling elite, together with its political power, to extend this discipline to increasing numbers of the ruler's subjects and dependants. On one occasion, about 1687, when the ruler had been excommunicated, he was ordered as penance to persuade three hundred of his subjects to adopt holy matrimony. In the event four hundred were presented, and a further six hundred immediately followed their example (Merolla, 1692: 227–34). By that time it was accepted that all the *mani*, the governors and headmen of major towns and villages, should be "legitimately married" or be deprived of their office "lest they should set bad examples to the common people" (ibid., 149).

Later, at the height of the delicate diplomatic negotiations with the Portuguese, the missionaries decided to launch a further offensive on the matrimonial front. Wishing to train and place teachers in every district to instruct the people and prepare them for Christian marriage, the missionaries gathered the ruler, the electors, the war captains, and all the elders into their church, where they pointed out to these leaders the responsibility they had before God towards their subjects, whose "souls were being lost by their negligence." To this appeal the Capuchins added the threat that, if these orders were not promulgated, they would leave and go to other more fruitful fields. Touched probably both by the threat and the appeal, the ruler and his councillors swore that they wished to live as good Christians, and immediately promulgated the necessary orders. The missionaries and teachers, in company with the ruler or one of the elders, then went out to search for those whom they regarded as living in "concubinage," and in 1689 in Mbanza Soyo alone more than a thousand marriages were celebrated. Three years later the missionaries in Soyo confidently expected that, with the help of a zealous new ruler, Giovanni Barreto da Silva, "soon everyone would be married."[8]

These expectations were widely over optimistic, and the missionaries in general failed totally to appreciate the nature and values of African marriage. Yet the evidence suggests that the principles enunciated in canon law were beginning to become as much respected in Soyo as they were in parts of contemporary Europe, where, as in Soyo, practice often failed to match principle. In the remoter parts of rural Catholic Europe in the eighteenth century, probably a majority of the villagers still lived together without being married according to canon law (Chadwick, 1981: 149), so it would hardly have been surprising if among the masses in Soyo the new rules of marriage were often more honored in the breach than in the observance. Nevertheless, the degree to which the missionaries were able to exert pressure towards an acceptance of canon-law marriage is an extraordinary sign of the extent of their influence on the ruling elite and on the lives of at least those people of Soyo who lived within easy reach of Mbanza Soyo.

The Interaction of Christianity and Indigenous Religion

For the missionaries the other touchstone of Soyo Christianity was the question of the continuing attachment of the people to the shrines, charms, and other elements of their religion. The Capuchins' approach was one of straightforward confrontation. Encountering the

---

8. SC Africa II, f.314–15 and 573v, Angelo Francesco da Milano to Prefect, Luanda, March 4, 1690 and April 15, 1692.

literate civilizations of Asia, some seventeenth-century missionaries had begun to appreciate the necessity of attempting to enter into a dialogue with alien cultures; in tropical Africa, recognition of the values of African institutions and beliefs was to prove far more elusive. Identifying most African rituals as the works of the devil, the Capuchins generally demanded total renunciation. If a nominal Christian continued impenitently to officiate over these rituals, they considered it perfectly just that he or she should be exiled into slavery across the Atlantic (Merolla, 1692: 106). The missionaries assumed that conflict between the new and old religions was inevitable and total. The evidence suggests that some Soyo converts may have agreed with them, and that a few of these were prepared, at least in private, to accept wholeheartedly a radical break with customary beliefs and practices.

While Andrea da Pavia was in Soyo a general assembly of the people was called "with the consent and intervention of the Prince." The question for debate was whether they "wished to observe the laws of God or their superstitious ceremonies." The reply was given that "they firmly believed in God and in everything that was taught them, but that they also believed in their ceremonies and vain observances." Afterwards, many came in private to protest against what had been said in public, and these alone were admitted to the sacraments.[9] Besides these committed members of the elite and populace, another group of people who were almost totally identified with the Capuchins were the slaves of the mission, who maintained the hostel, served as medical aids in the hospital (ibid., 399), and accompanied the missionaries on their visitations. Shortly after his arrival in Soyo, Fra Girolamo found that the slaves of the mission did not hesitate to lay hold of a hostile *nganga*, having no fear of his supernatural powers because they themselves wore medals "given to them by us as preservatives against sorcery" (ibid., 105).

The hostile *nganga* represented the other extreme of the religious spectrum in Soyo. When Cavazzi visited the area in 1663 he found that there was still a determined resistance against the Christian ruler and his wife. A church had been burnt in Soyo, a hostile charm had been placed against the ruler's wife, and guards were mounted

---

9. SOCG 514, f.471v, "Compendiosa relatione."

in the churches to prevent "some superstitious Christians' from dig-
ging up and transporting corpses "into the bush to the graves of their
ancestors" (Cavazzi, 1687: VII, 123, 856; Wilson, 1978: 343–44). By the
1680s, however, the *nganga* in Soyo were very much on the defensive.
Fra Girolamo and his confreres led attacks on hidden shrines, and
the impression is given that traditional ritual experts carried on their
practices only at considerable risk to themselves, though, significantly
enough, when the missionary and ruler were in dispute over the slave
trade, "the magicians and sorcerers" sought to exacerbate the situation (Merolla, 1692: 209).

In between these two extremes of Soyo religious commitment
there was, as the reply of the ruler and the general assembly to Fra
Andrea indicated, a whole range of people for whom the concept of
religious conflict was minimal or even absent. They believed in God
and "everything that was taught them," but they also held to their
own rituals. For them the new faith was part of a religious spectrum
in which they continued to find relevance in many of the old beliefs
and practices. Shortly before Fra Girolamo arrived in Soyo, the ruler,
Antonio I Barreto da Silva, had administered an oath to many of his
subjects, some of whom, however, were able to stage a public protest
against this act during Fra Girolamo's first sermon (ibid., 89–93). Antonio I repented that evening, and this eclectic attitude to religion did
not generally involve the ruler and people of Soyo in deliberate syncretism, in a conscious attempt to take elements of Christianity and
create a new and distinct amalgam of beliefs. In the first decade of the
eighteenth century such an attempt did emerge in Kongo around the
young, prophetic figure of Dona Beatrice and the Antonine movement,
but the people of Soyo, save in the remote south, were hostile to emissaries of this syncretistic sect (Cuvelier 1953: 159, 171, 228). In Soyo the
interaction between religious beliefs was less dramatic, the process of
change being gradual and cumulative.

The situation in Soyo in the late seventeenth century seems to have
borne a striking resemblance to that of Kongo in the second half of the
twentieth century where as reported by Janzen and MacGaffey, "very
few people think of themselves as non-Christian and "conversion" is
no longer an issue" (1974: 16). In such a situation most individuals

were not continually confronted with stark religious alternatives. There was a large middle ground of "ambivalent flexibility," and across this religious spectrum there was a process of "complex interaction and adaptation" (ibid., 4, 17). The problem for a historian faced with such a situation is to identify the broad direction of change in religious thought and practice. Of course Christianity was, in Balandier's phrase, "associated with traditional usages," but the crucial question is whether Christianity was being absorbed into an unchanged cosmology, "a system of thought that remains African and traditional rather than European and Christian" (ibid., 3), or whether the new religion, through its sacraments, liturgy, discipline, and literacy, possessed sources of strength which enabled it over time to exert a cumulative impact.

The evidence for late seventeenth-century Soyo suggests, as we have already seen, that among the ruling elite something of this cumulative influence can be clearly discerned. In this narrow compass Soyo Christians were constantly being confronted with the challenges presented by the new religion, and many of them were gaining new insights into its implications. For the populace at large the evidence is much less abundant. Here a distinction must be drawn between the situation in Mbanza Soyo with its immediate neighborhood, and the more distant areas of the region. The influence of the Capuchins was definitely concentrated on the capital. Because of the rains and the pattern of agricultural activity, the visits of the missionaries to distant rural areas were restricted to the months from May to September (Jadin, 1966: 292), and even then they could undertake such visits only if there was another priest who could stay behind to maintain the mission at Mbanza Soyo. On their relatively infrequent visits they encountered in rural Soyo an almost universal enthusiasm for baptism, whereas resistance to this rite was encountered in some areas of Kongo. The popularity of baptism indicates a readiness of the majority to accept at least a nominal Christian identification, a move which in the minds of the missionaries exposed these adherents to the dictates of canon law. Baptism by itself could, however, have been readily absorbed by most recipients into an unchanged folk cosmology. The jubilant acceptance of the rite even in the remoter parts of Soyo may therefore merely have testified to the absence of open hostility to Christian missionaries and their elite assistants.

Confessions, however, would seem to be another matter. The rite was by no means a formality: the investigations were often searching and prolonged, while absolution was withheld if the confessor was not convinced that penitence was sincere. Many Capuchin missionaries would have agreed with Fra Giovanni da Romano in regarding the confessional as the principal means of evangelism and of deepening the hold of Christian beliefs and discipline.[10] Like baptism, confession could be seen as essentially a rite of purification and as such highly congruent to Kongo religious practice. Unlike baptism, however, it must have been, at least in most cases, an ordeal not lightly entered upon. Willingness to submit to confession could be a good indication of popular attitudes. When Fra Girolamo visited Kitombo more than a decade after the battle with the Portuguese there he found that some people had not confessed since then on account of "the great provocation" (Merolla, 1692: 127). Among the many hundreds of confessions heard annually by the Capuchins in Soyo some, especially in the outer rural districts, may have been fleeting encounters with little permanent effects, but the readiness of many of the people of Soyo to present themselves for this sacrament, even walking five or six days to do so (ibid., 135), would seem to indicate an increasingly wide and deep commitment to the new religion.

Even in folk rituals, a new significance was becoming apparent. The ancestors, for instance, were beginning to be seen as synonymous with the holy souls of Catholic tradition. Fra Andrea da Pavia reported how, after his arrival in Soyo in 1688, he went to bed as usual on the eve of All Souls but was roused almost immediately by many people singing at the top of their voices. Informed by the mission's slaves that this was merely the normal devotions for the dead, he joined the torch-lit processions which visited the churches in the town and also the cemeteries where the graves were illuminated by many candles. "Everyone was chanting prayers in their language," and Fra Andrea went on to assist them with great enthusiasm. Two hours before daybreak

---

10. Giovanni Belotti da Romano, "Avvertimenti salutevoli . . ." f.287. Mss in Biblioteca Radini-Tedeschi, Bergamo.

he sounded the church bells, sang the office, celebrated Mass, and then led out another procession to the graves where he intoned the responses for the dead. The whole night passed in this manner, for sleep was quite impossible. The next day, when all the ceremonies had finished, everyone came with their baskets "each offering alms for the dead," so that the mission distributed ten tons of fruit and other gifts (Jadin, 1970: 440-1). The sacrifices for the ancestors had become alms for the church's poor; yet, it will be recalled, at the time of Cavazzi's visit only a generation earlier the ruler of Soyo had had to place guards to prevent the reburial of Christians in ancestral cemeteries.

Fra Andrea also glimpsed something of the anguish and dilemma of the majority of Soyo Christians as, faced with the Capuchins' rigid missiology, they attempted to explore and appropriate for themselves these new religious horizons. When he reported to the Congregation of Propaganda Fide the response of the general assembly called to debate "superstitious ceremonies" (see above), he went on to ask "if in some respects they could be excused, for in their ceremonies they do not make an explicit, or implicit, pact with the devil, but have a simple faith, from which one tries to raise them as much as one can."[11] His question raised an issue of fundamental missiological significance. His assessment of Soyo rituals in this passage, if not in all his writings, showed far more understanding than that exhibited by most of his confreres, at least in their published works. As he said, this was no devil worship. Indeed he seems to have begun to grasp the fact that their beliefs and rituals represented not only a basic acceptance of supernatural powers but also a continuous attempt to summon their assistance in the constant conflict with evil, however that might be defined. Fra Andrea's final phrase might even imply that he was perhaps ready to take the first vital step towards a recognition of the positive, fundamental values in Soyo religion.

His report was submitted to the cardinals of Propaganda Fide on April 6, 1693, by Cardinal Gaspare Carpegna, a great canon lawyer. Carpegna was to be an assiduous participant in the congregation appointed in 1704 to consider the momentous issue of Chinese rites which involved similar missiological problems, so it is interesting to

---

11. SOCG 514, f.471v, "Compendiosa relatione."

note that a decade earlier he was fairly sympathetic to the problems raised by Fra Andrea. While insisting that "superstitions" should be combated through the confessional, Carpegna went on to suggest that certain sacred rites such as benediction could be introduced to take the place of "superstitions."[12] The path towards adaptation was not wholly closed, and it might have developed had these Soyo Christians been permitted to foster their own Catholic priesthood. A Capuchin did later advocate the construction of a seminary (Jadin, 1964: 443–44), but in Soyo the highest post in the church effectively open to local people remained that of interpreter.

The Mission, the Rulers, and the Slave Trade

This lack of an indigenous priesthood seriously hampered any prospect of a fruitful theological dialogue, and undoubtedly jeopardized the future development of Christianity in Soyo. A more immediate cause of grave tension between the Capuchins and the rulers of Soyo arose from the Atlantic slave trade, which provoked a continued and deepening crisis in the relations of church and state. Acting on a mistaken interpretation of instructions from Propaganda Fide (Gray, forthcoming), the Capuchins condemned the sale of baptized slaves to English or other heretical traders. Fra Girolamo twice excommunicated Antonio I, although he himself recognized the dangers of employing this drastic sanction (Merolla, 1692: 220). Some of his successors seem almost to have gloried in their power of interference and their ability to humiliate publicly the rulers of Soyo (Zucchelli, 1712: 160–73). Despite the bitter resentment that these theocratic pretensions must have aroused, Antonio II sent a cool, humble petition to Propaganda Fide. Written on October 4, 1701, his letter appealed over the heads of the Capuchins to what he hoped would prove an impartial authority. To the Capuchin insistence that he sold slaves only to the Portuguese or to those Protestants who traded with Catholic ports, the ruler pointed out that the Portuguese would provide him with neither powder nor arms necessary "for our defense against our enemies," and that Protestants trading with Catholic ports were but few in number. Antonio

---

12. SOCG 514, f.472–472v, Comments by Cardinal Carpegna.

II failed, however, to mention that the trade also supplied him and his court with valued luxury imports, and that strategical considerations were not his sole motive. He, like European Christians involved in the trade, was ensnared in an immense structure of evil. Instead he stressed the necessity of preserving "my principality and the peace of my people," and he asked permission to conduct this trade without danger of excommunication, for "I am a Catholic Prince and desire the accomplishment of my salvation."[13]

The interior, reflective beliefs of individuals are almost totally excluded from the records. Yet as one reads how Antonio II served the mission in his youth, rising to the rank of interpreter, and how, despite his sharp disagreements with the Capuchins over the slave trade, he continued "faithfully to promote the apostolate" (Cuvelier, 1953: 180, 289), one is prepared to accept, not as a mere phrase penned by a secretary well trained in ecclesiastical correspondence but as an expression of a deeply held conviction, the claim that he was "a Catholic prince" and that he desired "the accomplishment of [his] salvation."

Conclusion

The records of the late seventeenth century do not therefore depict Christianity in Soyo as affecting "only a slim minority" or as being "weakly established': the judgment of contemporaries might rather have been that it was vigorous, expanding, and in some respects almost arrogantly triumphant. One can perceive the ruling institution becomingly increasingly dependent on legitimation by recognized Christian ritual experts; an elite, trained and recruited through exposure to an extremely rigorous religious discipline; a gradual imposition of radically new practices concerning marriage; and the main public festivals becoming centered around the Christian calendar, with the Mass as perhaps the principal ritual focus in Soyo life. One can see Christianity and canon law as features distinguishing Soyo from its northern neighbors. One can even begin to glimpse something of the difficulties and anguish in which the people of Soyo were involved as they

---

13. SC Africa III, f.288–288v, Antonio Barreto de Silva to Cardinals of Propaganda Fide, Sonho, October 4, 1701: "ser eu principe Catholico, e dezejar o acerto da minha salvação."

explored the implications of this Christian identity, while remaining subject to the jurisdiction of aliens who understood but a small part of this tension and conflict.

In such a situation the cumulative weight of a literate, universal tradition was considerable. The process of religious interaction was dynamic, though its direction could change. Christianity was then, and has ever been, "in constant danger" (Balandier, 1968: 255), whether in long-established Christian territories, such as seventeenth-century Italy or France, or on the distant frontiers of overseas missions. Some grounds for deep anxiety had already appeared in Soyo. There was the ominous reluctance to raise an indigenous priesthood. Most obviously there were the tensions arising out of the slave trade, with both European and African Christians enmeshed in the system. With a terrible irony, missionaries and rulers were quarrelling to the point of repeated excommunications over an aspect of this evil whose importance was already, in the considered judgment of the Holy Office as handed down in 1686, paling into insignificance compared with the violation of human rights which the whole system involved (Gray, 1981: 37-9). Here indeed the Christian community in Soyo appears as a frail and fragile vessel to confront the greed and cruelty of several continents orchestrated by Europe. The dangers to the faith were manifold, and these few decades in the late seventeenth century may have constituted for Soyo the deepest point of identification with Christendom. At some subsequent period the impetus slackened, the direction of religious change appears to have altered. One should not, however, allow this later story to determine our assessment of what was happening in the seventeenth century. Church historians should not fall, any more than others, into the trap of Whig interpretations; rather they should recall Ranke's dictum that every generation is equidistant from eternity. The meaning and message of salvation has ever to be discovered anew.

6

Christian Traces and a Franciscan Mission in the Central Sudan, 1700–1711

Merely as an exploit, the first recorded trans-Saharan crossing to a Hausa city by Europeans would seem to deserve more attention than it has yet received. The story was first recounted in an early eighteenth-century manuscript history of the Franciscan order;[1] echoes of it were published in 1818;[2] and a fuller account, based on records in Tripoli, finally appeared in 1924.[3] The mission's records in Rome add detail to these outlines; they also reveal an impressive, if somewhat garbled, accumulation of evidence pointing to the persistence of Christian symbols among kingdoms to the south of Bornu and the Hausa states at the turn of the seventeenth century: a fact the relevance of which for African history possibly extends to ancient Benin on the one hand, and to Christian Nubia on the other.

On December 14, 1700, the cardinals of Propaganda Fide, the Vatican Congregation established in 1622 to supervise Catholic missionary activity, considered a memorandum proposing a mission to the Kingdom of Bornu, "where there are many Christians, little or uninstructed in the faith, with virtually only the name of Christians." The writer, Fr. Maurizio da Lucca, who for seven years had been prefect of the Franciscan mission in Tripoli, went on to assure the cardinals that among the Negro slaves brought from Bornu via the Fezzan "there were many who say that they are Christians." Possibly, this information did not appear wildly improbable to the cardinals, for Propaganda

---

1. A. M. de Turre, *Orbis Seraphicus*, ed, A. Chiappini, II, pars. ii (Quaracchi-Firenze, 1945), Liber Octavus "De Novissimus Apostolicis Missionibus ad regna Fezzàn, Bornò Nubiae et Gorolfae in Africa," 312–33.

2. *Quarterly Review* (1818), quoted in R. Hallett, *The Penetration of Africa* I (1965), 102–3.

3. C. Bergna, *La Missione Francescana in Libia* (Tripoli, 1924).

was already actively engaged in attempting to succor Christian remnants in the Eastern Sudan, and the legend of Prester John still influenced their worldview. Fr. Maurizio's proposals were therefore readily accepted, and a small financial subsidy was allocated for sending two Franciscans to Bornu.[4]

Fr. Damiano da Rivoli, an elderly, accomplished Arabist with some knowledge of medicine, who was appointed prefect of the new mission, found on his arrival at Tripoli that the route to the Fezzan and Bornu was blocked by fighting and pestilence. After several months' delay he decided to travel up the Nile to Sennar, in the hope of joining there the alternative caravan route to Bornu. He reached the Fung capital on November 11, 1703, and subsequently established contact with a caravan leader, "a robust fakir [*un santone*], sixty-two years old, a native of Bornò," who told him that the only Christians in Bornu were three representatives "who looked after the affairs of the Christians." He asserted that there was "a village inhabited by Christians, close to which flowed the River Niger [*il fiume negro*], not far from the city of Bornò." With a certain relish, one feels, he went on to describe how the inhabitants of this "village" produced wine from vines and possessed "fruits in abundance, corn and vegetables [*erbe*] of every kind." Halfway between the "city" of Bornu and this "village" there was a weekly market frequented by Muslims and Christians, where, "when the Muslims of the city wanted to drink wine, they went to drink their fill." The leader added "that the Christians flourished and that they had their graves in the middle of their village, surrounded by walls." He invited the missionary to join the caravan, which took sixty days to reach Bornu from Sennar, "ten[5] of which were in the desert," but Fr. Damiano was warned by "various Muslim acquaintances in Sennar" not to go, "as both Muslims and Christians who went with that caravan, would

---

4. Archives of Propaganda Fide (A.P.F.), Scr. Cong. Gen. 536, ff. 458, 461. Copy of memorandum by Fr. Maurizio da Lucca, presented by Cardinal Sacripante to the General Congregation of December 14, 1700.

5. Another account gives thirteen days here (A.P.F. Scr. Cong. Gen. 557, f. 342). The figure of ten days strangely echoes the tenth-century account by Al Muhallabi of the distance between the kingdoms of Nuba and Zaghawa, quoted in R. Oliver and J. D. Fage, A Short History of Africa (Hammondsworth, 1962), 47.

be killed by its members," and so on May 26, 1704, he left Sennar to return to Tripoli via Cairo.[6]

In July 1705 Fr. Damiano, back in Tripoli, reported that the French consul, Claude Lemaire, would ask the ruler of the Fezzan to write on the mission's behalf "to his cousin the king of Bornò." Lemaire assured Fr. Damiano that he would be able to work with "Sultan Corurfa," a powerful king who fought the ruler of Bornu, a Christian together with "all the people of his kingdom." Fr. Damiano was also told that there was "another kingdom not far from Bornò, where they are neither Christian nor Muslim, and are easy to convert to any law which is taught them," so he formally asked Propaganda for permission to work in "the kingdom of Sultan Corurfa" and the non-Muslim areas if he found that there were no Christians in the Fezzan or Bornu.[7] Subsequently he met several Negro men and women who arrived from Bornò with two caravans from the Fezzan. He took the opportunity of questioning each one separately in Arabic, including a Negro slave in the house of the bey of Tripoli. He was told that "in Bornò there were no Christians; but that, nearby, there were many, who have their own king, though but poor Christians. They fight when there is no peace between the king of Gorolfa and that of Bornò, and the said Christians are strong in the tenacity of their faith, allowing themselves to be massacred rather than become Muslim." His informants added that the Christians lived comfortably in their country, "where there was abundance of vegetables, corn, and every type of fruit." Fr. Damiano reported that the caravans from Tripoli to the Fezzan took twenty-five days, and from the Fezzan to Bornu took ninety days, but that the road to the "kingdom of Gorolfa where the Christians are found" was somewhat shorter than this, being a little nearer to the Fezzan.[8]

---

6. A.P.F. Scr. Cong. Gen. 557, ff. 315, 324, 326–43. Copies of two memoranda by Fr. Damiano submitted after his return to Italy, and considered at General Congregation of February 22, 1707.

7. A.P.F. Scr. Cong. Gen. 552, ff. 422–23. Fr. Damiano da Rivoli to Prefect of Propaganda, Tripoli, July 4, 1705. Fr. Damiano in his later memoranda changed the spelling of "Corurfa" to "Gorolfa."

8. A.P.F. Scr. Cong. Gen. 557, ff. 315, 324. Memorandum by Fr. Damiano considered on February 22,. 1707.

This information was supplemented by Claude Lemaire. Already in 1686, during an earlier course of duty at Tripoli, he had reported that the king of Bornu allowed a great liberty of conscience, "so much so that a great number of his subjects are Christians'; and in 1698 Consul Delalande described how Muslim merchants, passing from the Fezzan to Mecca, brought with them Negroes from the country of Prester John, "who are originally Christians and who are distinguished from others by certain marks that they have on their faces."[9] Twenty years after his first report, Lemaire, by now on terms of close friendship with the ruler of the Fezzan, was able to correct his first impressions. He informed Propaganda that the "vast" kingdom of Bornu was completely Muslim, but that "the kingdom of Gourourfa is completely Christian, but only nominally. The king of that country is most powerful, and often wages war against that of Borneò [sic] in the name of religion."[10] Asked to amplify his remarks, Lemaire replied that there were but few Christians in Bornu Kingdom, "but in that of gouroufa [sic], there are more than one hundred thousand. . . . They have no more than the name, but this they guard at peril of their life," refusing to change their religion when enslaved by the King of Bornu. Yet as well as the name, at least one piece of Christian ritual seems to have been preserved, for he added that he had seen "several of them here who make the sign of the cross, but their language is different from that of other Negroes and they can be understood only by sign." He was assured that there was now peace, and that at that moment an ambassador from their king was in Bornu.[11]

Advanced in age and weakened by illness contracted on his journey to Sennar, Fr. Damiano was recalled to his province of Piedmont in April 1706. His place was taken by Fr. Carlo Maria di Genova, also experienced in medicine and surgery, who was then in Cairo waiting

9. Reports by Lemaire and Delalande quoted in P. Masson, *Histoire des établissements et du commerce française dans l'Afrique barbaresque, 1560–1793* (Paris, 1903), 178–79. I am most grateful to Mr. Robin Hallett of Oxford for drawing my attention to this reference and for those in notes 41 and 51.

10. A.P.F. Scr. Cong. Gen. 557, ff. 134–35. Lemaire to prefect of Propaganda, Tripoli, April 18, 1706.

11. A.P.F. Scr. Congressi. Barbaria 3, ff. 505–8. Same to same, Tripoli, May 25, 1707. An Italian translation is at Scr. Cong. Gen. 559, ff. 632–33.

to proceed to Ethiopia.[12] Before leaving for Tripoli, Fr. Carlo questioned two sons of the king of Bornu who were then passing through Cairo on their return from Mecca. They confirmed that in "the kingdom or province of Canorfa," there were people "who venerate the cross and erect it over the houses and churches, and that their king acts among them as high priest." From what the princes reported of their behavior and ceremonies, however, Fr. Carlo concluded that these people had "little knowledge of the holy law of Christ and of our rites."[13]

Eventually,[14] early in June 1710, Fr. Carlo and his companion, Fr. Severino da Silesia, a Bohemian with fluent Arabic, left Tripoli with a caravan for the Fezzan. They travelled under the protection of the bey of the Fezzan, whose favors had been enlisted with the assistance of Francesco Passinelli, a Venetian merchant at Tripoli, and because of the medical services which Fr. Carlo had already given to the bey's relatives. His knowledge of medicine was indeed the key to the whole undertaking, for, although "no Christians, particularly in religious orders, had ever passed by that route," Fr. Carlo was able to travel as "a doctor returning to the land of the blacks where I had once been."[15] On July 26 they reached the Fezzan, entering the capital, Murzuk, four days later. Well received by both bey and populace, they were, however, overtaken by a war scare and had to take refuge, together with the court, in the walled town of Traghen. Here Fr. Carlo was able to contact

---

12. A.P.F. Scr. Cong. Gen. 561, f. 23. Note from the Franciscan procurator, discussed on January 9, 1708.

13. A.P.F. Scr. Cong. Gen. 561, f. 25. Fr. Carlo Maria di Genova to Propaganda Cairo, July 28, 1707. C. Beccari, *Rerum Aethiopicarum Scriptores Occidentales*, xiv (Rome, 1914), 384, quotes a letter from the French consul in Cairo, January 18, 1707, which refers in passing to both Fr. Carlo ("mon chapelain") and to the visit of the princes of Bornu.

14. Fr. Carlo offended both the French consul and the prefect of the Tripoli Mission by his dilatoriness and the company he frequented: he was even accused of having proposed a toast in honor of the Queen of England. But he pleaded an interruption of the caravans, and he may well have thought that his unprecedented task demanded unorthodox friendships. (A.P.F. Scr. Cong. Gen. 569, f. 266, Poullard to Card. Sacripante, Tripoli, March 25, 1709; 571, f. 8, Fr. Francesco Maria di Sarzana to Prefect of Propaganda, Tripoli, January 19, 1710; 569, f. 264 and 572, f. 405, letters from Fr. Carlo to Propaganda, Tripoli, August 26, 1709 and May 18, 1710.)

15. A.P.F. Scr. Cong. Gen. 573, f. 41, Fr. Carlo to the prefect of Propaganda, Tripoli, June 9, 1710.

the son of the king of the "Tuargha nation,"[16] who arrived there with a caravan from Mecca. Won over by a small gift of medicines, this prince willingly agreed to accept the Franciscans into his caravan, and on October 17, 1710, Fr. Carlo wrote that they were hoping by this means to reach "Accades [i.e. Agades], gate and key of the Negro kingdoms," in order to pass on to "Garolfa," provided that they could obtain the permission of the king of Agades, "without which no white man, not even be he a Muslim, can pass into the Negro kingdoms."[17]

Two years later Fr. Francesco Maria di Sarzana, prefect of the mission in Tripoli, reported the end of their journey. On October 10, 1712, Aggi Milleit (Hajj Milad), a "Moorish merchant of Tripoli," a close and faithful friend of Fr. Carlo, who had accompanied him to the Fezzan and on to Agades, told Fr. Francesco, with obvious grief, how Fr. Carlo and his companion, prevented from proceeding to Bornu on account of the "great dangers of that route," had set out from Agades, with a small caravan of eight other traders, in a southwesterly direction[18] in order to enter the " kingdom of the Sudam." The sole survivor of this caravan on his return to Agades told Hajj Milad how, after arriving safely in Cassinà (Katsina),[19] one of the party had developed an illness from the "malignant and pestilential waters" which made "the body swell like those who have the dropsy." Fr. Carlo had tried in vain to operate, but ended by catching the infection himself and died eight days later. The ruler of Katsina seized Fr. Carlo's belongings and, in reply to the remonstrance of Fr. Severino, admonished him to become a Muslim. The lone missionary refused "this iniquitous proposal," and soon caught the same disease, dying thirteen days afterwards, in August 1711, according to Fr. Francesco.[20] On hearing this news in

---

16. Muhammad Agabba (1687–1721). Cf. Y. Urvoy, *Histoire des populations du Soudan Central* (Paris, 1936), 176–78.

17. A.P.F. Scr. Cong. Gen. 577, f. 125, Fr. Carlo to Card. Sacripante, Fezzano da Daraghen, October 17, 1710.

18. The text has "verso le parti di Lebechio." *Libéccio* = southwest wind.

19. Fr. Francesco has "harrivati al Sudam capitale di quel Regno, in una Terra chiamata Cassinà," but subsequently he refers to "il commandante di Cassinà."

20. A.P.F. Scr. Cong. Gen. 586, ff. 41–42. Fr. Francesco Maria di Sarzana to Prefect of Propaganda, Tripoli, October 14, 1712. A copy of this report must form the basis for the account in the *Quarterly Review* quoted in Hallett, op. cit. 103.

March 1713, the cardinals ordered the secretary of Propaganda to confer with the procurator of the Franciscans in order to send other missionaries, but no successors followed Fr. Carlo until 1845, when the congregation, considering whether to establish the Vicariate Apostolic of Central Africa, was in part spurred to action by a report from Tripoli of these earlier endeavors.[21]

Various conjectures have been made as to the location and identity of "Garolfa" or "Gourourfa," the Christian mirage which summoned the Franciscans across the Sahara. Fr. Francesco Maria di Sarzana thought quite simply that "Garolfa" was a synonym for Sudan; Fr. Chiappini and Fr. Robert Streit equate "Canorfa" with Kordofan.[22] Hausa and Bornu sources, however, seem to point unmistakably to the Kwararafa, or "Kororofa,"[23] or "Kornorfa,"[24] for the chronicles show that the Kwararafa, by the end of the seventeenth century, were a people who closely fit the missionaries' reports of a powerful kingdom at war with Bornu and the Hausa States. The first reference to the Kwararafa in the Kano Chronicle is in the reign of Yaji, possibly in the latter half of the fourteenth century. It may be not without significance that the chronicle reports that Yaji was the first ruler of Kano to accept Islam, and that he successfully attacked Santulo,[25] "the key to the south," sacking there "the place of their god." Afterward, when "all the pagan tribe," were subject to Yaji, "the Kwararafa alone refused to follow him," and they were forced, therefore, to pay a tribute in slaves.[26] The trib-

---

21. A.P.F. Acta 209, ff. 36–37, Fr. Venanzio di S. Venanzio to Prefect of Propaganda, Tripoli, February 6, 1845. The new vicariate, established in 1846, included the Central and Western Sudan, but its activities were restricted to the Nile; cf. R. Gray, *A History of the Southern Sudan, 1839–1889* (1961), 23–24.

22. Fr. Francesco in A.P.F. Scr. Cong. Gen. 586, f. 42. A Chiappini, op. cit. 313, n. 1; R. Streit and J. Dindinger, *Bibliotheca Missionum,* xvii (Freiburg, 1952), 60.

23. H. Barth, *Travels and Discoveries in North and Central Africa,* II (1857), 578.

24. "Kornorfa, which embraces about twenty divisions, ruled by one king, who often sallied forth upon Kanoo and Barnoo, and caused much desolation"—Muhammad Bello's description in Denham and Clapperton, *Narrative of Travels and Discoveries in Northern and Central Africa,* II, 3rd ed. (1828), 451.

25. "I have always taken this to be a hill called 'Santolo' some miles south-east of Kano, which I believe, like some other hills, was the residence of a particularly powerful iska in pre-Islamic times" (Professor H. F. C. Smith in a letter dated July 1, 1966).

26. H. R. Palmer, *Sudanese Memoirs,* III (Lagos, 1928), 104–6.

ute, or exchange of slaves in return for horses, apparently continued into the early fifteenth century,[27] but by about the end of the sixteenth century the Kwararafa began to take the offensive, possibly, it has even been suggested, with the aid of firearms obtained from the Guinea coast.[28] In the reign of Muhammad Zaki (for whom Palmer suggests the dates 1582–1618) they attacked Kano, whose inhabitants fled to Dawra, "with the result that the Kwararafa ate up the whole country," and during the late seventeenth century they entered and sacked Kano on two other occasions, the last occurring during the reign of Dadi.[29] In the same period, and shortly before Lemaire reported the first rumors of Christians, the ruler of Bornu, returning in 1667 from his third pilgrimage to Mecca, found his state under attack from both the Tuareg of Agades and the Kwararafa, "then at their apogee and the terror of all the Central Sudan."[30]

It is, of course, far harder to evaluate the references to Christian symbolism and ritual. The Jukun, who represent some of the principal survivors of the Kwararafa, have a divine kingship which, to Meek, forcibly recalled descriptions of ancient Egypt. In describing the kingship ritual, however, Meek himself drew several parallels with the Mass,[31] and his book contains clear evidence of the continued use and importance of the cross as a symbol. In his text his only references are to the ear disks worn by some women among the Kona Jukun, which were made "of hard wood with burnt-in designs, usually of triangles resembling a Maltese cross," and to the symbol of the widespread Aya cult, a mud pillar "surmounted by a cross lying flat and shaped like the letter X." But, surely, far more significant than these examples is

27. Ibid., 107.

28. C. K. Meek, *A Sudanese Kingdom* (1931), 28–29.

29. Palmer, op. cit. III, 116, 121–22.

30. Y. Urvoy, *Histoire de l'empire du Bornou* (Paris, 1949), 85.

31. Meek, op. cit. 153: "when the king of the Jukun daily drinks the ceremonial beer, he may be said to offer himself as a living sacrifice. The rites are, in fact, regarded by the Jukun congregation assembled in the precints in much the same way as a Catholic congregation regards a celebration of the Mass." Cf. also pp. 150, 158 n. i, 162, 256, and, although Meek did not draw the comparison, the use of holy water (p. 156), the washing of the hands after the meal (p. 161) and the burial "punctuated by sounds reminiscent of the responses of a choir in a vestry," p. 171.

the photograph of the king of the Jukun, which shows a row of Maltese crosses prominently displayed on his tunic and its sleeve.[32] Art historians are understandably skeptical as to the weight which should be attached to such evidence.[33] By itself the existence of a cross motif cannot of course be taken as evidence of even indirect Christian influence, and the Maltese cross shown in Meek's photograph may be an isolated example, as it does not occur on the robes worn by other Akus.[34] Professor Ryder has, however, recently drawn attention to the fact that a Maltese cross was one of the principal insignia sent by the Ogane to the Oba in fifteenth-century Benin, and has suggested that "the cross is of vital importance for the identification of the Ogane."[35] At the very least the new documentary evidence would seem to reinforce the theory that the cross was once a symbol of very considerable significance in the Niger-Benue area. One need not for a moment assert that in the late seventeenth century, or at any earlier period, the Kwararafa were a fully practicing Christian community—even the Franciscans would have hesitated to claim this; but some tenuous or indirect contact with Christianity, possibly representing the absorption of a small migrant minority into an ancestral Kwararafa culture, does seem to be at least a plausible hypothesis.

It may be objected that the Franciscans in their inquiries unconsciously persuaded their informants to confirm for them the existence of the "Christians" whom they were so anxiously seeking. Few if any of their informants can have had an intimate or first-hand knowledge of

---

32. Ibid., 19, 206, and plate I.

33. Mr. William Fagg of the British Museum writes that "the 'Maltese crosses' on the Aku of Wukari's clothing may be illusory, for the technique used is appliqué, in which the easiest designs are combinations of triangles, especially in 'solid' appliqué." (Letter dated June 1, 1966).

34. Mr. Arnold Rubin, who has undertaken field work among the Jukun, informs me that photographs of Agbumanu I, Ashumanu IV, and Agbumanu IV show a number of motifs on their robes, "but nowhere, as far as I can tell, anything resembling a Maltese cross." Down the sleeve worn by the present Aku is a motif somewhat resembling a Maltese cross, but "given the triangular basis of most of the other motifs," Mr. Rubin would be inclined to doubt whether it should be so interpreted. (Personal letter dated July 27, 1966.)

35. A. F. C. Ryder, "A reconsideration of the Ife–Benin relationship," *Journal of African History* VI (1965): 25–37.

Christian practice, and, to Muslim observers from Bornu, the complex ritual of the Kwararafa might well have seemed analogous to Christianity.[36] Against this, however, can perhaps be set the number and variety of the informants and, in particular, the report from the two Bornu princes in Cairo. Again, unlike the Franciscans, Consul Lemaire does not seem to have been unduly anxious to give importance to the trans-Saharan mission. In his correspondence with Propaganda he was at pains to emphasize his greater interest in the work among enslaved Europeans in Tripoli, and it was of course he who reported the only piece of eyewitness evidence: the sight of Kwararafa captives in Tripoli making the sign of the cross. There is also one other piece of unpublished, contemporary evidence from someone who was in no way connected with the Franciscan mission. At Tripoli in 1669 a French surgeon, taken captive the previous year, saw on several occasions the nephew of the king of Bornu, who had been brought as a slave to Tripoli during the disorders which had occurred while the king had been on pilgrimage. Some time subsequently the captive surgeon composed a brief "history of Bornu in the seventeenth century," in which he reported constant warfare between the Muslim ruler of Bornu and his neighbor the Christian "emperor of Ethiopia, who is called in Europe Prester-Jean," from whose lands the people of Bornu "carried off quantities of young persons of both sexes whom they conducted to Fezzan."[37] The author was obviously rather vague as to the geographical limits of Bornu—he considered that it touched Monomotapa in the south—but here again would seem to be an echo of the same phenomenon which the Franciscans were sent to report on and investigate.

The reports of these Frenchmen and the Franciscans are by no means the only references to possible Christian influences in the Central Sudan. From the account of the conversion of the Garamantes in the third year of the reign of Justinian (A.D. 569–70)[38] onward, there

---

36. I am grateful to Professor H. F. C. Smith and Mr. Arnold Rubin for their comments on an earlier draft.

37. Bibliothèque Nationale, Paris. MSS. franç. 12220, f. 318. This information is omitted from the extracts published by Ch. de la Roncière, "Une histoire du Bornou au XVIIe siècle par un Chirurgien français captif à Tripoli," *Revue d'histoire des colonies françaises* 7, ii (1919): 73–88.

38. U. Monneret de Villard, *Storia della Nubia Cristiana* (Rome, 1938), 207.

are a variety of allusions scattered in explorers' accounts and tribal traditions.[39] One of the most detailed accounts, though dependent like those of the Franciscans on hearsay evidence, came from a British naval officer, W. H. Smyth, who surveyed the North African coast in the early nineteenth century. Writing to the commander in chief, Malta, in February 1817, he reported having had

> several remarkable conversations relating to the existence of certain Christian tribes in the interior of Africa, and it would appear in the neighborhood of Wangara and Goober. They are described as a very muscular race of Negroes, but I cannot discover that any sign of the cross or other characteristic symbol has been observed and their tenets are so slightly impressed that on their arrival in the markets, they readily embrace Mahometanism. A French captain in the service of the Bashaw, who had resided at Tripoli twenty-five years, circumstantially related to me that several years ago, some of them were brought from the interior, and that twenty-eight of the finest being selected to be sent to Algiers, he was appointed to transport them thither. As he was bringing his vessel to an anchor an evening bell was heard on board one of the Christian ships, when to his infinite surprize those on deck manifested the utmost delight, and called up their companions, fervently embraced them, pointing at the same time towards the vessel the sound issued from, and repeating the word Campaan. As this appeared a corruption of the Italian, or more probably of the Latin itself, he made his interpreter inquire, touching their congratulations, and found that in their native town a large building occupied a central place, having a bell on it,[40] which every morning and evening summoned them to prayer, and that in this building there was neither idol, mat, nor divan, but that the priest exhorted them. Another curious fact is that the late bey of Bengazi,

---

39. H. Sölken, "Innerafrikanische Wege nach Benin," *Anthropos* 49 (1954): 914–95, lists examples relating to ten peoples connected with his "Kisra-Zaghawa-Barbar-Völker-kreis." His inclusion of Kanem-Bornu is not, however, justified by his sources, which include Streit's reference to the Franciscan mission. Other Zaghawa references are mentioned by Sir Richmond Palmer, The Bornu Sahara and Sudan (1936), 148. See also L. Frobenius, *The Voice of Africa* (English trans.), ii (1913), chapter xxix for Nupe, Borgu, and Yoruba.

40. When Yaji sacked the sacred place at Santulo (see above, note 25) he found a bell and two horns among the sacred relics; cf. the horned figure of the Christian king of Nubia in A. J. Arkell, *History of the Sudan to 1821*, 2nd ed. (1962), fig. 24, p. 193.

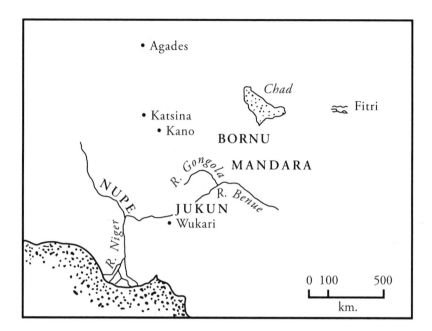

who in his boyhood was brought a slave to Tripoli, recollected some ceremony similar to the celebration of Mass, and the use of consecrated wine.[41]

The extent and variety of these references, reinforced by the detailed evidence of the Franciscans and Lemaire, suggest that Christian symbols, and possibly ritual, may have had a surprisingly widespread and persistent distribution in the Central Sudan and on its southern frontiers. In the case of the Tuareg of Air, with their monogamy, Christian-influenced vocabulary, the use of camel bells and of the cross as an ornament, this has long been recognized.[42] The reports of the use of the cross and of a "Coptic" descent in Gobir,[43] and the strong resem-

---

41. P.R.O. F.O. 76/11. W. H. Smyth to Rear-Admiral Penrose, Lebida, February 24. 1817, enclosed in Admiralty to Goulburn, May 8, 1817.

42. F. Rennell Rodd, *People of the Veil* (London, 1926), 275–79, 293–94.

43. Denham and Clapperton, op. cit. ii, 450; C. K, Meek, *The Northern Tribes of Nigeria*, i (1925), 72–73; S. J. Hogben and A. H. M. Kirk-Greene, *The Emirates of Northern Nigeria* (London: 1966), 368–69.

blance of the Nupe dagger hilts to the Agades cross,[44] are indications that this influence may have percolated southward, and the concept of a line of cultural influence stretching from North Africa to Benin has been propounded at length.[45] But the use of the Maltese cross was far more pronounced along the Nile than among the Tuareg,[46] and if, as would now seem probable, the Kwararafa were once renowned for their attachment to Christian symbols—in particular to the Maltese cross—and were a crucial link in its distribution, the evidence of some of their traditions points eastwards to Christian Nubia rather than northwards to Roman Africa.

Meek was unable to find any coherent body of Jukun historical traditions, and he attributes this "singular absence of interest or pride in the past" to the disintegration of the Kwararafa confederacy, which should probably be assigned to the eighteenth century, predating the final disruption caused by the Fulani conquests.[47] Palmer's reconstruction of the Jukun migration seems to rest therefore not on a commonly held corpus of Jukun tradition, but principally on one piece of recorded evidence: the celebrated version of the "Kisara" migration recorded by Mallam Sherif of Argungu, who, at Wukari in 1882,[48] was shown by Mallam Kura a book about the origin of "the unbelievers of Wukari, a people of no ordinary character." After recounting how the "tribe of Kisara" fled to the Nilotic Sudan from Egypt, the manuscript went on to trace a route from Darfur and Wadai, through what Palmer identifies as "the Fitri region, Mandara, and the Gongola region, to the

---

44. For Nupe, see Frobenius, op. cit. ii, 634–5. For an illustration of the Agades cross, see Rodd, op. cit., plates 36, 37.

45. Sölken, op. cit.

46. For examples of the Maltese cross in Nubia, see U. Monneret de Villard, *La Nubia Medievale*, IV (Cairo, 1957), plates cxvii, cxxix, cxxxiv-vi, cxl, clxvi, clxxvii, clxxxi–iii. See also the illustrations of Karanog (Nubia) pottery in Palmer, *The Bornu Sahara and Sudan*, 88, 167. I have not seen any clear illustrations of the Maltese cross among the Tuareg, though Palmer states (p. 167) that they call it "the market ornament." The Agades cross might well derive from the Maltese, but this would hardly explain the presence of clear examples of the Maltese cross far to the south among the Kwararafa and other peoples.

47. Meek, *A Sudanese Kingdom*, 21.

48. The comet mentioned in the text must have been that seen in Kano during September 1882.

Benue." [49] Archaeologists have recently found evidence of the influence of Christian Nubia in Darfur and the Chad area,[50] and there are two references to the existence of "Christians" directly along this route of the "Kisara" migration. In the Mandara Chronicle, "a record of the ancestors of the kings of Mandara, and their progress from the east hither," it is stated that they were "followers of Isa" and for that reason were forced to leave "Yaman," while in April 1823, when Denham accompanied an expedition from Bornu to Mandara, he was told that the Musgu captives brought to the capital of Mandara were "Christians."[51] Denham thought that the principal reason for this assertion was the willingness of the Musgu to eat dead horse flesh, but, taken together, these allusions constitute at least a hint that the "Kisara" may have left some Christian impact on peoples along their route east of the Benue. In the case of the Kwararafa, it would seem that the "Kisara" tradition may record the arrival of a small minority, and possibly it refers not to the beginning of state formation but to a relatively late absorption of a small Christian, or semi-Christian, element by peoples who had already constructed their basic version of a Sudanic state. Must we not, perhaps, reconsider Meek's conviction that "there is nothing to connect Kisra with Christ,"[52] and return to an earlier line of speculation?[53] The answer would seem to lie with the archaeologists.

Summary

In 1700, reports from Tripoli reached the congregation of Propaganda Fide in Rome that Christians, "little or uninstructed in the faith," were living in Bornu. Further enquiries revealed that these rumors related

---

49. Palmer's introduction to Meek, op. cit. xv; *Sudanese Memoirs*, II, 61-63.

50. A. J. Arkell, "A Christian Church and Monastery at Ain Farah, Darfur," *Kush* 7 (1959): 115-19; *Kush* 11 (1963): 315-19.

51. Palmer, *Sudanese Memoirs*, II, 96; Denham and Clapperton, op. cit. I, 294. The "Kisara" passed the rock of Balda in Musgu country.

52. Meek, *Northern Tribes*, I, 72.

53. Frobenius, op. cit., was the principal advocate of a link between the Kisra tradition and medieval Nubia. Recent reviews of the Christian element in the Kisra legends are in A. B. Mathews, "The Kisra Legend," *African Studies* 9 (1950): 144-47, and in an unpublished seminar paper at the Institute of Commonwealth Studies, London (AH 59/2), by J. D. Fage, "Some Myths, Legends, and Traditions of the Central and Western Sudan Relating to Immigrations from the North and East."

not to the kingdom of Bornu, but to a neighboring, rival kingdom, that of "Gourourfa" or "Carnorfa." Two sons of the ruler of Bornu, interviewed in Cairo, stated that in "Canorfa" there were people "who venerate the cross and erect it over the houses and churches," while the French consul at Tripoli reported how he had seen slaves from "Gouroufa" who made the sign of the cross. In June 1710, two Franciscans, attempting to establish contact with these "Christians," set out from Tripoli, passed through Murzuk and Agades, and were later reported to have died in Katsina in August 1711.

Hausa and Bornu sources indicate that these reports almost certainly referred to the Kwararafa, who on several occasions in the seventeenth century attacked Kano and Bornu. It is then pointed out that a Maltese cross was one of the motifs still used in the twentieth century as a decoration by an Aku of Wukari, a ruler of the Jukun, who are among the principal survivors of the Kwararafa. At least a section of the inhabitants of Wukari also preserved a clearly remembered tradition of having taken part in a migratory journey from the Nilotic Sudan to the Benue. It is suggested therefore that the reports of the French consul and the Franciscans, although garbled and consisting in the main of second-hand evidence, strengthen the possibility that the Maltese crosses used among the Jukun, in Nupe, and at Benin indicate an influence which emanated originally from Christian Nubia and is perhaps connected with the Kisra traditions.

7

The Catholic Church and National States in Western Europe during the Nineteenth and Twentieth Centuries, from a Perspective of Africa

In 1799 a young, hitherto unknown Camaldolese monk published in Rome what Wiseman was later to describe as "a large work of great merit, which gave proof of his extensive and varied learning." It carried the title *Il trionfo della Santa Sede e della Chiesa contro gli assalti dei Novatori respinti e combattuti colle stesse loro armi*. One might have expected that the innovators referred to in the title were the Jacobins and regicides of revolutionary France. The volume, however, has little or no trace of these contemporary events. The church in France is indeed singled out as the principal fount of the pernicious attacks which Don Mauro Cappellari was anxious to confute, but these stemmed from concepts of a rather earlier age, of Jansenist and Gallican complexion as reflected in the Italian writings of Pietro Tamburini, while the main thrust of Don Mauro's work is a detailed defense of papal infallibility. While Pius VII and Consalvi endeavored to restore an ancien régime, Don Mauro continued for more than twenty years to enjoy "the quiet obscurity" of a rich library, yet the ultramontane insight based on his earlier researches proved prophetic.[1]

Reflecting on the course of events in which the papacy was distanced from European nationalism and from the exercise of temporal power, a historian has suggested that this process enabled the Catholic Church to survive two world wars which might otherwise have destroyed its unity.[2] A prominent theologian, however, while conced-

---

1. Nicholas P. Wiseman, *Recollections of the Last Four Popes and of Rome in Their Times: Pius VII, Leo XII, Pius VIII, Gregory XVI* (London, 1858), 421 f. For Cappellari's work, I have used the edition published in Venice in 1832.

2. J. Derek Holmes, *The Triumph of the Holy See: A Short History of the Papacy in the Nineteenth Century* (London, 1978).

ing this point, has recently argued that the increasing centralization of papal control over the church has led to "the most dramatic transformation of the papal office in 2000 years of Christian history." Nicholas Lash suggests that the papal office has been transformed

> from court of last appeal to chief executive officer. . . this transformation was—from the production of the Code of Canon Law in 1917 to the system of concordats established throughout the first half of this century—deliberately planned and engineered. . . . Whatever one's assessment of the increasing power and influence over diocesan affairs of the Roman Curia and its network of nuncios, these things are recent innovations.[3]

This is an interesting thesis, highly relevant to our theme of the balance between local autonomy and centralization, between the universal and the congregational or *Volkskirche*. For it is this balance which is most clearly involved when one seeks to examine, in the comparative context of ecclesiastical history, the relationship of the papacy, compared to that of other churches, with the national states of Western Europe.

Someone, however, who has studied not his own European history but that of Africa, might bring a rather different perspective. An Africanist might well see some of the roots of what Lash sees as a revolutionary change in the role of the papacy to stretch back, not to the nineteenth century but at least to the creation of Propaganda Fide, and indeed well beyond this. It was the ancient Christian kingdom of Ethiopia which began in the fifteenth century to open the eyes of the papacy to the strategic importance of Africa in Rome's confrontation with the Ottoman threats in the Mediterranean. And it was appeals from Ethiopia, reinforced by those from the newly Christian kingdom of Kongo, which helped to influence Gregory XV's decision to create Propaganda Fide in 1622.[4] An Africanist might also underline the fact that the church, in its confrontation with colonialism, that almost inevita-

---

3. *The Tablet* (October 2, 1999).

4. Richard Gray, "The African Origins of the 'Missio Antiqua,'" in Vincenzo Criscuolo, ed., *Clavis Scientiae. Miscellanea di studi offerti a Isidoro Agudo da Villapadierna in occasione del suo 80o compleanno* (Bibliotheca Seraphico-Capuccina 60) (Rome, 1999), 405–23.

ble concomitant of European nationalism, was providentially already equipped with a potentially powerful bureaucratic instrument, so that the papacy could pursue a mission which differed at certain critical points from the aims of the colonial powers.

For its first two centuries Propaganda had sought, with only a modicum of success, to liberate the control of Catholic missions overseas from the patronal rights which had earlier been granted by the Renaissance papacy to the Iberian powers, and which Louis XIV and his successors in France sought in some ways to emulate. The sudden collapse of the ancien régimes presented Propaganda with a great opportunity, and it was Cappellari, appointed cardinal prefect of propaganda in 1826, and subsequently as Gregory XVI (1831–46), with his deep sense of the universality of the Church who notably helped to mobilize for the defense of the papacy the liberated energies of a global Christianity. The new missionary societies founded in the nineteenth century, especially those with a particular focus on Africa, were all far more intimately dependent on Propaganda than earlier missions, even including those of the seventeenth-century Capuchins. Propaganda now found itself with a host of eager, loyal ultramontane recruits.

In Africa the first major new Catholic missionary society was the Spiritans or transformed congregation of the Holy Ghost, which previously had trained French priests for work in the colonies of the ancien régime. In 1824 Propaganda recognized this long-established Congregation, assisting it in a gradual move from its dependence on the Gallican-inclined French monarchy. Far more important, however, was Propaganda's support for Francis Libermann, who was warmly received in Rome by Gregory XVI in 1840 and enabled to create another group of missionaries committed to work among Africans and slaves of African origin. Libermann's priests were entrusted with the recently established Vicariate of the Two Guineas, stretching vaguely along the West African coast from Senegal to the Orange River in southern Africa, and Propaganda assisted the union of these new missionaries with the ancient Congregation of the Holy Ghost.[5]

---

5. Paul Coulon, Paule Brasseur et al., *Libermann, 1802–1852. Une pensée et une mystique missionnaires (Histoire)* (Paris, 1988).

The creation of the Vicariate of the Two Guineas represented a major curtailment of ancient Portuguese Padroado claims, and a dramatic assertion of papal authority. Gregory XVI's attention was also drawn to the Egyptian Sudan and the existence of the navigable White Nile stretching a thousand miles south of Khartoum. In 1846 he created the Vicariate of Central Africa, with a vast territory stretching southwards to Ptolemy's fabled Mountains of the Moon. Here, however, he turned not to France but to subjects of the Austro-Hungarian Empire. A young Slovenian, Ignaz Knoblecher, trained in Propaganda's college in Rome, played a major role in the development of this mission. He was able to arouse a measure of support and interest in Vienna and directed the creation of two stations deep in the southern Sudan. Disease and violence cut short these first endeavors, but this initiative was maintained and gradually developed, amidst the tensions of the Risorgimento in Italy, by Daniele Comboni and his colleagues from Verona and the Tyrol.[6]

The papacy's influence over these new missionary initiatives was ultimately further enhanced by the fact that new independent sources of financial assistance for Catholic missions were rapidly becoming increasingly important. Previously overseas missions had been intimately dependent on logistical support from the governments of the ancien régimes, but a crucial distinguishing feature of modern missions were the networks of local associations whose numerous members regularly contributed small sums of money to mission work. Propaganda and Gregory XVI supported the most notable of these networks, the Association for the Propagation of the Faith founded in Lyons in 1822. The relationship between Propaganda and the association was delicate and not without tension, but gradually the papacy was acquiring for missions a means of logistical support independent of the European governments.

Just as Libermann had been personally assisted by Gregory XVI, so Comboni was encouraged by Pius IX, but when the European partition of Africa was beginning in earnest, Propaganda turned to Charles Lavigerie. In 1866 the young, brilliant, and ambitious Bishop

---

6. Gianpaolo Romanato, *Daniele Comboni, 1831–1881: l'Africa degli esploratori e dei missionari (Le vite)* (Milan, 1998).

of Nancy, renouncing a distinguished ecclesiastical career in France, had accepted the see of Algiers. He held that his new post was a door "opened by Providence" to a continent of "two hundred million souls," asking a friend "would you find in France a task more worthy to tempt the heart of a bishop?" Almost immediately Lavigerie challenged the French governor-general on an issue which, he considered, involved religious liberty. He found that he was supported not so much by the liberal element among the French episcopacy, including many of his former friends, but by Pius IX and the ultramontane bishops. Lavigerie's African experience was quickly leading him into the ultramontane camp, and he entrusted the Jesuits with the initial training of the novices of his newly formed Society of Missionaries of Africa (the White Fathers), instructing them to pay especial attention to the Ignatian emphasis on obedience.[7] Later, much later, supporting Leo XIII against Eugene Veuillot, he was to write to the latter arguing that "the sole rule of salvation and of life in the Church is to be with the pope, with the living pope whoever he may be," and when he obeyed Leo XIII with the celebrated toast of Algiers in November 1890, he risked losing much support among French Catholics, even endangering the survival of his missionary order.[8]

In 1878, when Propaganda was tentatively considering how to react to the foundation of the International African Association, Lavigerie hurriedly presented a memorandum, unleashing a force which deeply influenced the Catholic missionary impact in tropical Africa. Lavigerie argued that quick, decisive action was needed. Ignoring the claims of others, including those of Comboni and the Spiritans, the White Fathers were given by Propaganda a vast area stretching from Buganda southwards to Lake Malawi, and westwards ambiguously deep into the Congo. Here he encountered Leopold. The diplomatic skills of the King of the Belgians at least equalled those of Lavigerie. In 1885 the king insisted that missionaries in his Congo should be Belgian nationals or at least responsible to him. Rome sympathized

---

7. Xavier de Montclos, *Lavigerie, le Saint-Siège et l'Eglise. De l'avènement de Pie IX à l'avènement de Léon XIII 1846–1878* (Paris, 1965), 387, 480–83. See also François Renault, *Le Cardinal Lavigerie, 1925–1892* (Paris, 1992).

8. Renault, op. cit., 538 f.

since the vast majority of Belgians professed a Catholic allegiance, and although Lavigerie hastily agreed to establish a Belgian province of his society, he was forced to accept a drastic reduction in the size of the area entrusted to him. Nevertheless by establishing a Belgian province his society had been obliged to move out of the purely Francophone area, and this proved to be a vital step in the internationalization of the White Fathers. They were left with a huge, compact area in Bantu-speaking Africa, where, through them, Propaganda remained extremely influential.

Propaganda's partition of Africa in no way ceased with the colonial conquest of the continent. One of its vital weapons in preventing the missionary societies from exercising a monopoly of paternalist control over the large jurisdictions initially entrusted to them was the papacy's power to establish new ecclesiastical divisions in these missionary areas. In this way it could ensure that missionary societies, initially selected for their ability to work in a cooperative fashion with specific colonial governments, could later be persuaded to admit other, potentially more critical, missionaries into a given colonial territory. A most significant case for the Catholic Church in Africa was that of Zimbabwe. Here the English province of the Jesuits was entrusted with the Rhodesia mission both south and north of the Zambezi, where they encountered Lavigerie's White Fathers pressing southward. By the 1930s, however, it was already obvious that the small English province could not hope to supply sufficient recruits for this mission field. Their territory was therefore on several occasions divided, and among the new missions, two were to prove of critical importance during the war which led to Zimbabwe's independence in 1980. The dramatic public protest of Bishop Donal Lamont, a Carmelite but also an Irish nationalist born in Northern Ireland, and the firm policy of Bishop Alois Häne, fully supported by the Superior General of the Bethlehem Fathers from Immensee, succeeded in overriding the hesitations of the English Jesuits, some of whom had considerable sympathy for Smith's earlier illegal declaration of independence. The Catholics had therefore a considerable role in the transition to African rule in Zimbabwe. The Justice and Peace Commission, established by the bishops and consistently supported by Häne, investigated numerous cases of violence and oppression, and mainly through Catholic networks succeeded in publicizing internationally what was happening in the rural areas. Catholics led by Archbishop Chakaipa met Zimbabwean nationalists in Lusaka in August 1978 and facilitated ZANU's negotiators in the process which led to peace.[9] Racial reconciliation witnessed at least partially in Zimbabwe had an importance which spread far beyond its own territory. It played a part in the peaceful ending of the civil war in Mozambique. Even more significantly, it may well have been at least a minor influence in the extraordinary transfer of power in South Africa, which for so long had presented a terrible challenge to Christian authenticity in Africa and in the world at large.

The control of missionary societies, and the rupture between missions and specific colonial regimes, was not the only way in which Propaganda found itself in alliance with the movements for African liberation from colonial rule. Far more important was its emphasis on creating an indigenous priesthood equal to that of Catholic priests worldwide. This aim again went right back to the origins of the congregation, whose first secretary, Francesco Ingoli, had emphasized the importance of training indigenous priests and entrusting them with major responsibilities. In Africa in the nineteenth century, it was Propaganda which insisted that despite all the difficulties, seminaries for Africans should be established. In 1893 Cardinal Ledochowski admonished the White Fathers in Buganda that a mission which could produce martyrs could also produce priests, and the first two Ugandan priests were ordained in 1913. Until at least World War I, Protestant missions had far outstripped Catholics in their contribution to African education, that Achilles' heel of European colonialism. This vital Protestant input was seen particularly in those denominations, like the Presbyterians and the Methodists, whose internal organization fostered, and indeed depended on, the development of a sturdy, self-confident laity. This would provide in many countries, notably in Ghana and Malawi, much of the early leadership in the African challenge to colonial rule. In the late 1920s, given the opportunities

---

9. Ian Linden, *The Catholic Church and the Struggle for Zimbabwe* (London, 1980). See also Carl F. Hallencreutz, *Religion and Politics in Harare 1890–1980* (SMU 73) (Uppsala, 1998).

created by the British decision to subsidize missionary education as the cheapest option available, Hinsley, apostolic delegate to British Africa, even exhorted missionary leaders to neglect their churches in order to build up their schools.[10] Yet the overall Catholic insistence on the requirements of an indigenous clergy was to provide independent Africa with a distinctive element in civil society. African Catholic leadership was to be solidly based as an elite, disciplined cohort of men who had received an education which bore favorable comparison with any that was available in their countries. The requirements of an indigenous clergy were given absolute priority by Benedict XV ("Maximum Illud," 30.9.1919), and reiterated by Propaganda's Cardinal Van Rossum and by Pius XI. In 1932 and 1936 the apostolic delegate to the Belgian Congo insisted at plenary conferences with the missions on the equal training and treatment of African priests, and in 1939 the first African Catholic bishop since the sixteenth century was consecrated.

African Catholic bishops, in contrast to leaders of other churches in Africa, have thus an umbilical cord linking them firmly to the wider Church, though it is perhaps still far too early to see whether this will enable the Catholic Church to confront adequately the many challenges that face it on that continent. Blood ties and imagined ethnicities, as in the case of European nationalities, have at times proved far more potent politically than the water of baptism. The tragedy in Rwanda was the result of many factors; poverty and the pressure of population growth on limited resources were perhaps as significant as ethnic fears. Yet, as the secretary of the pastoral department of AMECEA wrote, "a Church that did not openly address its own ethnic tensions could not speak to society with a united and credible voice."[11] Shortly before the genocide started, Mrs. Odette Kakuze of the Rwanda Association of Christian Workers wrote an open letter to her bishops who were attending the Africa Synod in Rome. In no uncertain terms, she upbraided them for their affluent style of life which, she said, "increases the gap between you and us ordinary people." "You have," she continued, "to teach the Christians about democracy, nonviolence

---

10. Roland Oliver, *The Missionary Factor in East Africa* (London, 1952), 275.

11. Fr. Wolfgang Schonecke, "What Does the Rwanda Tragedy Say to AMECEA Churches?," AMECEA Documentation Service, Nairobi, September 15, 1994, 3.

and human rights, and help them live these values in their family and places of work. Religious leaders clearly ought to be the first ones to live and practice them."[12] Hers was a prophetic word.

On what is perhaps a deeper theological issue, the acceptance of the missiological premise of inculturation enshrined in the statements of the Synod of African Bishops and in the papal encyclical, should ensure that a universal church has the capacity to attend sympathetically to local needs. Perhaps foremost among these is the demand, traditionally so strong in many African cultures, that religion must have an immediate impact on the sufferings felt by so many individuals and by society at large. Often in Africa, where modern medicine is so seldom available to ordinary people, this demand is translated into a cry for spiritual healing. Such a cry can so easily sweep thousands into a local enthusiasm which is sometimes difficult to reconcile with the outlook and concerns of a universal Church. The option for the poor can take many forms. Yet a religion which seriously addresses popular fears, however deluded and irrational they may seem to products of the European Enlightenment, need not always reject established authority and lead to schism. One could long admire the original obedience and loyalty of Archbishop Milingo to Pope John Paul II, which helped resolve a potentially damaging crisis.

Equally challenging is the wider ecumenism, the relationships with believers of other religions. Of all the continents, Africa is an area of global significance where large numbers of Christians and Muslims meet in perhaps the most natural and also the most intense relationships. Often in African families one can find both Christian and Muslim members. In some parts of Africa, however, bishops, priests, and faithful are sometimes confronted with systematic religious persecution. In such cases of conflict, the insistence from Rome, by the Secretariat of State and more specifically by Cardinal Arinze and the Pontifical Council for Interreligious Dialogue, on the need for patience, mutual understanding, and restraint can appear at the local level to be pusillanimous and even opportunistic. Yet the necessity of appreciating all that is shared with those of other faiths is, especially in a nuclear age, a prophetic voice for humanity.

---

12. Op. cit. 6.

From an African perspective, the increasing influence of the papal Curia was not, by any means, a sudden revolutionary change initiated by Pius IX or Pius XII. Rather its roots stretched back at least to the sixteenth century when the papacy gradually began to grasp the significance presented by the existence of African Christian kingdoms in Ethiopia and Kongo. Nor could it be argued that this process of centralization has disastrously hampered the witness of the Catholic Church in Africa. Instead the principal policies pursued by Propaganda prevented the Church from being too closely identified with the colonial masters of the European missionaries, and the firm linkage with Rome may emerge as a vital asset assisting the church in its witness to Africa in the twenty-first century.

8

The Southern Sudan

In the Southern Sudan there is no ancient common language, no sharp ethnic frontier distinguishing southerners from their neighbors, no clear geographical boundaries demarcating its area, and, until recently, no wide sense of a shared culture or history uniting its peoples. Regional nationalism, insofar as it exists, is the product of the area's contact with the outside world over the last hundred years, and in any developed, conscious form it was restricted before the late 1960s to a relatively small number of educated southerners who were able to generalize from the experience of their peoples. To apply the label of "regional nationalism" to such a situation is therefore virtually to accept what was till very recently the standpoint of merely a minute southern elite. Elsewhere in independent Africa similar elites have inherited the administrative, educational, and military apparatus of the colonial regimes, and, armed with these powers, many have succeeded in maintaining and developing a nationalist impetus. Will a southern elite deprived of these resources, which in 1956 on independence largely fell into northern hands, be able to continue to nourish the spirit of regional nationalism? Or will this task no longer in the future depend on the efforts of this elite? Recently some evidence suggests that the present warfare in the south may now be forging a supratribal unity between ordinary southern warriors, herdsmen, and peasants, though it is far too soon for an outsider to discern whether this momentum will be able to reinforce a coherent separatist demand, or whether it will be dissipated in scattered guerrilla initiatives of declining activity. In the meantime northern Sudanese can argue that they are faced in the south not with regional nationalism, nor even with one minority problem, but with a large number of mutually antagonistic tribal minorities. This unresolved debate about the fundamental nature of the Southern Sudan would seem to distinguish its case from that of many of the other examples considered in this journal. Even the most dedicated southern patriot can point only to an embryonic regional nationalism, and, lacking the supports of language, race, or geography, his argument largely rests on the one particular interpretation of the area's recent history.

Before the conquest of the Northern Sudan by the Egyptians under Muhammad Ali in the first half of the nineteenth century, the peoples of the south had remained almost completely isolated from their northern, Muslim, Arabic-speaking neighbors. Although all settled life to the north depended on the Nile waters, the White Nile itself had remained unexplored. Instead it was the pagan Nilotic Shilluk, with their light canoes, who dominated this major stretch of the Nile. From their densely populated riverain kingdom extending from the ninth to the twelfth parallels, they had expanded northwards, settling on islands and regularly raiding far up the river, even reaching the junction with the Blue Nile at the site of modern Khartoum. Penetration overland was also fraught with difficulties. Behind the Shilluk, the Nuba mountains provided a series of fastnesses where a host of fragmented peoples preserved their ancient independence, while to the east, as further to the west on the Bahr el Arab, the swampy grasslands provided magnificent grazing grounds for the numerous Dinka and Nuer pastoralists who, attuned to the harsh opportunities of this homeland, were more than a match for the Baggara cattle owners of the steppes to the north. This balance of power was destroyed by the introduction of a boat-building industry by the Egyptians; ensconced in their sailing boats and armed with firearms, they no longer had to fear the Shilluk canoemen, and by 1841 an expedition sent by Muhammad Ali had discovered a navigable highway stretching as far as Juba, a thousand miles south of Khartoum. The swamps and the fierce, independent pastoralists were outflanked; a vast hinterland, rich in ivory and agricultural possibilities and covering between a quarter and a third of modern Sudan's total population, was suddenly exposed.

There are at least three different ways of looking at the subsequent contact between the outside world and the peoples of the south. In the first place one can adopt the viewpoint of many Europeans who have visited and worked in the area since 1841. One can assume that success—whether expressed in commercial profits, Christian evangelism, or the extension of a Pax Britannica—depends on enlisting the co-operation of southerners and harnessing their energies to the pursuit of these goals, however alien they might be to the traditional cultures of the area. Such a viewpoint, while recognizing the cultural gulf between northerner and southerner, tended to regard their different ways of life as of equal value, and, at least at times, has sought a reconciliation between north and south on a basis of human equality. But in the nineteenth and, it might now appear, in the twentieth century, success in these aims has proved illusory, and the history of the area, looked at from this liberal standpoint, presents vistas of almost unrelieved tragedy. Or one can view the discovery of this southern hinterland of Khartoum as initiating a dramatic extension of the ancient Arabic-Islamic frontier, as continuing a civilizing process which in the Northern Sudan stretched back to the arrival of nomadic Arab peoples from the seventh century onwards, later to be reinforced by the pilgrimage to Mecca and the lives and teaching of holy men from Egypt and the rest of the Muslim world. This process, then, involved the assimilation—forced or spontaneous—of the peoples of the south into the culture of the north, a transformation in many respects far more thorough, if perhaps more gradual, than that sought by many of the Europeans. Seen from this aspect the history of the south since 1841, though by no means representing an uninterrupted advance towards such an objective, has recorded perhaps at least as many successes as those gained by the Europeans in pursuit of their rather more limited goals, while for many Sudanese it presents the main or only hope of creating a united national state. Finally, one can see the history of the south as one of hostility and resistance to the forces of the outside world: a belligerence which stretches back to the Shilluk canoe-raiders of the eighteenth century and earlier, an opposition which even in the nineteenth century began to operate above narrow tribal boundaries, a response which now is most fully represented by the southern armies in the forests and swamps. The situation in the Sudan can be understood only if all three of these contrasting themes are taken into consideration, but at the moment it would be rash for an outsider to suggest which holds the key to the future. The records so far collected and scrutinized tell us far more about alien activities in the south than about either of the other two themes, and indeed these fluctuating, alien initiatives have until very recently shaped the principal chapters of the modern history of the area. The themes of Islamic assimilation and southern resistance can therefore best be considered after a brief survey of the failure of the outside world to shape developments in the Southern Sudan along the lines hoped for by the aliens.

The impulses leading to Europe's goals or toward an Egyptian modification of them have alternated sharply, tending to cancel out each other. A burst of energy in one direction has faltered and been succeeded by a contrary impetus. Muhammad Ali's discovery came too late in his reign for him to exploit it with vigor, and in the 1850s it was Austrian and Italian missionaries and a cosmopolitan bunch of traders who seized the opportunity of penetrating into the heart of Africa at a time when other European activities were virtually restricted to the coastal fringes of the continent. Disease and disillusionment soon sapped these initiatives; the missionaries withdrew from their stations in the south, and the traders, frustrated in their efforts to gain access to further supplies of ivory, resorted to the use of force. Instead of developing the entrepreneurial activities of the riverain tribesmen, the traders constructed a series of zeribas or fortified enclosures in the interior and manned them with Arab soldiers recruited from the north. Tribal jealousies and divisions in the south were then ruthlessly exploited, and raids for cattle and slaves became the economic basis of these settlements, the cattle being used to purchase ivory and the slaves to pay for the soldiers. Although this system was pioneered by Europeans, their trading enterprises were soon bought out by the Egyptian firm belonging to the al-Aqqad family, and the net legacy of Europe's first venture into the area was the establishment of violence as a normal relationship between the southern tribesmen and the outside world.[1]

The next major initiative came from Egypt, in the person of the Khedive Ismail, Muhammad Ali's grandson. Inspired by the accounts given to him by the explorers Speke and Grant of the advanced, densely populated, interlacustrine kingdoms of Buganda and Bunyoro, Ismail decided to send a lavishly equipped expedition to plant the Egyptian flag at the headwaters of the Nile and to capture the trade

---

1. These developments and those dealt with in the next paragraph are described in R. Gray, *A History of the Southern Sudan 1839–1889* (London, 1961).

of this area by placing steamers on Lakes Victoria and Albert. At one stroke the southern hinterland of Khartoum was to be extended to the equator. Yet by selecting Englishmen, first Baker and then Gordon, to command his forces in Equatoria, Ismail gave his undertaking a cosmopolitan flavor, and with its aims of suppressing the slave trade and of establishing a centralized, alien administration over many disparate peoples, his enterprise stood as a precursor of later European imperialism. Faced, however, with the established patterns of violence and southern hostility, neither Baker nor Gordon achieved anything substantial. Both Buganda and Bunyoro were easily able to resist the Egyptian forces, hampered as the latter were by their long and broken line of communication and by the fact that Ismail's numerous other enterprises had overtaxed Egypt's resources. By the 1870s it was also becoming evident that the real challenge to a peaceful development in the Southern Sudan lay not in the riverain stations—the scene of the activities of Baker and Gordon—but in the interior of the Bahr el Ghazal and across the Nile-Congo watershed. Here the zeribas were no longer primarily linked to the riverain route but formed part of an overland extension of the ancient caravan routes of Darfur and Kordofan. From El Obeid and other centers in the north, Arab traders rode southward to exchange firearms and other goods against slaves purchased from the zeribas' soldiery. By 1867 it was reliably estimated that 1800 slaves a year were being despatched northward by Zubair, a northern owner of one of the principal chains of zeribas, and in the late 1870s Sulaiman, Zubair's son, mounted a major rebellion against attempts to suppress this traffic. Although Sulaiman was defeated, he had been able to put about 15,000 troops in the field, and the overland contacts between the north and the Bahr el Ghazal persisted, while resentment at the administration's attempts to put down the slave trade from this area powerfully contributed to the support which the Mahdi received in his successful attempt to expel the Turco-Egyptian administration from the whole of the Sudan.

Faced with this succession of disasters, the British, following Kitchener's defeat of the Mahdists in 1898, could argue with much justification that the primary need of the Southern Sudan was for a gradual extension of peace throughout the area. Although on several occasions the imposition of the Pax Britannica involved the use of overwhelming force, the British success in this limited aim stood in striking contrast to the efforts of its predecessors. For the first time an ordered framework embraced all the peoples of the south, and events since 1955 have underlined the vital necessity and vulnerability of this achievement. The tragedy of British rule in the south was that so little was constructed on this sound foundation. Basically their inertia stemmed from the narrowness of British interests in the Sudan as a whole, for Britain was primarily concerned merely to prevent another power from threatening her position in Egypt by gaining access to the Nile waters. It was also assumed that the commitment in the Sudan could not be allowed to become a burden on the Egyptian, and still less the British, budget, so that the small sums available for development were concentrated on the cotton-growing Gezira scheme in the north, which, besides being the quickest means of increasing the Sudan's revenue, had the advantage of supplying raw material for a major British industry. Economic stagnation in the south was deepened by the attitudes of local British officials, in part the result of the conservatism of the "bog barons," the scattered district commissioners in the swamps who sympathized with the proud independence of those southerners who scornfully rejected the clothes and trappings of material progress. More fundamentally, British officials were uncertain as to whether the ultimate destiny of the south lay with Uganda and East Africa or with the north.[2] Christian missionaries were allowed to proselytize in the south and were entrusted with all the tasks of education, with but minimal government assistance until after the Second World War. The feeling that the south should be given an opportunity "to develop along its own lines" led not merely to the removal of northern Sudanese officials, clerks, and traders from the south, but also to the silencing of Arabic as an incipient lingua franca, and even to the prohibition of northern dress among southerners.[3] When eventually some funds became available for southern development, instead of improving communications with either East Africa

---

2. R. Hill, "Government and Christian Missions in the Anglo-Egyptian Sudan, 1899–1914," *Middle Eastern Studies* 1 (January 1965).

3. M. A. Rahim, *Imperialism and Nationalism in the Sudan* (London, 1969), 75–79.

or the north, protective self-sufficiency was aimed at in a scheme for the local production and marketing of cotton goods among the Zande on the remote Congo frontier. Slender success attended this attempt at economic autarky, and a Zande remarked with bitterness that the greatest European contribution to Zande welfare had been the introduction of mango trees planted from the seeds discarded by carriers from the Congo.[4]

The South therefore was completely unprepared for the complete reversal of British policy suddenly revealed in 1947. Hopeful of gaining Egyptian acquiescence in a continued British occupation of Suez, Britain decided to withdraw from the Sudan far more rapidly than had ever been envisaged. A few southerners were brusquely informed of this change at a small conference held at Juba in June 1947 which was attended by seventeen educated southerners and chiefs. After explaining the function of the proposed Legislative Assembly which was to prepare for Sudanese self-government, the civil secretary stood back and allowed northern spokesmen to persuade the southerners to participate in the assembly. The promise of the end of alien rule in the south and the hope of equal salaries with northerners won their agreement, but the bewilderment, fears, and doubts of this mere handful of southerners emerge clearly from the minutes of the conference. They were expressed most characteristically by Chief Lolik Lado who

> regretted that he was not ready for these discussions as he had not been able to consult his people before coming to Juba. He said however, that a girl who has been asked to marry a young man usually wants time to hear reports of that young man from other people before consenting; likewise before coming to any fixed decisions about their relations with the northerners. The ancestors of the northern Sudanese were not peace-loving and domesticated like cows. The younger generation claim that they mean no harm, but time would show what they would in fact do. He agreed to unification with the north but insisted on the southerners' need for protection and for further time to consider the matter in conference with the elders of the people.[5]

---

4. C. C. Reining, *The Zande Scheme* (Evanston, Ill., 1966), 72.

5. The proceedings of the conference are printed in Appendix 9 in M. O. Beshir, *The Southern Sudan* (London, 1968).

With the bare pretense, however, of southern consent to so fundamental a change, the British administration, swept along by Egyptian
and northern Sudanese pressure, was henceforth obliged to ignore
the danger warnings; suggestions of special safeguards for the south
were rejected, and the Sudan became independent on January 1, 1956.
The hopes and achievements of Europe once more faded into insignificance, while the legacy of their shortcomings was to become ever
more evident.

The new rulers of the Sudan, the northern politicians, adminis-
trators, and army officers, had no doubts as to the basis of Sudanese
national unity. For even in the south they had behind them a long, if
interrupted, tradition of Islamic assimilation. When the traders established their zeribas in the interior they introduced a plural society into
the south. Although their profits depended on violence, within the
immediate radius of the zeribas the slaves, wives, and collaborators
of the Arabs entered a radically new cultural community. By Gordon's
time this process had developed so far that as he saw the "semi-Native
semi-Arab by contact population of lads and women" in the stations
he became convinced that "no nation could uproot Egypt from these
lands even if they possessed them. Arabic must be the language of
these countries."[6] This assimilation also began to spread outwards
from the stations. Emin, Gordon's successor, noted how some Acholi
chiefs, overcoming their scorn for clothing of any kind, were adopting
Arab dress, and he described how one of them, "a thorough Dongolawi
in appearance and manners," sat on an *angareb* (a wooden bedstead
used in the north) and "regaled his guests with coffee," while near Juba
"all the chiefs of the neighborhood" attended the Islamic feast of Id al
Saghir in 1881.[7] Although only a small minority of southerners were
influenced by this new culture in the nineteenth century, and although
this process was largely halted during the Condominium, assimilation
of the south into Islam and Arab culture appeared to northerners to
be an inevitable and natural policy. "The Sudan," declared Ali Abdel

---

6. Gordon to Waller, January 29, 1875, and to his sister, October 22, 1875, quoted
in Gray, 113.

7. *Die Tagebücher von Dr Emin Pascha herausgegeben ... von Dr Franz Stuhlmann*
(Berlin, 1917), II, entries dated October 17–20, 1880, August 27, 1881.

Rahman, Minister of the Interior in 1958, "is an integral part of the Arab world and as such must accept the leadership of the two Islamic religious leaders of the Sudan; anybody dissenting from this view must quit the country."[8] Mission schools were immediately nationalized, and in 1964 all Christian missionaries were expelled from the south by the military regime. Their role was taken over by Islamic schools, and in 1966-67 considerable energy was expended on proposals for an Islamic constitution for the Sudan as a whole. The advance of Islam is, however, merely one aspect of this assimilation, which finds its deepest support in the conviction that the north is inherently superior to the south. Socially this is shown in the almost total reluctance to allow northern girls to marry southerners, although northerners in the south will of course marry or cohabit with southern girls; culturally this assumption of superiority, as the commission of inquiry into the southern disturbances of 1955 noted, is expressed in the use of the term *abid* (slave) applied to southerners, especially by uneducated northerners; politically it can be seen in a paternalism which ignores the aspirations of those southerners who are not prepared to accept that their destiny should be shaped by northerners. Hence in part the failure to reconvene the Round Table Conference of 1965-66—the only occasion when all southern and northern political parties have met on a basis of rough equality—and hence the recent statement by a northern Minister to visiting southern students that it was up to the minister of southern affairs "to consult the types of southerners he prefers."[9]

Since independence the technological gap between north and south has widened rather than narrowed. In the first ten years of independence the north increased its lead educationally with the addition of 45 secondary "streams" compared with only 3 added in the south. During the same period 483 northerners obtained commissions in the Army compared with 13 southerners, and 153 northerners were accepted for training as police officers as against 7 southerners.[10] With power so heavily weighted in favor of the north, assimilation into the

---

8. Quoted in J. Oduho and W. Deng, *The Problem of the Southern Sudan* (London, 1963), 38.

9. Quoted in *The Grass Curtain* 1 (May 1970): 13.

10. O. Albino, *The Sudan, A Southern Viewpoint* (London, 1970), 100-105.

Arab world may well prove to be much the most significant theme in the history of north-south relations; yet it is difficult to believe that at some stage the north will not have to come to terms with the other contrasted theme of southern resistance.

Muhammad Ali's expeditions of 1839–41 encountered not hostility but an ecstatic welcome from the riverain peoples to the south of the Shilluk. Cattle were sacrificed to these emissaries from the gods, and Knoblecher, one of the first missionaries to visit the area, described how tribesmen joyfully came down to the river and helped haul the boats through difficult passages in the swamps. In the subsequent clash of cultures, exacerbated by the rapacity of the traders, fear and suspicion soon replaced this open-hearted treatment, and, apart from the comparatively few inhabitants of the zeribas, southern reactions to the outside world were marked throughout the rest of the nineteenth century by withdrawal and hostility. By the 1880s, some of the narrow horizons of traditional tribal animosities were giving way to a fierce united resistance against the alien intruders. In 1884, Dinka and Nuer, under the leadership of a prophet called Donlutj, attacked the Egyptian station at Bor, and the following year Dinka, Aliab, and Mandari pastoralists aided the local Bari in a fierce attack on the stations at Lado and Rejaf.[11]

The British, entering after the Mahdist upheaval, were not faced by this supratribal resistance, but at a local level they often encountered determined opposition, and only in the 1920s were the Nuer eventually forced to accept alien rule. Having subdued this initial resistance, the British laissez-faire policy did little to foster supratribal institutions, nor did it arouse an active, widespread demand for self-rule; it was not until 1955, on the brink of independence, that southern opposition again erupted in the mutiny of the Equatoria Corps and the killing of northerners in the three southern provinces. This spontaneous uprising was supported by southerners of all tribal groups and religious affiliations: the commission of inquiry found that "some of the leaders of anti-northern propaganda are southern Muslims."[12] This

---

11. Emin, *Tagebücher*, III, December 26, 1884, October 14, 1885.

12. *Report of the Commission of Enquiry into the Disturbances in the Southern Sudan During August 1955* (Khartoum, 1956), 6.

widespread violence, however uncoordinated, blind, and destructive, revealed a deep determination in the south not to accept another period of alien rule, for self-government and Sudanization in 1954 had involved the replacement of British officials by northerners, only six southerners being appointed out of a total of eight hundred vacancies. This was the basic fact, together with fears of economic exploitation and cultural oppression, that lay behind both the mutiny and the subsequent demand by southern politicians for a federal-type constitution under which they hoped to gain a large measure of control over their own affairs. This demand for a federal constitution won support from other underprivileged groups in the Northern Sudan—notably from the Beja, Nuba, and Fur—and this growing unrest, this fear that the new state might dissolve into fragments and fall an easy prey to Egypt, was one of the factors leading to the military takeover by General Abboud in November 1958. In the south the military government firmly silenced all opposition to its rule, but it did nothing to alleviate the economic and other grievances of southerners. Northern traders monopolized government contracts in the south and expropriated fertile lands suitable for rice production or tea and coffee plantations. The south felt itself in the grip of an increasingly harsh and alien regime with no constitutional means of redress. Several prominent southern politicians were imprisoned and many of their colleagues were forced into exile, where they established the Sudan African National Union (SANU). In the south itself, desperate youths and men escaped into the bush where they linked up with remnants of the mutineers of 1955. In 1963 they announced the formation of the Anya-Nya, bands of freedom fighters, their name taken from the deadly poison of the Gabon viper, their arms seized from northern soldiers or from the Congolese "simbas."

Since then developments have tended to take place at two different, yet interacting, levels. On the one hand there have been the political initiatives and negotiations, the disputes among northern and southern politicians, and a few attempts to find a solution acceptable at least to the majority of thoughtful people on both sides. On the other hand there has been the stark military confrontation with its continuing stalemate, which divides the south into military garrisons and guerrilla-held territory, suffocating all hope of peaceful development. After the overthrow of Abboud's regime, in part provoked by the failure of the army's repressive southern policy, there was a brief respite in the south during which political opinions could again be voiced. In March 1965, the interim government led by Sir al Khatim al Khalifa convened the Round Table Conference attended by leading northern and southern politicians; but these leaders could not agree on a solution, and behind their disagreements there lurked the suspicion and fear that even if the politicians could reach a compromise, neither side could control the fighting in the south. The Anya-Nya, dispersed and hidden in the bush, were by no means amenable to decisions reached in Khartoum, while the massacre of southern civilians in Juba and Wau by northern soldiers in July 1965 tragically revealed the gulf between the government's apparently benevolent intentions in Khartoum and the continued military presence in the South. Following these events panic and anarchy swept the south, and one hundred thousand Southern refugees were reported to have crossed into neighboring countries. Despite subsequent changes in northern governments and the coup d'état in 1969 which brought into power General Nimeiry with a commitment to Marxist socialism rather than traditional Islam, the war in the South has continued its bitter course. Recent reports from visitors to Anya-Nya detachments describe how the bombing and reprisals are welding a deep unity among southern villagers and the Anya-Nya soldiers,[13] while the various southern groups have reportedly been brought together in July 1970 under a unified leadership of the Anya-Nya. Time alone will show whether this move represents merely another stage in a desperate but anachronistic defiance, or whether it is a milestone towards the achievement of southern independence, or even perhaps towards the recognition by both north and south that they each have much to contribute to the other.

---

13. E.g., A. Reed, "A Journey to a War," *The Grass Curtain* 1 (May 1970): 17.

9

Christianity, Colonialism, and Communications in Sub-Saharan Africa

For nearly a thousand years Islam was by far the more significant of the two world religions that have deeply influenced tropical Africa. It has been estimated, however, that since the mid-nineteenth century the number of Africans who claim a Christian identity has been doubling about every twelve years. If this trend continues, there may well be three hundred fifty million Christians in Africa before 2000 A.D. (Walls, 1976: 182). And this change is not merely a question of numbers. In 1870, apart from the ancient kingdom of Ethiopia and the settlements of Sierra Leone, Liberia, and South Africa, Christians were an insignificant minority in nearly all sub-Saharan societies. By 1970 Christianity had become the dominant religious influence among many African societies, and the social and political influence exerted by African Christians far exceeded that warranted merely by their numbers. During this period of unprecedented social and cultural change, at least until the early 1970s, it was Christianity rather than Islam that had made the greatest impact south of the Sahara.

Christianity and Colonialism

Like most generalizations dealing with so vast an area, this assertion concerning the comparative growth of Christianity and Islam undoubtedly requires many qualifications. But it also demands an explanation. Many observers would assume that the reason is fairly self-evident. The century 1870–1970 roughly coincided with the colonial period and its immediate aftermath. Christianity, it is argued, made its rapid advances precisely because its emissaries, the missionaries, were so closely linked with the whole apparatus of colonial rule.

153

This is an attractive thesis. Undoubtedly these links were close. For a variety of reasons many missionaries advocated imperial expansion during the latter part of the nineteenth century. Indeed, the principal aspect of this story debated among historians is whether this missionary advocacy effectively influenced the partition of Africa or whether the missions were merely manipulated by European statesmen for their own secular aims and ambitions.[1] In the twentieth century most missionaries cooperated with the colonial regimes, even if on occasions they criticized some colonial policies, with varying degrees of effectiveness. As the work of many African novelists has illustrated, for many Africans there was little if any difference between an administrator and a missionary.

Black Christian Initiatives

This explanation of the influence of Christianity in Africa overlooks, however, three fundamental considerations. In the first place, it incorrectly identifies Christianity in Africa with the Western missionary. It also ignores the extent to which the missions were able independently to initiate the modern communications revolution in black Africa and, thirdly, the ways in which this revolution has been intimately associated with Christian cosmology.

The whole thrust of recent research on this subject has exposed the extent to which the growth, expansion, and development of Christianity south of the Sahara have depended on, and been distinctively molded by, African initiatives. This is the most obvious in the case of those African churches that have separated from the missions or were founded independently. The prophets and ministers who led thousands of Africans into these movements were manifestly proclaiming that, for them, Christianity was no longer an alien intrusion but a faith that had become indigenous. The same process of indigenization can be clearly discerned within the mission-connected churches. Right from the start the expansion of Christianity in west Africa depended largely on Blacks. It was the Nova Scotian settlers of African descent who ensured that Freetown developed a distinctive Christian culture

1. See, for example, the different interpretations of Oliver (1952) and Robinson and Gallagher (1965) concerning the case of Uganda.

and who provided the reference group for the colonies of freed slaves (Peterson, 1969; Fyfe, 1962). It was these Sierra Leoneans who as ministers, teachers, and traders were the pioneer evangelists in southern Nigeria and the neighboring areas (Ajayi, 1965; Ayandele, 1966; Tasie, 1978). In the Gold Coast the first Methodist missionaries were originally summoned to the area by Fante Christians, while the Presbyterian church, founded by Basle and West Indian missionaries, soon developed an indigenous leadership which by World War I was strong enough to seize and retain control of the church's affairs (Bartels, 1965; Smith, 1966). In the interior of Africa south of the equator, although most of the pioneer mission stations were founded by whites, it was African catechists, teachers, traders, and migrant laborers who assimilated the faith and initiated villagers, kinsfolk, workmates, and strangers into this new identity.

Encounter with African Beliefs

African initiatives were not restricted to the work of these pioneer evangelists. The encounter between Christianity and indigenous beliefs, rituals, and customs involved a massive and continuous process of interpretation and reassessment. The traditional concerns, hopes, and fears of many Africans, often ignored or belittled by missionaries from an alien culture, asserted their claims on the new religion. Often, especially at first, this involved a distortion or misunderstanding of the nature of Christian teachings. In these cases the beliefs and symbols of the world religions were merely absorbed and taken over by the indigenous religions, which were themselves developing in response to social change (Horton, 1971). But the interaction was a dynamic two-way process. The long-term, cumulative advantage lay with the world religions with their sacred writings, literacy, large-scale organization, and universalist claims (Fisher, 1973), but in meeting African needs, both Christianity and Islam adopted new characteristics, discovered new insights, and themselves became indigenous.

This encounter assumed innumerable forms. One of its most dramatic aspects concerned the problem of evil, which for most Africans was most sharply represented by negative spiritual forces. The sins of anger, lust, envy, pride, and hatred were often personified in the activities of sorcerers and witches. At first the proclamation of Christ's salvation was interpreted by many African communities as implying the dramatic arrival of a spiritual power akin to the series of beneficent spirits, who, with their charms and shrines, had previously claimed to cleanse the community from the evil of witchcraft (Vansina, 1971). In 1882 a ruler of the Yao at Masasi in Tanzania "hailed as a grand and certain result of Christianity spreading into his country the fact that witchcraft would be driven out before it" (Stuart, 1974). Sometimes this saving aspect of "Christianity" assumed drastic and horrendous forms. In 1925 Tomo Nyirenda, who had been influenced by the millenarianism of Jehovah's Witnesses, embarked upon a career of identifying and slaughtering witches, but to the Lala people in Zambia he appeared as "before all else the bearer of Christianity . . . a Mission like any other" (Ranger, 1975: 45, 50). Here the Christian message of salvation was being interpreted in terms almost exclusively determined by traditional concepts, but later generations of Christians substantially modified their approach to the task of witchcraft eradication. Thirty years after Nyirenda, Alica Lenshina in Zambia sought to cleanse her Lumpa church from fears of witchcraft through baptism, prayer, and praise, and a similar transformation has been reported among the Xhosa in South Africa, where the reliance of Christians on prayer rather than on traditional diviners has assisted in a radical decline of specific accusations of witchcraft with their traumatic social consequences (Pauw, 1975).

Here, then, one can begin to perceive how successive generations of African Christians have brought Christianity into contact with traditional cosmologies, and how in this encounter Africans have helped the Christian churches to develop an effective concern with beliefs and phenomena that modern Western missionaries had been inclined to ignore. The same process occurred in another dimension of traditional belief. The incidence of sickness and infertility led Africans not merely to seek to eradicate witchcraft but also to have recourse for positive spiritual assistance through possession cults and other forms of spiritual healing. When African Christians began to read the New Testament they discovered that Christ and the apostles had also been heavily involved in spiritual healing. By the end of the nineteenth century most Western missionaries were emphasizing, and some were bringing, the benefits of medical science, but in a few cases Africans established direct links with those Pentecostalists who in North America and Europe were, at that very moment, renewing Western concern in the ministry of spiritual healing. In other cases, the links with Pentecostalists in the West were far more tenuous, but they helped to emphasize the universal significance of this African response to the Bible (Turner, 1967; Sundkler, 1976). The links with Western Pentecostalism seem, however, to have been nonexistent in some of the most spectacular African responses, as for example in the career and impact of the prophets William Wade Harris and Simon Kimbangu. The message and influence of these two men, which resulted in the formation of large Christian communities along the west African coast and in Zaire (Haliburton, 1971; Martin, 1975; Ustorf, 1975), illustrate the extent to which the call to purification and healing emerged almost automatically as a dominant aspect of the Gospel in Africa. Here African Christianity is proclaiming a Christian belief with universal relevance; indeed it is challenging that emphasis on technology which, as we shall see, has been so beloved in recent centuries by the West.

The reaction to fears of witchcraft and the ministry of healing are merely two ways in which the development of Christianity in sub-Saharan Africa since 1870 has depended not on alien intruders but on indigenous enterprise. Any assessment of the connections between Christianity and colonialism must therefore surely begin by recalling this basic fact: African Christianity is not the result primarily of a massive campaign of brainwashing by foreign missionaries. Whatever the missionaries may have thought, Africa was no tabula rasa. Aspects of Christianity were eagerly accepted and transformed by Africans because this faith was seen to meet not merely the exigencies of modernization but also at least some of the longstanding spiritual needs and demands of African societies. Christianity in Africa was never synonymous with the missionaries' understanding of the faith; the encounter with Africa involved a process of interaction in which Africa's distinctive characteristics and contributions have become ever increasingly prominent.

Modernization

The vital dimension of African initiative does not, however, explain by itself the rapidity of Christianity's recent growth in sub-Saharan Africa. It reveals the fallacy of equating this phenomenon with alien missionary activity or the mere influence of colonial rule, but it hardly illuminates the comparison with Islam. For in the century under consideration, the growth and expansion of Islam in Africa was, to an even greater extent than Christianity, the product of African rather than alien initiatives, and the encounter between Islam and black African societies involved at least as great a segment of indigenous beliefs. Africans found in Islam, just as much as in Christianity, a source of spiritual assistance when confronted with the problems of evil and suffering. Like Christianity, Islam also brought to black Africa a more vivid and complete picture of life after death than that possessed by most indigenous cosmologies (Gray, 1978). It is only when one turns to consider the progress of modernization, the comprehensive nature of recent social change in Africa, and the contribution of the revolution in communications, that the contact between the modern roles of Christianity and Islam begins to assume significance.

In order to appreciate the precise contribution of Christianity to modernization in Africa, it is necessary to take up again the question of the relationship of the missions to the colonial powers. We have already noted that for many Africans, confronted all too often with common white attitudes of racial pride, there was little if anything to distinguish a missionary from a colonial administrator, and most missionaries cooperated with the colonial regimes. Yet one of the most remarkable features of the modern missionary movement was its relative independence from the European colonial powers.

The Independence of Modern Missionaries

The early European missionaries in Africa, as in Asia or Latin America, had been intimately dependent on the support of secular rulers. Catholic missions from the fifteenth to the eighteenth centuries had operated largely under the patronage of the Spanish, Portuguese, and French crowns, while Protestants had been primarily concerned with providing chaplains for the trading forts and areas of European settlement. In contrast to these early activities, the modern movement, which began at the end of the eighteenth century, depended on the support and sacrifices of a much larger number of people for whom the industrial revolution was providing new levels of income. The new missionary societies, both Catholic and Protestant, depended as much on regular weekly offerings as on occasional large legacies. With these independent financial resources they were able to recruit and deploy their missionaries where the need was greatest or the opportunities most promising. Their policies and objectives could, if the missions chose, disregard the interests of the colonial powers, for their organization in the home base transcended national frontiers. Catholic missions were brought closely under the control of Propaganda Fide at Rome, and the Protestant societies developed an ecumenical, international network which at times could act as a powerful pressure group. In a few instances, as in the outstanding case of the Congo Independent State of Leopold II, missions could challenge and defeat a colonial power (Slade, 1959). For Africa as a whole, however, the consequences of this new-found independence of the missions were in no sphere more significant than in the revolutionary changes that were taking place in the techniques of communication in sub-Saharan Africa. Independent of the state, missions, albeit for their own interests, could introduce innovations of critical importance for Africans.

Missions and Communications

For the third and final point to be mentioned in refuting the thesis that the recent rapid growth of Christianity in black Africa was directly dependent on the establishment and extension of European colonial rule, is that such a proposition grossly exaggerates the significance of the colonial interlude in African history. As has been remarked elsewhere, there have been two great watersheds in the history of Africa during the last seven millenia, changes that have profoundly altered the whole social environment of most of the continent. The first was the transition to food production; the second was the modern revolution in the means of communication. This transformation "began, not with colonial rule, but with the steamers, railways, telegraph, vernacular bibles, and newspapers of the nineteenth century" (Gray, 1975: 1), and Christian missions were able often to play a decisive role in pioneering these momentous changes. Their early commitment to the alliance between Christianity and commerce, to eradicate the slave trade and to bring the interior into direct contact with the Christian world, led the missions to become foremost innovators. It was the missions and their humanitarian allies, who, under the leadership of Sir Thomas Fowell Buxton, campaigned for the opening up of the Niger; it was the missions, following in David Livingstone's footsteps, who placed their steamers on the navigable Congo and on Lakes Malawi and Tanganyika. But their material contribution was by no means limited to these major, well-known facts. Virtually every mission station brought with it examples of technological change. In some cases it was that ancient invention, the wheel, that they introduced. Thus the Verona missionaries, reestablishing the Catholic initiative in the southern Sudan in the early twentieth century, were horrified at the system of forced human porterage that radiated out from the riverhead at Wau. Instead they constructed oxcarts, and rejoiced in liberating man "from the shame of being used as a beast of burden" (Fusero, 1970: 127–28).

Literacy

The missions' link with more modern means of transport was, however, incidental to their main purpose. Nor was it their most important contribution to communications in Africa. Far more central and crucial was the role of Christianity as a proponent of literacy. Probably without exception, Protestants shared the aim of bringing the Bible to Africa. Because of their deep desire that African Christians should be able "to search the Scriptures," many Protestant missions even insisted that the acquisition of literacy was a prerequisite for baptism. While rejecting this stipulation as an unwarranted obstacle to membership of a Christian community, African Christian prophets equally proclaimed and manifested their reverence for God's word. It was with Bible in hand that the prophet Harris cast out evil, and the distinguishing mark of most African Christian prophets has been that they are men or women of the Bible. Catholic missions laid rather less emphasis on literacy. The catechism, rather than the Bible, was often for them the first priority, and in some missions in the early days, as with the White Fathers among the Bemba (Garvey, 1974), the catechism was mainly learned by rote, in much the same way as Muslim teaching had been communicated for centuries in the Koranic schools of black Africa.

Yet, whereas in sub-Saharan African Islam literacy had been restricted effectively to a relatively small number of learned Muslims, even Catholic missions powerfully contributed to the spread of literacy. Books of devotions, lives of the saints, and selections from the scriptures, as well as catechisms, were all translated fairly rapidly by Catholics. The Christian propagation of literacy involved a massive penetration into African languages. Unlike the Koran and the main Islamic works of learning, which had remained tightly anchored to the Arabic original, Christian teaching and literature became rapidly accessible in many African vernaculars. Pioneer missionaries quickly recognized the strategic significance of literacy. As an American missionary remarked: "Ours is the opportunity to provide the only literature they will have for many years to come. Would it not thrill you to think that you controlled the reading matter of an entire tribe?"[2] Such arrogantly paternal sentiments might well exaggerate the power that the production of this literature bestowed on missionaries, for the mission could not control the individual's interpretation of the Bible and Christian teaching, but his remarks underline the revolution in communications that their activity was initiating.

In order to introduce and exploit this new technique, all Christian missions found themselves in some degree committed to establishing schools. Their commitment varied from the rather reluctant provision of the most elementary classes, to the enthusiastic planning by Robert Laws in Malawi of courses he hoped would lead to a university curriculum (McCracken, 1977). Yet, whatever the attitude of different missions toward education, whether they viewed it as a diversion from their evangelistic aims or an integral means of creating a new

---

2. I owe this quotation from H. S. Dulp, a pioneer missionary in Bornu province, Nigeria, to Mr. T. M. B. Mapuranga, who had been researching the history of the mission of the Church of the Brethren in Lardin Gabas.

Christian community, African demand for education soon ensured that the provision and maintenance of schools rapidly became the distinctive activity of Christians in Africa (Ekechi, 1971). And because the missions could mobilize funds and teachers independently of state support, they were able in many cases to provide this crucial service to Africa long before the colonial regimes sought to control this process. When at last colonial rulers awoke to the incipient dangers and challenge to their authority posed by what one of them, the governor-general of Nigeria, termed this "extraordinary irruption of hedge-schools" (Clifford, in Jones, 1922: 175), the African renaissance had already begun. The colonial powers could not turn back the clock; missionary education had become the Achilles' heel of colonialism.

Communications and Cosmology

Christianity had thus powerfully contributed to the radical transformation of communications in sub-Saharan Africa. Its participation in this revolutionary process was not, however, limited to the mere provision of new techniques, be they steamers or mass literacy. It was intimately involved with these changes at a deeper, cosmological basis. And it is perhaps at this level that one can perceive the most striking contrast with Islam. Much earlier, Muslims had developed the vital trans-Saharan communications, and had subsequently been responsible for bringing black Africa into contact with the civilizations of North Africa and the Middle East. Islam had thus been closely concerned with the social and political changes associated with long-distance trade, but this commerce had been limited in its economic impact. Muslims had not introduced a new technology. In tropical Africa, with its parasitic diseases, modernization and the communications revolution had to await the arrival not merely of the plow and the wheel, but of steam power, and internal combustion engine, and electronics. The new technology, which at first sight bestowed on its Western possessors something of the status of gods, had been the consequence in Europe of a cosmological revolution, a profound and radical change in the way men regarded nature and the universe. In its origins this scientific revolution, which lay behind the inventions and new technology, had owed something to early Islamic and ancient Greek thought, but essentially it had developed in Christendom. Early Western science had been built on the Christian belief in the potential and freedom of man within God's creation, and, in its turn, Christianity, alone of the world religions, had been forced, albeit gradually and hesitantly, to come to terms with the claims and assumptions of the scientists. The results can clearly be seen in the changing world-view of Christian missionaries in Africa. Whereas in the sixteenth and seventeenth centuries European missionaries, in accord with African cosmologies, believed that spiritual forces were responsible for most of the events determining the course of human life, by the nineteenth and twentieth centuries this wide range of causation had been considerably curtailed. Modern missionaries therefore generally had little patience with fears of witchcraft, and they relied on pills almost as much as on prayer for a defense against illness. Simultaneously, missionaries claimed that the secrets and wonder of the new inventions could rightly be understood only in the light of the freedom and order inherent in the Christian revelation. Or, to put it in popular parlance, the Bible had made Europe powerful. Many Westerners, missionaries included, forgetting the universal implications of this insight, went on to assume that their technological superiority was inherently linked, not with science, but with Caucasian ethnic origins, so that for them Christianity became part of a white man's package of "civilization" to be thrust on Africans with varying degrees of force. But despite these absurd aberrations, the fact remained that for most Africans, confronted with the turmoil of modernization initiated and intensified by the communications revolution, Christianity alone presented a set of beliefs and ideas which, at one end of the spectrum embraced their traditional spiritual needs and concerns, at the other enabled them to reach out and comprehend some of the new forces that were so radically altering their whole environment.

10

Popular Theologies in Africa:
A Report on a Workshop on Small Christian
Communities in Southern Africa

The development of small Christian communities is a central focus of theological debate in Africa as elsewhere, but their significance far transcends purely ecclesiastical concerns. These local groups of believers, scattered across remote rural areas or concentrated in urban slums, are found in varying forms in every Christian denomination in Africa. They represent both a powerful reserve of resistance, preserving African cultural values and insights, and, at the same time, an immense potential for social and economic change. A workshop at the School of Oriental and African Studies, University of London, recently considered two major statements on this theme. One was presented by Bishop Patrick Kalilombe, WF, Third World Lecturer at the Selly Oak Colleges. As Bishop of Lilongwe, he had been one of the principal architects of the concept of small Christian communities among Roman Catholics in Africa. The other was a document, *Speaking for Ourselves*, published by the Institute of Contextual Theology (Box 32047, Braamfontein, 2017 South Africa), which reports on a pilot study conducted in South Africa by Archbishop N. H. Ngada and other members of the Church of the Spirit and the Church of the People, those African churches which have sometimes been called separatist or prophetic.

The role of small, or basic, Christian communities caught the world's headlines with the instruction issued in Rome on August 6, 1984, by the Congregation for the Doctrine of the Faith. The instruction depicts how the theses of the theologies of liberation

> are widely popularized in a simplified form, in formation sessions or in what are called "base groups" which lack the necessary catechetical and theological preparation as well as the capacity for discern-

ment. Thus these theses are accepted by generous men and women without any critical judgment being made.[1]

The actual situation in Africa may have been far from the minds of those who issued the instruction. Nevertheless the implications are seen as of universal application, and Africanists must ask to what extent this picture accurately reflects developments in Africa. One major aspect is the spontaneity of African Christian communities. As regards Catholics, official recognition of these communities and attempts by the African hierarchies to foster them developed relatively late. Bishop Kalilombe, and other bishops in Africa, saw that many of the structures and institutions brought by Western missionaries were largely irrelevant to the African situation. These imports hardly touched the mass of the people. This was true not merely of Catholics. One of the dominant facts of church history in Africa is that the parish, or other formal ecclesiastical division, has so seldom provided the structure of the local Christian communities. The widespread response of Africans to Christianity developed far beyond the immediate neighborhood of the mission station. Typically the parish in Africa comprised a vast area which the ordained priests or ministers could not hope to weld into a community with close personal and permanent ties between its individual members. Yet in every Christian denomination, small nuclei of believers have developed into such communities, often almost unknown to the missionaries. Seen in this light, the spontaneity and initiatives so graphically described in *Speaking for Ourselves* are representative of much of the experience of many African Christians, both in the mission-connected churches and in those of independent origin. Whereas in Europe small Christian communities have tended to be marginal in the life of the churches as a whole, in Africa they have perhaps been central to the development of Christianity.

We need to know much more about the membership and organization of these varied communities before we can adequately assess their contemporary contribution and potential. We need to hear more of their experience as centers of worship and theological reflection. It is precisely here that *Speaking for Ourselves* is so fascinating a document.

---

1. The translated text was published in *The Tablet* (September 1984), section xi, par. 15.

It describes how members of the Spirit Churches have been meeting at Tsakane in the Transvaal since 1980 to investigate and articulate their theology and to develop a theological training system. As an experiment in training, they formed a group of twelve men and women who developed a method of systematic discussion, reports Archibishop Ngada, asking

> ourselves questions about our experience of faith. . . . At times we had heated debates and all of us felt that we were learning and discovering so much more than we had ever expected.

To these discussions was added research through interviews with members of the churches, which produced some revealing memories and records of spontaneous development. Here then from the Transvaal is a vivid picture of theological discussion full of active discernment and critical judgment.

Bishop Kalilombe also emphasized the contribution of small Christian communities to social development. Theological reflection at the grassroots is, he maintains, "potentially a revolutionary and explosive enterprise." It involves a process of conversion. The common members must "regain confidence in themselves as full citizens of Christ's church." This enables them to

> rid themselves of the inhibiting attitudes of fatalism and passivity. . . . Only then can they begin to struggle for liberation and embark on projects of self-reliance and genuine development.

Such theological reflection is essentially a communal enterprise. It takes forms which are unusual and unexpected to Western observers, "like songs, stories, proverbs, artistic and symbolic expressions, drama, celebrations etc."[2] Here again we are confronted with a picture far removed from the passive, uncritical reception of theses passed down to the local communities from outside.

The primary contribution of small Christian communities to African social development is therefore their role in raising peoples' consciousness, in reactivating the springs of communal action and

---

2. P. A. Kalilombe, "Doing Theology at the Grassroots: A Challenge for Professional Theologians," paper presented to the Second General Assembly of the Ecumenical Association of African Theologians, Nairobi, December 1984.

initiative. We need, however, to examine and discover what practical forms and directions are taken by this renewed power. Some communities may start with charity towards the sick and disabled. Some also engage in projects of mutual aid, such as work on road-making or a communal farm. Do such activities then lead onwards to reflection on the causes of poverty, famine, oppression, and injustice? M-F. Perrin Jassy has emphasized the significance of such acts of communal endeavor as the vital first steps in overcoming passivity and dependence.[3] But is it the case that in Africa small Christian communities have confronted the problems of poverty by mobilizing self-help, and that generally speaking they have not attempted to challenge inequities or consciously to transform their social environment? Any communal activity, however, begins to carry with it political implications. In those rural and urban areas where these communities are involved in development, to what extent has this activity brought them into contact with agencies and organizations operating on a wider, national scale? And has this contact been marked by a positive cooperation, or does it carry the seeds of conflict with powers which seek to control or even monopolize such development?

These questions of social and economic development lead then into an issue of fundamental significance: in what ways do these small Christian communities constitute alternative structures? There is an obvious ecclesiastical dimension to this question, for their vitality calls into question many established concepts concerning church leadership and organization. But is there also, in Africa, a political dimension? Do these communities provide their members with an identity which ultimately can challenge political absolutism, ethnic fanaticism, and oppressive structures? Is grassroots theology proving to be in Africa, as Bishop Kalilombe suggests, "a revolutionary and explosive enterprise"? As is intended on such occasions, the SOAS workshop raised more questions than answers. We were, however, deeply interested in two themes underlined by the writers of *Speaking for Ourselves*.

The first was their emphasis on the role of the ancestors in the lives of their communities. The authors describe how as they read the Bible,

---

3. Marie-France Perrin Jassy, *Face au changement; former des communautés de base* (Bandundu, 1981), 56–61.

they discovered that, like them, "the people of the Bible had a great respect for their forefathers." Moreover, they soon realized "that there was nothing at all in the Bible about the European customs and Western traditions that we had been taught." As a result, they began to experience liberation. "Why could we not maintain our African customs and be perfectly good Christians at the same time? The Spirit of God was beginning to stir in us." Increasingly they appreciated the radical distinction between culture and religion. They began to argue that "the customary way of commemorating and making contact with the spirits of our ancestors is a family affair, not a religious service."

These observations led the workshop to reflect on the significance of burials in contemporary Africa and in the life of African communities. More than at any other event or situation, identities in Africa are proclaimed and established at burials. For not everyone becomes an "ancestor," and one of the essential qualifications is an honorable funeral. We were reminded that, at an earlier seminar at SOAS, we had heard how among the Venda, in the extreme north of the Transvaal, the task of organizing burials is firmly in the hands of the women leaders of local communities, and how burials there form a unique ecumenical occasion.[4] The workshop heard from Bishop Kalilombe how, in Malawi, the refusal of a local Christian community to make arrangements for the burial of a politician had provided the clearest possible assertion of an alternative identity. The community had mounted a manifest and unanswerable challenge to the legitimacy of specific political actions, a challenge which had been thoroughly understood by even the least sophisticated. The determination of Venda women at the grassroots to retain control of this ultimate sanction is mirrored on a far larger and grander scale in the speeches of Bishop Tutu and others, and in the massive attendances at the funerals of the victims of police and other violence in the South African townships. Respect for the dead who are still vividly alive, honor for forebears, the reciprocal support of the ancestors are still right at the heart of African societies as political insights and demands are articulated and communicated today.

---

4. See also D. F. Eiffe, "The Structure, Character and Growth of the R. C. Church in Venda in the 1980s" (Master's thesis, SOAS, 1984).

The workshop also began to consider the implications of the concern with spiritual healing which is so prominent in the activities of many Christian communities in Africa. The Holy Spirit is acknowledged to be "the central focal point" of the theology expressed in *Speaking for Ourselves*:

> The Spirit is our teacher and our guide in everything. It is the Spirit who assures us that the Bible comes from God. It is the Spirit who instructed our founders to found a new Church. It is the Spirit who inspires our prophets and calls our leaders to service in the Church. It is the Spirit who heals us when we are ill.

In Africa, more than anywhere else, small Christian communities have preeminently begun as loci of healing. "We know," continues the statement,

> that there are evil spirits or demons and that they can take possession of a person and that they can cause illnesses. But we believe that the Spirit of God is more powerful than any other spirit.

It is this dual conviction, shared in common with so many New Testament writers, which helps to give these communities their strength and influence in Africa today. It is a power which carries manifest secular consequences at the local, grassroots level. Dispute-solving, the airing of accusations so many of which carry supernatural implications, the resolution of bitter quarrels, and the healing of communal tensions were among the principal functions of elders, diviners, headmen, and rulers. These functions and the authority which they carry are now increasingly borne by the leaders of small Christian communities. In this sense they already provide alternative social structures, albeit of a highly fragmented nature. But if these communities, basing themselves now on their understanding of the Bible, begin by confronting their traditional concepts of evil, do some of them also go on to challenge evil in its wider and more modern forms.? Are they led by the Spirit to perceive new dimensions of social evil? Can their new-found symbols of salvation also be seen to have a bearing on the forces of injustice which confront so many of these poorest of the poor?

The authors of *Speaking for Ourselves* are quite certain that they have experienced healing and salvation "*now* and not only in the afterlife." The theology and worship of their communities are very definitely oriented towards the problems of daily living as experienced by their members. "Our peoples know what it means to be oppressed, exploited and crushed." They also know that "racial discrimination and oppression is rejected by the Bible."

> And so what do our people do about it? They join political organisations or trade unions and take part in the struggle for our liberation. But it is a matter of individual choice. . . . The "Churches of the People" and the political organizations or trade unions of the people have different roles to play. It is often the same people who belong to both. . . . We will have to do more study on this matter of religion and politics.

This plea for further study and reflection was also the main conclusion of the SOAS workshop. We hope that students in African universities and theological colleges will engage in similar fieldwork, interviews, and research, helping the members of small Christian communities to tell their story and to communicate their insights. Perhaps a means could then be found to enable their findings to be reviewed with church leaders, theologians, and other academics. For we are convinced that these communities spread out across all Christian denominations possess a profound significance in contemporary Africa. They may indeed turn out to be one of the institutions most powerfully shaping the future of the continent.

11

Bengt Sundkler's
African Encounters

The key to Bengt's unique contribution to the study of Christianity in Africa must surely lie in the extraordinary breadth and depth of his ecumenical encounters. It is highly significant that it was the life of a great African Christian which first decided Bengt to orientate himself toward Africa. Previously he had thought of China, which was, as he recalled to me some twenty years ago, "the great place" for a young man intent on missionary work in the early 1930s. I am fairly certain that he never met Kwegyir Aggrey personally, but the impact of the Ghanaian's personality, mediated through Edwin Smith's biography, decisively influenced him. Aggrey had swept through Anglophone Africa in the 1920s as an apostle of racial cooperation, a modern vindication of much that missionaries, like Smith exposed to settler Africa, were attempting to achieve.[1] Aggrey's intellectual achievements, curiosity and ability, and even more his personality, with its self-control, insight, humor, and sensitivity, to the qualities and feelings of others, manifestly appealed to the young Swede, who was in turn to exemplify these qualities in his career as missionary and scholar in Africa.

Undoubtedly many different considerations induced Bengt as a young missionary to turn his attention to the study of Bantu prophets in his southern African field. It is wholly characteristic of him, however, that in the 1970s, when looking back to the origins of this study, he himself selected as the decisive factor a crucial encounter at a "weekday Church service at Ceza, Zululand." After the service, an old Zulu woman confided to him that, since he had chosen a hymn too strong for her, she had had to go out, for she thought, until disabused by him, that she was not allowed to shake in his church.[2] Much of the

---

1. E. W. Smith, *Aggrey of Africa: A Study in Black and White* (London, 1929).
2. B. Sundkler, *Zulu Zion and Some Swazi Zionists,* Studia Missionalia Upsaliensia XXIX,(Lund, 1976), 7.

171

book is concerned with a sociological analysis of the racial, political, and economic factors which contributed to the proliferation of African independent churches in South Africa. But it is also wholly in tune with his deepest instincts as a scholar that, as a theologian and historian, he enthusiastically endorsed the robust proclamation of a very distinguished Swedish academic that "disinterested social science is pure nonsense. It never existed, and it never will exist."[3]

Today Sundkler's analysis in *Bantu Prophets* has been amplified and corrected by subsequent scholars. Even the principal typological distinction between Ethiopians and Zionists put forward in his book, and which for long dominated academic discussions of these African churches, has been modified and at times replaced.

One can be certain, however, that in a hundred years' time *Bantu Prophets* will still be consulted for its information concerning some of the pioneer leaders of these churches. Typically he claimed that the splendid, close-up photographs "contribute to a fuller understanding of the personalities" discussed in the book; but these impressive photographs are totally eclipsed by his word portraits, the fruit of brilliant observation, perceptions, and descriptions. Mainly on account of these descriptions, the book was a decisive landmark in the study of Christianity in Africa. It opened up to the wider, previously hostile audience, the motivations, aspirations, and something of the potential of the profoundly significant movement and phenomenon represented by these leaders.

If the sociological and typological dimensions of *Bantu Prophets* have been modified by other scholars, its basic theological stance was challenged and changed by Bengt himself. When writing the book, he had been deeply concerned by the threat of what he saw as syncretism. "The syncretistic sect," he had then concluded, "becomes the bridge over which Africans are brought back to heathenism. . . . It can be shown how individuals and groups have passed step by step from a mission church to an Ethiopian church, and from the Ethiopians to the Zionists, and how at last via the bridge of nativistic Zionism they

---

3. G. Myrdal, *An American Dilemma: The Negro Problem and Modem Democracy*, quoted in B. G. M. Sundkler, *The Bantu Prophets in South Africa* (London, 1948), 16,

have returned to the African animism from where they once started."[4] In 1948, when he returned to Uppsala University as professor of ecclesiastical and missionary history, he was already known as a keen and challenging ecumenist, anxious to revitalize the Scandinavian role in the international missions of the emerging postwar world. In his inaugural lecture there, he had what was then considered to be the audacity to suggest that the young churches would bring "a renewing elixir" to theological research. But in that lecture, he also showed himself to be gravely fearful of the consequences of syncretism, "the gnosticism of our time."[5]

Many factors gradually assisted Bengt to place his fears of syncretism in a calmer, broader perspective. Among these factors were his major contributions to the study of the development of ecumenism, which resulted in his great biography of Nathan Soderblom and his detailed exploration of the origins of the Church of South India.[6] There were also renewed contacts with Africa north of the Limpopo, which enabled him to witness again the intellectual achievements and the deep theological commitments of many different African Christians. In 1953, Bengt Sundkler and an advisory team set out to survey the pastoral and theological problems facing the churches during the decolonization of black Africa. The team notably included Christian Baeta, the Ghanaian Presbyterian who had already made his mark on the international missionary scene in 1938 at Tambaram when Bengt was still merely settling in at Ceza. The result, published in 1961, was a fascinating series of encounters with African pastors and teachers. His concluding chapter calling for a reconsideration of Christian theology within the context of developing African cultures showed far less fear of syncretism.[7] Equally important, perhaps, was his return to Bukoba as Bishop at the time of Tanzania's transition to independence. Bengt had originally been rushed to the area when the German missionaries there had been interned during the Second World War. His return

---

4. Sundkler. *Bantu Prophets*, 297.

5. Jonas Jonson, "Between the Scylla of Syncretism and the Charybdis of a Self-appointed Ghetto," in *Studia Misswnalia Upsaliensia* 39 (1984): 46.

6. *Nathan Soderblom: His Life and Work* (Lund, 1968); *The Church of South India* (London, 1954).

7. *The Christian Ministry in Africa* (London, 1961).

in 1961–64 enabled him to obtain an intimate understanding of the area and of different generations of church members. In preparing his account of this experience, he was able to consult not only his own notes and observations but also a host of autobiographical data placed at his disposal by the many African converts and Christian leaders whose confidence he had gained. His account is particularly interesting on the challenges and conflicts which faced the first generation of converts. He discovered the importance of dreams in their lives and realized that many of the members of his diocese shared much in common with the prophets and their followers in Zululand.[8]

On several visits to southern Africa and periods of field research there, he continued his study of the Zulu and Swazi independent churches. He renewed and extended his encounters with their leaders and congregations. Another great Swedish Africanist, Axel-Ivar Berglund, has given us an unforgettable account of the quality of these encounters. He recounts how, after many years, an old Zulu woman recalled the way in which Bengt had questioned her when she had been baptized by one of the prophets. "I tell you," she said, "he amazed me very much. For he neither scolded nor dismissed. We shared as if we were of the same family, speaking nicely to one another without any bad words."[9] So when Bengt came in the 1970s to reconsider his theological conclusions regarding the work of these prophets and the life of their churches, he realized that his fears of syncretism had subsided and he was ready, tentatively, to welcome them also as members of the same family. Concentrating on the history of these churches and especially on the inimitable biographical portraits of their leaders, he acknowledged that "to those in the movement, Zion meant newness of life, health and wholeness, a new identity. If it was a bridge, it appeared to them as a bridge to the future. . . . There are a number of Zionist churches which in intention and confession are as loyal to Jesus the Christ as Mission-related churches. . . . The Church of Christ is not uniform but universal."[10]

---

8. *Bara Bulwba: Kyrka oeh miljo i Tanzania* (Stockholm, 1974); English edition *Bara Bukoba: Church and Community in Tanzania* (London 1980).

9. Axel-Ivar Berglund, "Bengt Sundkler, Prophet among Prophets," *Studia Missionalia Upsaliensia* 39 (1984): 27.

10. Sundkler, *Zulu Zion and Some Swazi Zionists*, 305, 316–17.

Those of us who have been privileged to see drafts of the magnum opus which so happily occupied Bengt during more than the last twenty years of his life, know that its greatest distinguishing feature is again the depth and breadth of his ecumenical understanding and sympathies. While the reassessment of Zion was taking place in Bengt's thought, his ecumenical sympathies were expanding in another direction. Traditionally Rome had been seen as another example of the dangers of syncretism. I forget whether Bengt ever personally met, as opposed to seeing, hearing, and reading, John XXIII. Certainly this pope's photograph occupied a very prominent place in his home in Uppsala, and the deep humanity and faith of this man of peasant stock from Bergamo spoke to Bengt's heart in much the same way as those Zionist men and women had done. I would surmise that it was the encounter with Pope John's thought and personality, even more perhaps than the theologies expressed at Vatican II, which enabled Bengt to see through at least some of his fears in the case of Rome. I remember his warm, excited, almost astounded appreciation of the way in which in the 1970s he had been welcomed in Rome by the members of the Capuchin historical institute to their early morning Eucharists, just as I remember how they later enthusiastically recalled his participation in their life and studies. Certainly his draft history of the Christian movement in Africa is marked by a marvelous, almost astonishing degree of ecumenical insights, embracing the whole spectrum of African Christianity and of Christian missionary activities on that continent. All of us must hope that Christopher Steed and the Cambridge University Press will very soon be able to give us this remarkable book, the testament of an outstanding scholar who himself took a leading role in many of the more recent developments described in it.

Sources

1. "The African Origins of the *Missio Antiqua*." Published in Clavis Scientiae (Rome: Instituto Storico dei Cappuccini, 1999).

2. "A Kongo Princess, the Kongo Ambassadors, and the Papacy." Published in *Journal of Religion in Africa* 29, no. 2 (1999): 140–54. Used with permission.

3. "Ingoli, the Collector of Portugal, the *Gran Gusto* of Urban VIII, and the Atlantic Slave Trade. Published in W. Henkle, ed., *Ecclesiae Memoria: Miscellanea in onore del R. P. Josef Metzler O.M.I.* (Rome, 1991).

4. "The Papacy and Africa in the Seventeenth Century." Published in *Il Cristianesimo nel mondo atlantico nel secolo XVII* (Vatican City: Libreria Editrice Vaticana, 1997). Copyright © Libreria Editrice Vaticana. Used with permission.

5. "*Come Vero Prencipe Catolico:* The Capuchins and the Rulers of Soyo in the Late Seventeenth Century." Published in *Africa* 53, no. 3 (1983): 39–54. Copyright © 1983 International African Institute. Reprinted with permission of Cambridge University Press.

6. "Christian Traces and a Franciscan Mission in the Central Sudan, 1700–1711." Published in *Journal of African History* 8, no. 3 (1967): 383–93. Reprinted with permission of Cambridge University Press.

7. "Catholic Church and National States in Western Europe during the Nineteenth and Twentieth Centuries from a Perspective of Africa." Published in *Kirchliche Zeitgeschichte, Internationale Halbjahresschrift für Theologie und Geschichtswissenschaft* 14, no. 1 (2001).

8. "The Southern Sudan." Published in *Journal of Contemporary History* 6, no. 1 (1971): 108–20. Used with permission.

9. "Christianity, Colonialism, and Communications in Sub-Saharan Africa." Published in *Journal of Black Studies* 13, no. 1 (September 1982): 59–72. Used with permission.

10. "Popular Theologies in Africa: A Report on a Workshop on Small Christian Communities in Southern Africa." Published in *African Affairs* 85, no. 338 (January 1986): 49–54. Reprinted with permission of the Royal African Society and *African Affairs*.

11. "Bengt Sundkler's African Encounters." Published in *Journal of Religion in Africa* 25, Fasc. 4 (November 1995): 342–46. Used with permission.

Bibliography

Archival References

Acta (in archive of Propaganda Fide) 7, f. 132, No. 27 of September 6, 1630.

Acta 7, f. 174v.

Acta 209, ff. 36–7, Fr. Venanzio di S. Venanzio to Prefect of Propaganda, Tripoli, February 6, 1845.

Archivio Segreto Vaticano, Miscellaneorum Armaria (= ASV, Arm.) I, 91, f. 215, Draft petition, January 1607.

ASV, Arm. I, 91, f. 214, Minutes of a letter by Antonio Manuele, 11.V.1607.

ASV, Arm. I, 91, f. 220, Diego de la Encarnación to ambassador, Alcalá, 8.VI.1607.

ASV, Arm. I, 91, f. 253, Depostion by Archbishop of Saragoza, 25.X.1607.

ASV, Arm. I, 91, f. 229, Pedro de la Madre de Dios to the Ambassador, 24.VII.1607.

ASV, Arm. I, 91, f. 241, Certificate signed by the provincial, 10.X.1607.

Biblioteca Apostolica Vaticana, Codices Urbinates Latini (BAV, Urb. Lat.) 837, f.144.

BAV, Urb. Lat. 837, f. 147r–v.

BAV, Urb. Lat. 837, f. 464, Relatione.

BAV, Urb. Lat. 1062, f. 334, Avviso of 11.VI.1594.

BAV, Urb. Lat. 1076, f. 5v–6, Avvisi di Roma, 5.1.1608.

BAV, Urb. Lat. 1076 Pt. 1, f.19, Avvisi di Roma, 9.1.1608.

BAV, Codices Vatican Library. (Vat. Lat.) 6723, ff. 2–7v, Relazione d'Etiopia.

BAV, Vat. Lat. 6723, f. 6v, Unpublished memorandum written by Girolamo Vecchietti.

BAV, Vat. Lat. 12516, f. 43v, a report almost certainly drawing on information from Biondi, amongst others.

BAV, Vat. Lat. 12516, f. 122.

Biblioteca Vaticana, Codex Ottobonianus (B. V. Ottob.) 2536, f. 150, Ingoli to Agucchi, 28 December 28, 1630.

B. V. Ottob. 2536 f. 154, Minutes of Propaganda Fide committee meeting, December 18, 1630.

Bibliothèque Nationale, Paris. MSS. franc. 12220, f. 318.

Fondo Confalonieri, Vatican archives (Confalonieri) 27, f. 178v–179 Biondi to Aldobrandino, 11.V.1596.

Confalonieri 27, ff. 203, 213, 227 and 238, Biondi to Aldobrandino, letters concerning Vieira's plans and movements, 31.VIII.1596 to 15.III.1597.

Confalonieri 28, f. 401, Biondi to Archbishop of Evora, 27.XI.1595.

Confalonieri 28, f. 495v, Biondi to Alvaro II, 18.IX.1596.

Confalonieri 28, f. 566v, Biondi to nuncio, 27.XI.1595.

Confalonieri 28, f. 678–678v, Biondi to Silvio Antoniano, 31.VIII. 1596.

Confalonieri 43, f. 96v, Borghese to Collector, 12.X.1611.

Confalonieri, Alvaro II to Paul V, 27.III.1613, in Brásio, v.6, 132.

Confalonieri, Aytona to King, 14.X.1608, in Brásio, v.5, 473–5.

Confalonieri, Borghese to Carafa, 12.X.1611, in Brásio, v.6, 42–3.

Confalonieri, Giacinto's report of 20.VIII.1652 and Garcia's decree, in Brásio, v.11, 216–30.

Confalonieri, José de Melo's report of 17.IX.1608, in Brásio, v.5, 461–2.

Confalonieri, Philip II to Requesens, 12.VII.1566, in Setton, *The Papacy,* 910.

Confalonieri, Memorial by Bonaventura d'Alessano to Propaganda Fide, 4.VIII.1649.

Confalonieri, Vat., Papal brief of 30.V.1648, in Brásio, v.10, 166–8.

Confalonieri, Serafino da Cortona to the Capuchin Provincial in Tuscany, 15.V.1652, in Brásio, v.11, 191.

Fondo di Vienna 56, f. 101, archive of Propaganda Fide.

Lettere (in archive of Propaganda Fide) 10, f. 8.

Lettere 10, f. 28–28v.

Lettere 10, f. 83–83v.

Orden de los Carmelitas Descalzos (OCD) archives in Rome, 281e Cartapaccio f. 27–27v.

Scritture Originali riferite nelle Congregazioni, Angola (in archive of Propaganda Fide), V. fol. 180, Memorandum by Bernardino Ignazio d'Asti, December 12, 1749.

Scritture Originali riferite nelle Congregazioni, Barbaria 3, ff. 505–8, Lemaire to prefect of Propaganda, Tripoli, May 25, 1707. An Italian translation is at SOCG. 559, ff. 632–3.

Scritture Originali riferite nelle Congregazioni Generali (SOCG) 98, f. 53.

SOCG 98, f. 77–79.

SOCG 98, f. 91–93.

SOCG 98, f. 96–96v.

SOCG 98 f. 97v.

SOCG 98, f. 98v.

SOCG 98, f. 107. Ingoli to Vives, September 18, 1630 with notes added by Vives.

SOCG 131, f. 385–386v.

SOCG 131, f. 387v.

SOCG 250, f. 28. An unsigned memorandum, probably by Serafino da Cortona in late 1659 or 1660, entitled "Delli schiavi che si comprano e vendono nel Regno di Congo e come si possono Li Christiani vendere dopo Battezzati," ff.26–9.

SOCG 514, f. 471v, "compendiosa relatione . . . data da me F. Andrea de Pavia" considered on 6.IV.1693.

SOCG 536, ff. 458, 461, Copy of memorandum by Fr. Maurizio da Lucca, presented by Cardinal Sacripante to the General Congregation of December 1700.

SOCG 552, ff. 422–3, Fr. Damiano da Rivoli to Prefect of Propaganda, Tripoli, July 4, 1705.

SOCG 557, ff. 134–5, Lemaire to prefect of Propaganda, Tripoli, April 18, 1706.

SOCG 557, ff. 315, 324, 326–43. Copies of two memoranda by Fr. Damiano submitted after his return to Italy, and considered at the General Congregation of February 22, 1707.

SOCG 557, f. 342.

SOCG 561, f. 23, Note from the Franciscan procurator, discussed on January 9, 1708.

SOCG 561, f. 25, Fr. Carlo Maria di Genova to Propaganda Cairo, July 28, 1707.

SOCG 569, f. 264, Letters from Fr. Carlo to Propaganda, Tripoli, August 26, 1709.

SOCG 569, f. 266, Poullard to Cardinal Sacripante, Tripoli, March 25, 1709.

SOCG 571, f. 8, Fr. Francesco Maria di Sarzana to Prefect of Propaganda, Tripoli, January 19, 1710.

SOCG 572, f. 405, Letters from Fr. Carlo to Propaganda, Tripoli, May 18, 1710.

SOCG 573, f. 41, Fr. Carlo to the prefect of Propaganda, Tripoli, June 9, 1710.

SOCG 577, f. 125, Fr. Carlo to Cardinal Sacripante, Fezzano da Daraghen, October 17, 1710.

SOCG 586, ff. 41–2, Fr. Francesco Maria di Sarzana to Prefect of Propaganda, Tripoli, October 14, 1712.

Bibliographic References

Ajayi, J. F. Ade. *Christian Missions in Nigeria, 1841–1891: The Making of a New Elite*. London: Longmans, 1965.

Ajayi, J. F. Ade, and Michael Crowder, eds. *History of West Africa*, I. London: Longman, 1971.

Albergati. "Relatione delle missioni fatte per l'Asia, Africa e Brasil," Lisbon, March 4, 1623. 1, f. 414–17, Congregazione Particolari in archive of Propaganda Fide.

Albino, Oliver. *The Sudan, A Southern Viewpoint*. London: Oxford University Press, 1970.

Analecta Ordinis Capuccinorum, v.13, 1897.

Aregay, Merid Wolde. *The Legacy of Jesuit Missionary Activities in Ethiopia from 1555 to 1632*. In *The Missionary Factor in Ethiopia*. Ed. Getatchew Haile et al. Frankfurt/M: Peter Lang, 1998.

Aregay, Merid Wolde, and Girma Beshah, *The Question of the Union of the Churches in Luso-Ethiopian Relations, 1500–1632*. Lisbon: Junta de Investigações do Ultramar and Centro de Estudes Históricos Ultramarinos, 1964.

Arkell, Anthony John. "A Christian Church and Monastery at Ain Farah, Darfur, *Kush* 7 (1959).

———. *History of the Sudan to 1821*. 2nd ed. London: The Athlone Press, 1962.

Ayandele, E. A. *The Missionary Impact on Modern Nigeria, 1842–1914*. London: Longmans, 1966.

Bal, Willy. *Description du Royaume de Congo et des contries environnantes*. Trans. F. Pigafetta. Louvain, Paris: Nauwelaerts, 1963.

Balandier, G. *Daily Life in the Kingdom of Kongo from the Sixteenth to the Eighteenth Century*. English trans. London: George Allen and Unwin, 1968.

Barth, Heinrich. *Travels and Discoveries in North and Central Africa, II*. New York: Harper & Brothers, 1857.

Bartels, F. L. *The Roots of Ghana Methodism*. Cambridge: Cambridge University Press, 1965.

Beccari, Camillo, ed. *Rerum Aethiopicarum Scriptores Occidentales*. 14 Rome, 1914.

Berglund, Axel-Ivar. "Bengt Sundkler, Prophet among Prophets." *Studia Missionalia Upsaliensia* 39 (1984).

Bergna, C. *La Missione Francescana in Libia*. Tripoli, 1924.

Beshir, Mohamed Omer. *The Southern Sudan*. London: C. Hurst and Co., 1968.

Bluche, François. *Louis XIV*. English trans. London: Oxford University Press, 1990.

Bonaventura d'Alessano. 4.VIII.1649, SOCG 249, f.38–43.

Bontinck, François. "Jean-Baptiste Vives, Ambassadeur des Rois de Congo auprés du Saint Siège." *Revue du Clerge Africain* 7 (1952): 258–64.

———. ed. and trans. *Brève relation de la foundation de la mission . . . au Kongo*. Louvain: Nauwelaerts, 1964.

———. "Les Carmes Dechaux au royaume de Kongo (1584–1587)." *Zaïre-Afrique* 262 (1992): 113–23.

Brásio, Antonio. *Monumenta Missionaria Africana. Africa Ocidental.* (I serie). Vols. III–VI. Lisbon: 1954–1955.

Briggs, Robin. *Communities of Belief: Cultural and Social Tension in Early Modern France.* London: Oxford University Press, 1989.

Buenaventura de Carrocera. "Dos relaciones inéditas sobre la Misión Capuchina del Congo. *Collectanea Franciscana* 16–7 (1946–47): 102–24.

Buri, Vincenzo. "L'unione della chiesa copta con Roma sotto Clemente VII." *Orientalia Christiana* xxiii/2, 72 (Rome, 1931): 237–39.

Caraman, Philip. *The Lost Empire.* London: Sidgwick and Jackson, 1985.

Castellucci, A. "Mons. Giambattista Vives." In *Alma Mater*, II. Rome; 1920.

————. "Il risveglio dell'attivita missionaria e le prime origini della S. C. de Propaganda Fide. In *La Conferenze al Laterano, Marzo-Aprile 1923* (Rome, 1924).

Cavazzi de Montecuccolo, João Antonio. *Descrição Historica dos tres reinos do Congo, Matamba e Angola.* Trans. Graciano Maria de Leguzzano. Lisbon, 1965.

Cavazzi, Giovanni Antonio da Montecuccolo. *Istorica descrizione de tre Regni Congo. Matamba, et Angola .* Bologna: Giacomo Monti, 1687.

Chadwick, O. *The Popes and European Revolution.* Oxford: Clarendon Press, 1981.

Coulon, Paul, and Paule Brasseur et al. *Libermann, 1802–1852: Une pensée et une mystique missionnaires (Histoire).* Paris: Cerf, 1988.

Curtin, Philip D. *The Atlantic Slave Trade: A Census.* Madison: University of Wisconsin Press, 1969.

Cuvelier, Jean, and Louis Jadin. *L'ancien Congo d'apris les archives romaines (1518–1640).* Brussels: Academie royale des Sciences colonials, 1954. Section des sciences morales et politiques. Memoires, 36, fasc 2.

D'Agostino, Enzo. *I Vescovi di Gerace-Locri.* Chiaravalle Centrale, 1981.

Dapper, O. *Beschreibung von Africa.* German trans. Amsterdam: Jacob von Meurs, 1670.

Denham, Major Dixon, and Captain Hugh Clapperton. *Narrative of Travels and Discoveries in Northern and Central Africa, II.* 3rd ed. London: John Murray, 1828.

Die Tagebiicher von Dr Emin Pascha herausgegeben . . . von Dr Franz Stuhlmann. Berlin, 1917, v.2, entries dated October 17–20, 1880 and August 27, 1881.

Eiffe, D. F. "The Structure, Character and Growth of the R.C. Church in Venda in the 1980s." Masters's dissertation, SOAS 1984.

Ekchi, F. K. *Missionary Enterprise and Rivalry in Igboland, 1857-1914.* London: Cass, 1971.

Elliott, John Huxtable. *The Count-Duke of Olivares.* New Haven: Yale University Press, 1986.

Fage, John Donnelly. "Some Myths, Legends, and Traditions of the Central and Western Sudan Relating to Immigrations from the North and East," unpublished seminar paper, Institute of Commonwealth Studies, London (AH 59/2).

Fagg, William. Letter dated June 1, 1966.

Filesi, Teobaldo. *Le relazioni tra il regno del Congo e la Sede Apostolica nel XVI secolo.* Como: Cairoli, 1968.

———. *Roma e Congo all'inizio del 1600. Nuove Testimonianze.* Como: Cairoli, 1970.

Filesi, Teobaldo, and Isidoro de Villapadierna. *La "Missio Antiqua" dei Cappuccini nel Congo.* Rome: Istituto Storico Cappuccini, 1978.

Fisher, H. J. "Conversion Reconsidered: Some Historical Aspects of Religious Conversion in Black Africa." *Africa* 43, no. 1 (1973): 27-40.

Florencio del Nifio Jesius. *La Orden de Santa Teresa, la Fundación de la Propaganda Fide y las Misiones Carmelitanas.* Madrid, 1923.

Frobenius, Leo. *The Voice of Africa.* Eng. trans., II. London: Hutchinson, 1913.

Fusero, C. *Antonio Vignato nell'Africa di ieri.* Bologna: Editrice Nigrizia, 1970.

Fyfe, C. *A History of Sierra Leone.* London: Oxford University Press, 1962.

Garvey, B. "The Development of the White Fathers' Mission Among the Bemba-Speaking Peoples, 1891-1964." PhD diss. University of London, 1974.

Gracián, Jerónimo. *Zelo de la propagacio de la Fe.* Madrid, 1616.

Gordon to Waller, January 29, 1875, and to his sister, October 22, 1875, quoted in Gray, *A History,* 113.

Gray, Richard. *A History of the Southern Sudan 1839-1889.* London: Oxford University Press, 1961.

———, ed. *The Cambridge History of Africa.* Vol. 40, Cambridge: Cambridge University. Press, 1975.

———. "Christianity and Religious Change in Africa." *African Affairs* 77 (1978): 89-100.

———. "The Vatican and the Atlantic Slave Trade." *History Today* 31 (March 1981): 37-39.

———. "The Papacy and the Atlantic Slave Trade: Lourenço da Silva, the Capuchins and the Decisions of the Holy Office." *Past and Present* 115 (1987): 52-68, reprinted in *Black Christians and White Missionaries.*

———. *Black Christians and White Missionaries.* New Haven and London: Yale University Press, 1990.

———. "Ingoli, the Collector of Portugal, the "Gran Gusto" of Urban VIII and the Atlantic Slave Trade." In *Ecclesiae Memoria. Miscellanea in onore del R. P. Josef Metzler O.M.I.* Ed. W. Henkle. Rome, 1991.

———. "The Papacy and Africa in the Seventeenth Century." *Il Cristianesimo nel mondo atlantico nel secolo XVII.* Pontificio Comitato di Scienze Storiche, Atti e Documenti, 6. Vatican City: Libreria Editrice Vaticana, 1997.

———. "A Kongo Princess, the Kongo Ambassadors and the Papacy." *Journal of religion in Africa* 29, no. 2 (1999): 140–54.

———. "The African Origins of the *Missio Antiqua.*" In Vincenzo Criscuolo, ed., *Clavis Scientiae. Miscellanea di studi offerti a Isidoro Agudo da Villapadierna in occasione del suo 80° compleanno.* Bibliotheca Seraphico-Capuccina 60 (1999): 405–23.

———. "Fra Girolamo Merolla da Sorrento, the Congregation of Propaganda Fide and the Atlantic Slave Trade." In *La Conoscenza dell' Asia e dell' Africa in Italia nei secoli xviii e xix.* Ed. M. Taddei. Naples: Istituto Universitario Orientale (forthcoming).

Haliburton, G .M. *The Prophet Harris.* London: Longmans, 1971.

Hallencreutz, Carl F. *Religion and Politics in Harare 1890–1980 (SMU 73).* Uppsala, 1998.

Hallett, Robin. *The Penetration of Africa.* I. London, Routledge & K. Paul, 1965.

Hastings, Adrian. *The Church in Africa 1450–1950.* Oxford: Clarendon Press, 1994.

———. "The Christianity of Pedro IV of the Kongo, The Pacific (1695–1718)." *Journal of Religion in Africa* 28, no. 2 (1998): 145–59.

Heldman, Marilyn E. "A Chalice from Venice for Emperor Dawit of Ethiopia." *Bulletin of School of Oriental and African Studies* 53 (1990).

Hildebrand, Pére. *Le martyr Georges de Geel.* Antwerp, 1940.

Hill, R. "Government and Christian Missions in the Anglo-Egyptian Sudan, 1899–1914." *Middle Eastern Studies* 1 (January 1965).

Hilton, Anne. *The Kingdom of Kongo.* London: Oxford University Press, 1985.

Hogben, S. J., and A. H. M. Kirk-Greene. *The Emirates of Northern Nigeria.* London: Oxford University Press, 1966.

Holmes, J. Derek. *The Triumph of the Holy See: A Short History of the Papacy in the Nineteenth Century.* London: Burns and Oates, 1978.

Holt, P. M. "Egypt, the Funj and Darfur." In *Cambridge History of Africa.* Vol. 4, c.1600–c.1790. Cambridge: Cambridge University Press, 1975, 14–57.

Horton, R. "African Conversion." *Africa* 41, no. 2 (1971): 85–108.

Isichei, Elizabeth Allo. *A History of Christianity in Africa: From Antiquity to the Present.* Grand Rapids, Mich.: William B. Eerdmans Publishing Co., 1995.

Jadin, Louis. "Le clergé séculier et les Capucins du Congo et d'Angola aux xvie et xviie siècles." *Bulletin de l'Institut historique belge de Rome* 36 (1964): 185–483.

———. "Rivalités luso-néerlandaises au Sohio, Congo 1600–1675." *Bull. Inst. hist. belge de Rome* 37 (1966): 137–360.

———. "Andrea da Pavia au Congo, à Lisbonne à Madère." Journal d'un missionaire capucin, 1685–1702," *Bull. Inst. hist. belge de Rome* 41 (1970): 375–592.

———. "L'oeuvre missionnaire en Afrique noire." In *Sacrae Congregationis de Propaganda Fide Memoria Rerum.* Ed. J. Metzler. I/2. Rome: Herder, 1971.

Jassy, Marie-France Perrin. *Face au changement; former des communautès de base.* Bandundu: Ceeba Publications, 1981.

Janzen, J. M., and W. MacGaffey. *An Anthology of Kongo Religion.* Lawrence: University of Kansas, Publications in Anthropology 5, 1974.

Jonson, Jonas. "Between the Scylla of Syncretism and the Charybdis of a Self-appointed Ghetto." *Studia Missionalia Upsaliensia* 39 (1984).

Joseph de Santa Teresa. *Reforma de los Descalzos.* Madrid, 1684.

Kakuze, Odette. Open letter to African bishops.

Kalilombe, Patrick Augustine. "Doing Theology at the Grassroots: A Challenge for Professional Theologians." Paper presented to the Second General Assembly of the Ecumenical Association of African Theologians, Nairobi, December 1984.

Kowalsky, N. "Juan Bautista Vives." In *Enciclopedia Cattolica XII.* Città del Vaticano, 1954.

———. "Il testamento di Mons. Ingoli primo segretario della Sacra Congregatione 'de Propaganda Fide.' " In *Neue Zeitschrift für Missionswissenschaft* 19 (1963).

Landen, Ian. *The Catholic Church and the Struggle for Zimbabwe.* London, 1980.

Lash, Nicholas. "Pius XII's Radical Moves." *The Tablet,* October 2, 1999.

Lefevre, Renato. "Presenze etiopiche in Italia prima del Concilio di Firenze del 1439." *Rassegna di studi etiopici* 23 (1967–68).

Lopetegui, Leon. "San Francisco de Borgia y el plan misional de San Pio V." *Archivum Historicum Societatis Iesu* 11 (1942).

MacGaffey, Wyatt. *Custom and Government in the Lower Congo.* Berkeley: University of California Press, 1970.

———. "The Religious Commissions of the Bakongo." *Man* (1970) (N.S.) V(l). 27–38.

———. *Religion and Society in Central Africa.* Chicago: Chicago University Press, 1986.

Mariano d'Alatri, ed. *Santi e Santità nell'' Ordine Cappuccino* I. Rome: Postulazione Generale dei Cappuccini, 1980.

Martin, M. *Kimbangu.* Oxford: Blackwell, 1975.

Masson, Paul. *Histoire des établissements et du commerce française dans l'Afrique barbaresque, 1560–1793.* Paris, 1903.

Mateo de Anguiano. *Misiones capuchinas en Africa. I. La mision del Congo.* With introduction and notes by Buenaventura de Carrocera. Madrid, 1950.

Mathews, A. B. "The Kisra Legend." *African Studies* 9 (1950).

Maxwell, John Francis. *Slavery and the Catholic Church.* Chichester: Barry Rose Publishing, 1975.

McCracken, J. *Politics and Christianity in Malawi 1875–1940.* Cambridge: Cambridge University Press, 1977.

Meek, Charles Kingsley. *The Northern Tribes of Nigeria, I.* London: Routledge, 1925.

———. *A Sudanese Kingdom.* London: Kegan, Paul, Trench, Trabner, 1931.

Memoria Reru, Josef, ed. *Sacrae Congregationis de Propaganda Fide Memoria Rerum 11.* Rome: Herder, 1971.

Merolla, Girolamo da Sorrento. *Breve, e succinta relatione del viaggio nel Regno di Congo.* Naples: Francesco Mollo, 1692.

Monica, Sor M. *La gran controversia del siglo XVI acerca del dominio español en América.* Madrid: Ediciones Cultura Hispanica, 1952.

Montclos, de Xavier. *Lavigerie, le Saint-Siège et l'Eglise. De l'avènement de Pie IX à l'avènement de Lèon XIII 1846–1878.* Paris: E. de Boccard, 1965.

Moroni, Gaetano. *Dizionario di erudizione ecclesiastica.* Venice, 1841.

Myrdal, Gunnar. *An American Dilemma: The Negro Problem and Modern Democracy.* New York: Harper & Brothers, 1944.

Oduho, Joseph, and William Deng, *The Problem of the Southern Sudan.* London: Oxford University Press, 1963.

O'Fahey, Rex Seán. "The Growth and Development of Keira Sultanate of Dār Fūr," PhDd diss. London, 1972.

Oliver, Roland. *The Missionary Factor in East Africa.* London: Longmans Green, 1952.

Oliver, Roland, and J. D. Fage. *A Short History of Africa*. Harmondsworth: Penguin African Library, 1962.

Palmer, Herbert Richmond. *Sudanese Memoirs, III*. Lagos, 1928.

———. *The Bornu Sahara and Sudan*. London: John Murray, 1936.

Pastor, Ludwig von. *The History of the Popes*. English trans. London: J. Hodges, 1891–1953.

Pauw, B. A. *Christianity and Xhosa Tradition*. Cape Town: Oxford University Press, 1975.

Peers, Edgar Allison. *Mother of Carmel*. London: SCM. Press, 1945.

Peterson, J. *Province of Freedom: A History of Sierra Leone, 1787–1870*. London: Faber, 1969.

Piazza, Calogero. *La Missione del Soyo (1713–1716) nella relazione inedita di Giuseppe da Modena OFM Cap.* Rome: L'Italia Francescana, 1973.

———. *La prefettura apostolica del Congo alla metà del XVII secolo. La relazione inedita di Girolamo da Montesarchio*. Milan: Giuffrè, 1976.

Piras, G. *La Congregazione e il Collegio di Propaganda Fide di J. B. Vives, G. Leonardi a M. de Funes*. Rome, 1976.

Prudhomme, Claude. *Stratégie missionaire du Saint-Siège sous Leon XIII (1878–1903)*. Rome: École française de Rome, 1994.

Quarterly Review (1818), quoted in R. Hallett, *The Penetration of Africa* 1 (1965).

Rahim, Muddathir Abdel. *Imperialism and Nationalism in the Sudan*. London: Oxford University Press, 1969.

Ranger, T. O. "The Mwana Lesa Movement of 1925." In *Themes in the Christian History of Central Africa*. Ed. T. O. Ranger and J. Weller. London: Heinemann, 1975.

Reed, A. "A Journey to a War," *The Grass Curtain* 1 (May 1970).

Reining, Conrad. C. *The Zande Scheme: An Anthropological Case Study of Economic Development in Africa*. Evanston Ill.: Northwestern University Press, 1966.

Renault, François. *Le Cardinal Lavigerie, 1825–1892*. Paris, 1992.

——— Open letter to Eugene Veuillot, 538 f.

Report of the Commission of Enquiry into the Disturbances in the Southern Sudan During August 1955. Khartoum, 1956.

Robinson, R., and J. Gallagher. *Africa and the Victorians*. London: Macmillan, 1965.

Robreo, R. "Vives y María, Jaun Bautista." In *Diccionario de historia eclesiastica de España* IV. Madrid, 1975.

Rodd, Francis James Rennell. *People of the Veil*. London: MacMillan, 1926.

Rodrigues, F. *História da Comanhia de Jesus na Assistência de Portugal.* I/2 Porto, 1931.

Rogers, Francis Millet. *O Sonho de unidade entre cristaõs ocidentais e orientais no século XV.* Bahia, 1960.

———. *The Travels of the Infante Dom Pedro of Portugal.* Cambridge Mass.: Harvard University Press, 1961.

———. *The Quest for Eastern Christians: Travels and Rumor in the Age of Discovery.* Minneapolis: University of Minnesota Press, 1962.

Romanato, Gianpaolo. *Daniele Comboni, 1831–1881: l'Africa degli esploratori dei missionary (Le vite).* Milan, 1998.

Roncière, Ch. de la. "Une histoire du Bornou au XVIIᵉ siècle par un Chirurgien français captif à Tripoli,. *Revue d'histoire des colonies françaises* 7, no. 2i (1919).

———. *La décourverte de l'Afrique au Moyen Age.* Cairo, 1924–7, II, 115s.

Rubin, Arnold. Personal letter dated July 27, 1966.

Ryder, Alan Frederick Charles. "A Reconsideration of the Ife-Benin Relationship." *Journal of African History* 6 (1965).

Schonecke, Fr. Wolfgang. "What Does the Rwanda Tragedy Say to AMECEA Churches?" AMECEA Documentation Service, Nairobi (September 15, 1994): 3.

Sérouet, Pierre. *Jean de Brétigny (1556–1634). Aux origines du Carmel de France, de Belgique et du Congo.* Louvain: Bibliotheque de la Revue d'histoire ecclesiastique, 1974.

Serrano, Luciano. *Correspondencia diplomática entre España y la Santa Sede durante el pontificado de S. Pio V.* Madrid, 1914.

Setton, Kenneth Meyer. *The Papacy and the Levant.* IV. Philadelphia: The American Philosophical Society, 1984.

S. Ignatii de Loyola Soc. Jesu fundatoris epistolae et instructions. Rome: Monumenta Ignatiana, Ser. Ia, II, 1904, 304s.

Slade, R. N. *English-Speaking Missions in the Congo Independent State (1878–1908).* Brussels: Institut Royal Colonial Belge, 1959.

Smith, Edwin W. *Aggrey of Africa: A Study in Black and White.* London: Student Christian Movement, 1929.

Smith, H. F. C. A letter dated July 1, 1966.

Smith, N. *The Presbyterian Church of Ghana, 1835–1960.* Accra: Ghana Universities Press, 1966.

Sölken, Heinz. "Innerafrikanische Wege nach Benin." *Anthropos* 49 (1954).

Stow, Kenneth R. *Taxation, Community and State: The Jews and the Fiscal Foundations of the Early Modern Papal State.* Stuttgart: Hiersemann, 1982).

Streit, Robert, and Johannes Dindinger. *Bibliotheca Missionum, XVII.* Freiburg, 1952.

Stuart, R. G. "Christianity and the Chewa: the Anglican Case, 1885–1950." PhD diss., University of London, 1974.

Suau, P. *Histoire de S. Franfois de Borgia.* Paris: Beauchesne, 1910.

Sundkler, Bengt G. M. *The Bantu Prophets in South Africa.* London: Oxford University Press, 1948.

———. *The Church of South India.* London: Oxford University Press, 1954.

———. *The Christian Ministry in Africa.* London: Oxford University Press, 1961.

———. *Nathan Soderblom: His Life and Work.* Lund: Gleerups, 1968.

———. *Bara Bukoba: Kyrka och miljo i Tanzania.* Stockholm, 1974. English edition *Bara Bukoba: church and community in Tanzania.* London: Oxford University Press, 1980.

———. *Zulu Zion and Some Swazi Zionists.* London: Oxford University Press, 1976.

Taddesse Tamrat. *Church and State in Ethiopia 1270–1527.* London: Oxford University Press, 1972.

Tagebücher, Emin. v.3, December 26, 1884 and October 14, 1885.

Tasie, G. O. M. *Christian Missionary Enterprise in the Niger Delta, 1864–1918.* Leiden: Brill, 1978.

Thornton, John K. "The Kingdom of Kongo in the Era of the Civil Wars, 1641–1718." PhD diss. Los Angeles, University of California, 1979.

———. *The Kongolese Saint Anthony: Dona Beatriz Kimpa Vita and the Antonian Movement, 1684–1706.* Cambridge: Cambridge University Press, 1998.

Turner, H. W. *African Independent Church.* 2 vols. Oxford: Clarendon, 1967.

Turre, Antonio Maria de. (ed. A. Chiappini). *Orbis Seraphicus,* v.2, pars. 2 Quaracchi-Firenze, 1945. Liber Octavus "De Novissimus Apostolicis Missionibus ad regna Fezzán, Bornó Nubiae et Gorolfae in Africa," pp. 312–33.

Unzalu, Juan de. "El Prelado Romano, Monseñor Juan Bautista Vives." In *Agencia Fides,* 1.VI.1946, n.770, and 15.VI.1946, n.772.

Urvoy, Yves. *Histoire des populations du Soudan Central.* Paris: Librarie Larose, 1936.

————. *Histoire de l'empire du Bornou.* Paris: Memoirs de l'Institut Français d'Afrique Noire, 1949.

Ustorf, W. *Afrikanische Initiative. Das aktive Leiden des Propheten Simon Kimbangu.* Bern: Lang, 1975.

Vansina, Jan. "Les mouvements religieux Kuba (Kasai) a l'epoque coloniale." *Etudes d'Histoire Africaine* 2 (1971): 155–87.

————. *Paths in the Rainforests: Toward a History of Political Tradition in Equatorial Africa.* Madison: University of Wisconsin Press, 1990.

Villard, Ugo. Monneret de. Rome: Storia della Nubia Cristiana, 1938.

————. *La Nubia Medievale.* IV Cairo: Imprimerie de l'Institut Francais d'Archaeologie, 1957.

"W. H. Smyth to Rear-Admiral Penrose," Lebida, February 24, 1817, P.R.O. F.O. 76/II, enclosed in Admiralty to Goulburn, May 8, 1817.

Walls, A. F. "Towards Understanding Africa's Place in Christian History." In *Religion in a Pluralistic Society.* Leiden: Brill, 1976.

Wilks, Ivor. "The Rise of the Akwamu Empire, 1650–1710." *Transactions Historical Society of Ghana* (1957): 3, 2, 130.

Wilson, A. "The Kingdom of Kongo to the Mid Seventeenth Century." PhD diss. University of London, 1978.

Wing, Joseph. *Études Bakongo.* 1. Brussels: Geomaere, 1921.

Wiseman, Nicholas Patrick Stephen. *Recollections of the Last Four Popes and of Rome in Their Times: Pius VII, Leo XII, Pius VIII, Gregory XVI.* London: Hurst and Blackett, 1858.

Witte, C. M. de. "Une ambassade éthiopienne à Rome en 1450." *Orientalia Christiana Periodica* 21 (1956).

Zucchelli, Antonio da Gradisca. *Relazioni del viaggio, e Missione di Congo nell' Etiopia Inferiore Occidentale.* Venice: Bartolomeo Giavarina, 1712

Index

193